Hausa Tales and Traditions
Volume III

Hausa Tales and Traditions

An English Translation of
Tatsuniyoyi Na Hausa
Originally compiled by Frank Edgar

Translated and edited by
NEIL SKINNER

Volume III

The University of Wisconsin Press

Published 1977
The University of Wisconsin Press
Box 1379, Madison, Wisconsin 53701
The University of Wisconsin Press, Ltd
70 Great Russell Street, London

Produced and distributed *on demand* by
University Microfilms International
Ann Arbor, Michigan 48106

Printed in the United States of America

Library of Congress Cataloging in Publication Data

Edgar, Frank, d. 1937.
    Hausa tales and traditions.

    (Monograph publishing on demand: imprint series)
    Originally published as Litafina Tatsuniyoyi na Hausa,
Belfast, W. Erskine Mayne, 1911-1913.
    1. Tales, Hausa. 2. Folk-lore, Hausa. I. Skinner,
Neil, ed. II. Title.

GR360.H3E313   1969b   398.2'09669'5   76-53657
ISBN 0-299-07460-9 (v. 3)

Contents

Contents

Introduction

The contents of this volume are residual. They are what is left after the tales, the <u>tatsuniyoyi</u> that Edgar published in Hausa have been extracted, classified and printed in the first two volumes of this translation. Some attempt at giving this heterogeneous mass meaningful form has been made, as a glance at the Contents page will show: it has been rearranged and classified, partly by form (e.g. Proverbs, Riddles) and partly by content (i.e. Kebbi Traditions have been separated from Kano Traditions). Nevertheless, the whole remains somewhat shapeless--as was the original Hausa version. Burdon and Edgar employed malams to write down all and anything that might be of interest and that could be used to provide reading material in Roman script, both for British officers wishing to learn the language, and for the younger generation of Hausas, for whom a knowledge of Roman script could provide the key to entry into the modern world.

It is of interest here to note that in 1903--seven years before he handed his collection over to Edgar for publication--Burdon was leading the opposition to Lugard's proposal made on the advice of Walter Miller and Canon Robinson to stop using Arabic in official correspondence in favor of Hausa. Burdon wrote "to the educated man Arabic is the only method of written communication. Why should he desert a language of which he has made a life's study, for one in which rules for neither grammar nor spelling exist, nor even written material to serve as standard?"* Lugard made his decision, in favor of Hausa-- and Roman script--and so modern Hausa literature was born. The loyalty with which Burdon followed his chief's decision has material expression in these pages. Lugard's recognition of that loyalty is summed up in his minute in 1906 that he "had never met a more conscientious and devoted officer."*

---

*Kaduna archives.

Introduction

The unifying factor in this collection is surely the unity of Hausa culture as such. In this volume we have examples from history, religion, law and the traditional literature of proverb, riddle and praise-song, in addition to anthropological comment by Hausas on their own culture and that of some of their neighbors. If we except the trivia of Part XIV, which were perhaps hardly worth preserving, the remainder presents a good selection of the knowledge of Hausa malams of sixty years ago, and as such is surely worth preserving.

In a work of this size and diversity, there will be many errors. I have tried, wherever I had doubts about the translation or suspected corruption in the original text to indicate this by a footnote or at the least by a question-mark. As references are given to the Hausa text, those with access to this and a knowledge of the language can pursue such doubtful points and, it is hoped, clear them up. The references are made thus: I/, II/ or III/ refer to the volumes of Edgar; /23 or /LXX refer to the number of the item, Arabic numerals to items from the early part of each volume, the tatsuniyoyi, Roman numerals to those from the second half of each volume, the labarai. See Concordance on page 363.

One section of the original has not been included. This is a Hausa version of the Maliki legal code (I/LXXXVII There seemed little point in including the translation of a translation, especially when an English version (Ruxton, F. H. Maliki Law. London. (Luzac). 1916) is available; and a bilingual (Arabic and Hausa) version also (Gaskiya Corporation, Zaria. Risala ta Abdullahi Ibn Abi Zaid da kuma Fassararta da Hausa c. 1962-3). A few pages are also translated in ABR 2 (p. 116 etc.).

I acknowledge with gratitude help given by Malam Ahmadu Ingawa with many difficult points of meaning throughout this volume; by Malam Na'ibi Wali for help over difficulties with the legal material; and for Mr. Ali Jahadhmi and Hajj Ahmad Baba of Zaria for advice on the Hadiths.

Neil Skinner
The University of Wisconsin

Glossary

acca (sometimes, in older style, acha)

Small cereal, _Digitaria_ exilis; not now part of H. diet, but grown on the Plateau by non-H. tribes.

Babambade

A member of a Fulani clan which specializes in singing the praises (_roƙo_) of members of the ruling houses.

baushe

Tree of the _terminalia_ family, whose wood is used for bows and cudgels.

bori

Cult of spirit-possession. References to this may be found throughout BABA. See also King, A.V. in African Language Studies VI, 1965, p. 105, and Greenberg, J. H., _Influence of Islam on a Sudanese Religion_. Monographs of American Ethnological Society X, 1946. For its manifestations in Tripoli in 1913 among Hausas there, see Tremearne, A. J. M.. _The Ban of the Bori_ (London, 1914). There are also unpublished reports by Alexander, D. (1909) and Harries, P. G. (1929) in the Kaduna Archives (File S.N.P. 4789/1909, Acc. No. 726).

Glossary

bukka	Temporary shelter, beehive in shape, made by nomad Fulani of a frame of sticks covered with leaves or grass. In the text this is sometimes translated "booth" or "shelter".
cediya	*Ficus Thonningii*, grown for both shade and fruit.
dan kama	A type of strolling minstrel.
dinya	*Vitex Cienkowskii*, a tree whose plum-like fruit are used for a number of purposes.
doka	1. A pad on top of the head into which the hair is plaited by some women. 2. The tree *Isoberlinia doka*.
durumi	*Ficus syringifolia*, grown for both shade and fruit.
faifai	Plaited, disc-shaped, mat, slightly concave, which is used for covering vessels; made with grass covered with dyed strips of the young dum-palm. A very common household object, the connotations of the word have extended to cover other objects of similar shape, such as gramophone records.

fura

The usual morning meal, pref-
erably of millet, mixed with
buttermilk and "drunk". It's
preparation involves pounding,
winnowing; pounding, winnowing--
5 or 6 times; washing; back into
the mortar for a last pounding;
making into balls and putting into boiling water; taking out and
pounding again until quite smooth;
rolling in flour; putting into a
calabash with buttermilk and
mashing.

gawasa

Gingerbread-plum tree, _Parinarium
macrophyllum_.

gawo

Acacia albida, which has the unusual property of bearing foliage
during the dry season, but not
during the rains; hence its
kirari, _ka ƙi ruwan Allah_ ("you
reject God's rain").

geza

Various species of _Combretum_.

goge

A large fiddle played with a bow.

haza wassalamu

"This with peace"--see Trans-
lator's Introduction in Vol. I.

imam (Ar.) (H. limam)

The chief _malam_ of the village
or town, who leads the prayers
at the Friday mosque.

jekadiya

Female messenger of a king or
notable (being female she has
access to purdah compounds).

Glossary

kabido	Doubled matting worn over the head as a short cape to protect the body from rain, especially by Fulani herdsmen.
kalgo	_Bauhinia reticulata_.
kirari	"Praise-songs," epithets, personal slogans or theme tunes.
kurna	_Zizyphus spina-Christi_.
magajiya	Title of the chief prostitute (H. _karuwa_ which strictly = any mature woman not married-- see BABA, p. 25), having a number of other social roles in addition.
Maguje	See Introduction to Section 2 of Vol. I.
maiwa	_Pennisetum spicatum_ millet.
malam	Muslim cleric, the standard of whose scholarship varies from a nodding acquaintance with the Koran to an extensive knowledge of the Book, the Hadiths and the Maliki legal treatises. At the lower levels he is much involved in the traffic in charms (see Trimingham, _Islam in W. Africa_).
maroki	Praise-singer, panegyrist, "beggar-minstrel".

Glossary

miya   Soup or gravy, poured over <u>tuwo</u> before eating; usually <u>romo</u>, "broth" thickened with various condiments, such as <u>daddawa</u> and baobab leaves.

nakiya   Sweetmeat made of pounded guinea-corn (or other grain) mixed with honey, and peppers.

shari'a   The Muslim law.

tambari   A hemispherical drum of various sizes, usually beaten only for kings.

tsarance   This is defined in BABA as "institutionalized love-making between unmarried youths and girls." In TATS it has sometimes been left untranslated, sometimes rendered as "dating" or "courting".

tuwo   The usual evening meal--the Hausa food <u>par excellence</u>--taken with <u>miya</u> and "eaten". Millet, guinea-corn, or--less commonly--maize is used. As with <u>fura</u>, it involves 5 or 6 poundings and winnowings; and washing, before proceeding to cook. The rougher flour is put into the boiling water first; later the finer flour. Various stages of simmer and cool follow, before dishing out into a wooden bowl. Then the <u>miya</u>, which has been prepared separately, is poured over; and, probably, groundnut oil, which has been heated, added on top.

Glossary

'yan kama   Pl. of dan kama q.v.

yari   Official in charge of prisoners, whom he kept in a cell in his compound.

zagi   One of the retainers of a king, whose function is to walk before him (or sometimes run) when he is riding. He carries usually, as a mark of his office, a red blanket over his shoulder. The number that a king has varies in accordance with his status.

zana   Thick grass screen, used for fencing or for roofing (between framework and outer thatch). A single zana might be 8' x 12', made of stout, feathery grass.

Abbreviations

ABR   Abraham, R. C., <u>Dictionary of the Hausa Language</u>. London. 1962.

Ar.   Arabic.

ABR 2   Abraham, R. C., <u>Hausa Literature and the Hausa Sound System</u>. London. 1959.

BABA   Smith, Mary, <u>Baba of Karo</u>. London. 1964.

BARG   Bargery, G. P., <u>Hausa-English Dictionary</u>. Oxford. 1951.

H   Hausa.

J   Johnston, H. A. S., <u>Selection of Hausa Stories</u>. Oxford. 1966.

LDDNY   <u>Labaru Na Da da Na Yanzu</u>. Education Department, Lagos. 1931.

M   Mischlich, A., <u>Neue Màrchen Aus Afrika</u>. Leipzig. 1929.

I
Shehu Usumanu Dan Fodio, The Reformer

--AND YUNFA, KING OF GOBIR (II/LXVI)

During the time that Shehu Dan Fodio was living at Ruggar Fakko, the King of Gobir being at Alkalawa, they were both in the same country; and people were continually trying to turn Yunfa against Shehu Dan Fodio, saying to him "Do you see that malam, that is living at Ruggar Fakko?--well, if you don't kill him, he'll take from you all that you now rule." "Is that so?" said Yunfa thoughtfully.

Then Yunfa had them dig him a well close to where he usually sat. And when they had dug it, they cleared away all the earth and taking it away outside the compound, threw it there. Then they fetched peeled hemp stalks and a skin mat, and with them covered the mouth of the well.

Presently Shehu Dan Fodio arrived. Says Yunfa, King of Gobir "Sit over here, malam. There's a mat for you." So Shehu went over and sat himself down; and Yunfa's people, his guards gathered, prepared to see Shehu Dan Fodio fall down the well, whereupon they in-

1

tended taking stones and hurling them in on to him, to
kill him. But, as they watched, he didn't fall into
the well; and he and the King of Gobir finished their
exchange of courtesies. Both of them rose; and so Shehu
Dan Fodio returned home.

On another occasion* word was brought to the King
of Gobir, Yunfa, that one of his cows was with calf, and
it was suggested that he should summon his malam. They
gathered the <u>bori</u> - men from the town, who said "Her calf
will be a female." But when Shehu came along, he said
that she would produce a bull-calf. At which the <u>bori</u>-
men said "Well, if that cow produces a bull-calf, Yunfa,
King of Gobir, you may kill us," and they went on "But
if she produces a female calf, then you must kill your
malam." "Very well" said Yunfa, King of Gobir, "Do you
hear that, malam?" "Yes, King of Gobir, I heard" answered Shehu.

Well, in due course the cow produced--a female calf.
They took it and shut it away and then sent someone to
fetch the malam. They fetched him and asked him "Malam,
what did the <u>bori</u>-men say on that last occasion?" Shehu
answered "Why do you ask? They said that if the cow
produced a bull-calf, they, the <u>bori</u>-men were to be
killed; if a female calf, they said that I was to be
killed." "Right" they said, "Well--as you shall see,
she has produced a female calf." Someone then went and
let the calf out--and there they saw a bull-calf! After
this, they didn't kill the <u>bori</u>-men, but were much a-
mazed at what had happened.

Then there was a horse, that kicked like a mule**.
And they suggested to the king that he should get his
malam to come and give this horse a thorough inspection,
"For if the horse takes it into his head to kick him,
we shall be rid of him." Now this horse would let no
one approach him, much less stroke him. But the malam
went up to him and stroked the whole of it, even right
under its stomach; and it didn't even put its ears
back, let alone kick or bite. And so the malam returned
home, to Ruggar Fakko, and resumed his life there. That's
all that I have heard of that account.

_____

*Cf. I/XLIX
**<u>Lit</u>. "like a scorpion"--for a scorpion "kicks" in H.

--AND HIS PEOPLE* (I/XXIX)

When Shehu Usumanu had come to power, Umaru-duniya came
to him, with Sulaimana Sulluɓawa and Aidaka, and they
asked him to give them flags. Said he to them "Let us
make prayer on your behalf" and he prayed for them.
Then he said "Go to Bello and let him pray for you."
"Certainly" said they. But when they reached Bello's
compound, he espied them coming, and getting up went
into the compound.

They arrived and made formal greeting, and were
told "He's inside." They waited a little, but as he
didn't come out, Sulaimana Sulluɓawa and Aidaka got up
and went off. But Umaru-duniya was of a grateful nature
and said to himself "However tasty the tuwo, it's the
better for some oil" and he stayed till the early afternoon, when Bello came out and saw him. "How about this
man?" says he, and the other answered "I am Umaru" and
told him his story. Then Bello said "Here's a prayer
for you." And though he was the youngest of the three,
Bello said "If God wills it, you will be greater than
they."

Then they returned (to the city) and the other
two were there before him. Sulaimana Sulluɓawa went
in by the Goga Gate, saw the compound of a wealthy man,
and thinking it was the Sultan's place, entered. Meanwhile Aidaka went in by the Aidaka Gate**, and he too
saw the compound of a wealthy man, and went in, thinking
it was the Sultan's place. Then, when Umaru-duniya
arrived, he too went in by the Aidaka Gate, on the west
of the city, and going on came to the compound of the
wealthy man. But he passed it and reaching the Sultan's
compound, went in there. This was on the Wednesday.

On the Thursday morning they all gathered at
Sulaimana's compound, to congratulate him. For he had

---

*Edgar's note reads "this MS is very badly written
   and expressed, and is very sketchy history."
**Deleting the full-stop after ƙofar.

received the land of Maradi, also Tasawa and eastwards
from the city to Daura. Time passed and the son of
Umaru-duniya came to pay his respects to him, and
Sulaimana said to him "I give you Shinkafi to give to
your followers." Then he gave Aidaka* Kafin Mashi and
Yanhoho and Kaita and other districts. And Sulaimana
saw the great extent of his districts, but, in fact, if
he sent his messengers to Maradi, it was if they had a
beautiful woman, but one whom you had to get out and
win possession of.

For then the pagans of Maradi said to each other
"What shall we do about this?" Now some of the sons of
the Habe king were at Karofi, enslaved. But his eldest
son was at Damagaram, whither he had fled with his possessions. And the pagans of Maradi sent to him saying
"Come, so that we may make you our king." But he answered "Since you want to make me your king, you can
send me the head of Adamu, the messenger who is sent
to you--otherwise I won't come." "Very well" said they.

So they sent to the King of Sullubawa, to send his
messenger to collect money. And he sent Adamu. When
he came, they killed him and cutting off his head, sent
it to Dan Kasawa. Then he came to Maradi and the pagans
of Maradi made him ruler of Katsina.

Then Dan Kasawa ransomed his younger brother,
Darauda, also Dan Mafedi and Dan Mari from Karofi.

And that was how a state of hostilities arose in
Maradi. So the King of Sullubawa had very little land
under his control, while Umaru-duniya had a large area,
and was the greatest of them. Moreover the hostilities
continued, without peace being established, until the
time of Mazadu, who was called "Maza-waje" King of
Katsina at Maradi.

And after him too, there was no peace till the
days of Kure, Dan Barmo, King of Katsina at Maradi.
It is he who is now Madarunfa at Maradi.

---

*This translation a little stretches the Hausa but I
  can see no other.

TWO VARIANT TRADITIONS (II/XLII)

When Shehu Dan Fodio appeared on the scene, he visited
Silame. There he asked whether there wasn't anyone who
knew where Kanta's tomb was. He was told that no one
knew--save only an old man who had been present at the
burial.

So they sent and asked him, and he said yes, certainly he knew; there were twelve tombs*. "Very well"
said Shehu, "I want you to take me there." But the old
man said that he wasn't able to get there, he wasn't
even able to leave his hut. "We'll put you on a camel"
said Shehu. "All right" said the old man, and Shehu
said "And I--indeed, if you take me there, not only you
but your children will gain great honor." "All right"
said the old man, "We'll go in the morning. Good night."

But morning came and they went along--and found
that he had died.

A TALE OF MALAM SHEHU
DAN FODIO** (II/XLII)

After Malam Shehu Dan Fodio appeared on the scene, he
came to Silame, and there asked for someone who knew
where Kanta was buried. And an old man, who was unable
to leave his hut, said that he knew. Says Shehu "Let
us go. Take me there." But the other said "I can't
walk."

Says Shehu "All right! You there, lift him up and
put him on a horse or a camel, and take him along." So
they picked him up and put him on a mare. And they took
him to Gungu, and there he showed them where Kanta's
tomb was, and they took him back to his home[+].

---

*See II/XLVI.

**See II/XLVI.

[+]I have not tried to render <u>kai</u> which seems redundant
and may have been inserted in error.

HOW HIS SON, BUHARI, CAME TO
LEAVE SOKOTO (I/XXV)

Buhari was the son of Shehu and what made him go away
was jealousy of his relative. He went away when his
father, Shehu, built Dogondaji for his grandson, Bara'u,
while Buhari was at Tambawel. When Buhari died, his
son Umaru succeeded to the title. He was succeeded by
his son, Haruna. But when Haruna died, a dispute arose
over whether his younger brother or a son of his elder
brother should succeed. His nephew did succeed, and
after him Haruna's younger brother*.

--AND THE TUAREG (II/C)

In Shehu's time the camels of a certain Tuareg went
astray. And their owner set off searching for them,
and eventually reached where Shehu dan Fodio was. He
found him sitting with two others reading the Koran.
Says the Tuareg "Malams, I'm looking for my camels, five
of them that have strayed. It is now a whole month I've
been following their traces, seeking them, and I still
haven't found them."
    Then Shehu said "Friend, look! There are your
camels there." And the Tuareg looked and said "So they
are!" And again Shehu said "Hurry and go to where your
beasts are." "All right" said the Tuareg, but he said
to himself "I need not hurry, for look how near they
are." And he travelled slowly on--and eventually the
sun set and he still hadn't reached where his camels
were, nor could he even see them. So he went back to
Shehu dan Fodio, and said "Those camels--I didn't find
them, malam." And Shehu answered "Oh, there are your
camels--look, over there! They haven't moved away at
all." And the Tuareg looked and saw his camels quite
close, and set off once more, following their tracks.
But he didn't come up with his camels for another thirty
days. Then at length he reached them.

---

*The Hausa, through its brevity, is obscure here.

So the Tuareg took hold of his camels and mounted, and went back to Shehu dan Fodio, and said "Look, malam, here are my camels, and I had to travel for thirty days before I reached them. And now another thirty days have passed, which makes sixty days in all since I left you. Malam, accept my sincerest thanks, and may God bless you! And now I must be getting home, so goodbye." And taking the road again, he went off. That's all.

ABOUT SHEHU USUMANU (I/LIV)

At the start of his career Shehu was in Gwandu, then in Sifawa, and then in Sokoto. Here I will mention fifteen things. When he was at Faru*, five of them happened. And when he had performed them to the glory of God, ten thousand people were themselves giving glory to God. And when Shehu asked what they were saying, he was told "They are praying for you, that you may achieve victory at this time."

God gave him knowledge of five things: first, the Holy War; second, the appointment of a Sultan to lead the faithful; third, that God was on his side against his enemies; fourth, the appointment of kings to the different towns; fifth, that he was not to have the opportunity to visit the House of God, as he wished. Then there were five things that God gave him knowledge of at Dagyal (?Degel): first, when he left Faru, that he should take the left road on his emigration; second, that his emigration should be during the month of Dhu 'lqa'ida; third, that his helpers were the men of Kwanni, and the Sullubawa clan, and the men of Yabo; fourth, the king he was to fight was Yunfa; fifth, he was commanded to send to the people of the Sudan, to inform them that calamity would descend on them, if they didn't become Muslims. And he sent letters to them, wherever he travelled.

---

*Reading Faru for faru which makes no sense.

Then there were five, after he had emigrated.
First, the seditious spirit that affects rulers affected his own son at Sabon Gari. Then he besought
God to prevent strife between them, and his prayer was
granted.

Second, there was the quarrel that arose between
his son and his brother of Gwandu. Again he besought
God, and this too subsided.

Third, the quarrel that arose between them, at
Sifawa. Malam Usumanu prayed, but his prayer wasn't
answered--until he had prayed for three years. Then
his prayer was heard, at the time he left Sifawa for
Sokoto.

Fourth, after he had come to Sokoto, he besought
God that strife might not arise between his descendants,
for he knew that this was a thing that often happens
between the sons of rulers who have inherited their
fathers' titles.

Fifth, if, however, this last had to occur in fact,
he besought God that it might not happen for three (years)
after his rule*--so that his case might be exactly the
same as that of the Messenger of God--in that the number of years that elapsed before strife arose among his
people was three years, that is during the caliphate of
Umar, son of al Khattab** (for it was said of Umar that
he closed the doors of strife, so that it was kept from
men's hearts). While Umar was alive, Uthman, son of
'Afan--the fourth caliph⁺--shut the door of strife, and
no sword was drawn among the faithful--but only during
his lifetime. When he was killed, fighting broke out
among the faithful, and killing, so that in one year
thirty-five thousand people were killed. And since the
sword was raised against the faithful, it will not be
lowered till the Day of Judgment. And these were the
five gifts that Shehu said he had received of God, after his emigration; God revealed these to him and he
gave his thanks to God in this world and the next.

---

*The Hausa is obscure, but the general drift fairly clear.
**He seems to have ignored Abubakar.
⁺Actually the third, but the fourth leader of the faith-
ful.

A MIRACLE* (I/LI)

We had this story of a miracle of Shehu from a man
called Dodo.

Once a trader was on his way back from Gwanja**
with his cola-nuts, two donkey-loads, travelling in a
caravan. They had reached the bank of the Niger, and
the people were being brought over. All the caravan
was safely over and only he remained.

The ferryman returned for him, and putting his
cola-nuts on board, they set out. But when they reached
midstream, a wind got up and the boat began to roll, as
if it would overturn with them. Then the trader exclaimed "Shehu, son of Fodio, help us!"

As he said that, there appeared a man in the middle
of the water close to the boat, who seized its prow and
righted it, and it ceased to roll.

Now at the time that the trader had called on
Shehu's name, Shehu was sitting with his courtiers.
Suddenly the people there saw him get up and go into
the compound. Then after a while he came forth again
to his courtiers and sat down. Then said the people to
him "Malam, we see that your gown and trousers are somewhat wet--have you dipped them in water?" And he answered "Before twenty days have passed, you will see
the reason why they are wet."

Meanwhile the trader, when he had safely crossed
the Niger, said "By God's grace, the day I get to Sokoto,
I will give Shehu five calabashes of large+ cola-nuts."

When they reached Sokoto, they stopped at the camp
for travellers, and there he sorted out three calabashes

---

*There is a different version of this in Imam, Magana
  Jari Ce, I. No. 27. For another English version, see
  J. p. 124. For a Somali analogue, see Andrzejewski
  at African Lang. Studies XV (1974) p. 31.
**Region of Ashanti.
+For marsa see goro in BARG (which conflicts with
  ABR).

of cola-nuts and added fifty assorted cola-nuts, and
went off to Shehu's compound with them. He obtained
permission to come before Shehu and going in, greeted
him. After they had exchanged greetings, he produced
the cola-nuts and said "Malam, here are alms." But
Shehu said "Oh no! That wasn't our arrangement. When
you got across the river you said that when you reached
Sokoto you would give me five calabashes of cola-nuts,
and large ones too. Why have you brought me three
calabashes and fifty nuts only? And the fifty, moreover,
are a mixed lot."

Then said Shehu to the people "You see this man?
It was he I went to the Niger to help, when their boat
was rolling and like to upset; and when I came back you
asked how my gown had got wet. I told you that before
twenty days I would tell you the reason. Well--here's
the reason, this man made the promise of his own accord.
And now, see, he has departed from it!"

Then the trader rose and returning to the camp
sorted out five calabashes of large cola-nuts, and taking
them to Shehu told him that he was sorry, and Shehu said
"I forgive you," and having said a prayer for him, he
told him "From here all the way to the city of Kano, not
even the cry of a bird will disturb your journey through
the bush, by God's grace."

The trader set out and made his way to Kano, and
nothing troubled him. That's how it was. Finis.

A VARIANT ON THE LAST (III/IV)

Once long ago, some traders had been to Gwanja and
brought back cola-nuts. Returning they had reached the
Niger, where the Gungu people* were the ferrymen. The
caravan, a large one, arrived and continued being taken
across from morning until the sun set. So they rested
for the night, and next morning began ferrying them over
again--until they were all across except for one man.

-----

*Presuming Gungawa (with capital letter) to be the
  correct reading.

This man had been helped into the canoe, and they were in the middle of the river, when a wind arose. Then the boat began to rock so much that it looked as if it would overturn in the water.

Then the trader began to say over and over "Shehu dan Fodio, help us! Shehu dan Fodio, help us!"

Now Shehu dan Fodio had a gathering of malams to whom he was teaching the Book away in Sokoto, and he suddenly said "Students, I am called somewhere."

And then Shehu dan Fodio went in a twinkling to the bank of the Niger and entered the water; grasped the edge of the canoe and, drawing it after him, so reached the bank.

Then the trader said "Praise be to God! I thank God, I thank the Messenger of God, I thank His Messenger, and I thank Shehu dan Fodio. Moreover, with God's grace, when I get to Sokoto, I will give Shehu dan Fodio twenty calabashes of cola-nuts."

Then Shehu dan Fodio returned to his pupils here, in Sokoto. And his pupils saw that as he came, he was wringing water from his gown.

His pupils asked him "Malam, has water been spilt over you?" "No" he answered, "It was one of God's servants, who was on the verge of drowning away in the Niger, and he called me. So I went and grasped the prow of the canoe--and it reached the bank safely."

He went on "But you're here and you'll see him presently when he comes. He'll be here before ten days are past."

Ten days passed and the trader arrived. He took out fifteen calabashes of cola-nuts, and said to himself "When I was back there by the Niger I said that on the day I reached Sokoto I would give Shehu dan Fodio twenty calabashes of cola-nuts, but I'll just take him fifteen now."

So the trader came to the entrance of the compound of Shehu dan Fodio. His students were gathered there, and the trader made formal greeting, and went on to say "Is the malam at hand?" "Yes" said the students.

Then Shehu dan Fodio told them to invite him in, and the trader entered. "Servant of God" said Shehu dan Fodio, "Did you arrive today?" "Yes" said the trader, "May God pardon you, malam.*"

"There" said Shehu (turning to the others), "You see the man who called me that day." And the trader said "Here are fifteen calabashes of cola-nuts that I've brought you." But Shehu answered "Twenty was what you said you would bring me, when you were on the bank of the Niger. You said that whenever it pleased God to bring you to Sokoto, you would give me twenty calabashes-- and now, see, you have brought me fifteen. Don't think I'm not grateful. May God give you his blessing, but give me two more calabashes to divide among my students. Then you can take the rest of your cola-nuts to sell."

Then the trader said "Very well. I give your students five calabashes." "No" said Shehu dan Fodio, "Just give the two I said--they'll be enough; for the rest-- take your property and sell it." And so he brought two more calabashes and gave them to the pupils of Shehu dan Fodio.

The trader went off with the rest of his cola-nuts, overjoyed that Shehu dan Fodio had given him his blessing. That's all. This with peace.

---

*A formulaic style of address to a malam (perhaps the origin is the malam's habit of himself frequently saying "I seek pardon of God.").

II

Sultans of Sokoto, Their Viziers and Fief-Holders

SULTAN MUHAMMADU BELLO AND THE PAGAN* (II/XLI)

It is said that once upon a time at Kwaido, in the land of Argungu, a pagan had three of his family taken (as slaves). He followed them till he came right to where Sultan Muhammadu Bello was. Says the pagan "Sultan, I've had three of my family taken and brought here." To which the Sultan answered "Then go you, and bring back three others to replace them**."

The pagan departed, and the same day bought the heads of two nanny-goats, and of one billy, complete

---

*Cf. III/73 which perhaps casts doubts on the authenticity of this account.

**The Hausa is lit. "three heads" or "three individuals," kai having both meanings. The point of the story depends on this double meaning which I have been unable to render in the English.

with beard. These he brought along. Says the Sultan
"Pagan, you've been very quick to get them." "I've
got them though" said the pagan, "And including a
bearded one." "Very well. Bring them in, and let's
see them." So the pagan fetched a goatskin bag, and
untied it and shook out its contents. The Sultan
laughed and said "People's heads was what I said, not
billy-goats' heads."

At which the pagan addressed the courtiers "You
were here. What did you hear the Sultan say?" And
they said "The Sultan didn't specify. All he said was
that you were to bring three heads--that was all."
"Right" said the pagan, "And here they are; I've brought
them." Then said the Sultan "Give him back the goats'
heads, and give him his three children too. The pagan
has spoken truly" said the Sultan. So they gave him
his three children and he went off with them.

VIZIER HALILU AND HIS WIFE, DAUGHTER OF
ABDULLAHI, EMIR OF KANO (II/XIX)

Halilu, Vizier of Sokoto, who was the father of Rufa'i
(among others) married the daughter of Abdullahi, Emir
of Kano. But when she was brought to his compound,
forty days passed and he never went to her hut. Then,
on the forty-first day, a storm came, and the bride
said to her slave-girl "Shut the door. My learned
husband is not going to come to my hut. Let us go
and lie down to sleep, for he is angry with me." And
they did so.

But Halilu came after all, and found that they
had shut the door. And he remained there, being unwilling to return to his own part of the compound; nor
was he willing to open the door; or to say anything,
for he felt that to do so would be unworthy. But that
it would be just as unworthy to return to his own part
of the compound. Now he was wearing a thin, heavily
indigoed gown, and he just sat there. And presently
the storm burst in a torrent of rain.

And there he sat until it grew light next morning.
Nor was it until the slave-girl opened the door that
she saw Halilu, the Vizier, sitting there--completely
drenched by the rain. The girl fell to her knees,
saying "Oh dear, how can this be! Here's the master
at the door of our hut, and he's quite drenched!" And
his wife came quickly out and she too fell to her knees,
declaring how sorry she was. As for him, he rose and
went to his own part of the compound, and there went
and stripped off the gown, and his trousers and shoes,
and put on fresh ones. And from there he went to where
his retainers awaited him.

After this the bride sent, saying that they should
go and tell her father, the Emir of Kano, that her husband was angry with her, not having visited her hut for
forty days. And that she had not closed the hut all
that time--until the forty-first day, when a storm had
come. Then she had closed the hut up, and she and her
slave-girl had gone in. That then her husband, Halilu
the Vizier, had come. But that, finding they had closed
the hut, he still didn't open the door--or even speak;
nor did he return to his own part of the compound. The
storm had broken, as he sat there, and he was soaked by
the rain. That this had gone on right until it was
light. And, when he heard this, the Emir of Kano said
"Very well! Bring me ten kitbags, with burnouses in;
and another ten with black and blue check gowns; and
ten kitbags of turbans; and ten leather flasks with
Maria Theresa dollars; and ten leather flasks full of
silver; and five leather flasks full of gold." And
they collected together all these things, and the Emir
of Kano said "Pick them all up and take them to Vizier
Halilu, as a cure for his cold; tell him please to be
patient, and not to take the matter to heart--for it
was the ignorance of youth. I beg him not to take the
matter to heart." That's the end of that account. This
with peace.

VIZIER HALILU AND THE SHARIF (II/XX)

Halilu, Vizier of Sokoto, had a guest from the East--
a Sharif, who came to visit him. And the Vizier ordered that he be taken and lodged. And it was done.

And daily the master of the house where the Sharif
lodged would buy the buttermilk for him which was then
mixed in with his <u>fura</u>. But one day his host said
"Sharif, won't you assist me in the purchase of buttermilk. For three months now you've let me buy buttermilk for you." But the Sharif answered "But, sir, I
haven't any money." And the other answered "Oh, but
you are always going to Halilu the Vizier--ask him for
some money for buttermilk. You go and pay your respects
to him every day. Now, today when you go, you ask him
for money for buttermilk." "Very well" said the Sharif.

So the Sharif went along to pay his respects to
Vizier Halilu. He greeted him and said "God give you
long life, Vizier, sir. Please, of your generosity,
give me money that I may buy buttermilk daily." "Very
well, Sharif, I see" said the Vizier, and he dismissed
him. The Sharif returned to his lodging, and so another night passed. In the morning he again went along
and paid his respects, and so back to his lodging.
Again next morning he came along and greeted the Vizier,
and said "God give you long life, Vizier, sir, but--may
I remind you about the money for buttermilk." "Very
well, Sharif, I've noted your request" said the Vizier
and dismissed him. And the Sharif returned to his
lodgings and another night passed. Next morning back
he went again, and again greeted the Vizier. And when
he left the Vizier's compound, he went strolling through
·the town.

Presently some people came with money--twenty mat
bags of cowries--which they were about to take into
the Vizier's compound, when he said "Hey! That money
there--take it to the Sharif to buy buttermilk with--
he asked for money for that." So they went, but found
the Sharif out. And they put the bags in his hut and
left them there. Shortly after that another eighty

mat bags of money were brought, which they were about
to take into the Vizier's compound, when he said "Hey!
Just take that money to where the Sharif is staying--
to buy buttermilk with; for he asked me for money for
that." And so that money too was taken, and the Sharif's
hut was full to the brim with money--on the bed and
under the bed and heaped high right to the door of the
hut. Presently another thirty bags of money were brought
to the Vizier. "Stop!" says he, "Don't take that money
in. Go back and take it to the Sharif, so he can buy
buttermilk; he asked me for money for that." And it
was taken to the compound where the Sharif was staying.

Then the master of the compound where the Sharif
lodged went into the town, seeking the Sharif, until he
found him. The Sharif returned to his lodging, and the
people said to him "Quick, make haste and go to Halilu
the Vizier and tell him that you are sorry, and ask him
to stop." Well, the Sharif went into the compound,
meaning to get his turban--and saw the money, in heaps.
Then he stuck his head into his hut, and saw bags of it.
And he would have run quickly to the Vizier to tell him
that he was sorry, but all the Sharif could do was say
again and again at the top of his voice "Help! Vizier!
Hee-hee*, money!" And he went on saying this, until
they seized him and tied him up--for the Sharif was mad.
The sight of the money had been too much for him. That's
all. This with peace.

VIZIER HALILU AND UWAR-DAJE (II/XXI)

Uwar-Daje was a daughter of Shehu dan Fodio, who, one
morning when it rained**, sent a message to Vizier
Halilu, saying "Tell the Vizier that I send him the
compliments of the season (of heavy rain)$^{+}$." When he

---

*I think that ha is a nonsense word to indicate that
  he was raving.
**Evening rain is, of course, the norm, except at the
  wettest part of the rains.
$^{+}$sc. "and expect a present in return".

heard this, the Vizier turned to his <u>jekadiya</u> and said
"Did you hear that? Uwar-Daje has sent to give me the
compliments of the season." "May your life be prolonged,
malam" answered the <u>jekadiya</u>, "Then we'll have to give
her the presents of the season, won't we?" "Yes,
<u>jekadiya</u>" he answered, "Now we must give Uwar-Daje the
presents of the season."

He went on "Go and fetch ten grass bags for clothes
and take them to her" and it was done. Again he said
"Fetch ten grass bags full of burnouses and take them to
her." And again "Fetch ten grass bags of lengths of
indigoed cloth, and take them to her." They did so.
"Fetch ten mat bags of money and take them to her" and
they did so. "Fetch ten grass bags of cloths and take
them to her." And again "Fetch ten grass bags of
burnouses and take them to her." Again he said "Fetch
ten grass bags of lengths of indigoed cloth and take
them to her." And once more "Fetch ten mat bags of
money and take them to her." - To these he added a mare,
four slave-girls and a slave-lad to cut grass for the
mare.

Then at length Uwar-Daje had her horse saddled and
came along at a gallop, till she reached the entrance
to the compound of Vizier Halilu. She dismounted, and
went and threw herself on the ground before him, saying
"Vizier Halilu, I am sorry for what I did." "Very well"
he answered, "I understand." That's all. This with
peace.

HALILU, VIZIER OF SOKOTO AND HIS SERVANT (II/XIII)

Once one of the servants of Halilu, Vizier of Sokoto,
asked him for some perfume. "Give me your flask" said
the Vizier, and the man did so. Next day, the Vizier
said to his servant "Didn't you ask me for perfume?"
"Yes" the other replied. "Then give me your flask" said
the Vizier, and the man fetched another and gave it to
him.

Next day again Vizier Halilu said to his servant
"But didn't you ask me for perfume?" "Yes" he answered.
"Then give me your flask," and he fetched one and gave
it to his master. Ten times in all this happened. But
on the eleventh day, when the Vizier again asked "Didn't
you ask me for perfume?" and being told "Yes," said
"Give me your flask," the servant said "May your life
be prolonged, but I haven't got one." Then said Vizier
Halilu "Well, that's where your good luck ends then.
But I wish you'd managed to keep giving me flasks for
three months!" For--do you know what?--the Vizier had
had every one of those flasks filled to the brim with
scent.

     Then the Vizier said to his _jekadiya_ "Bring me the
flasks of perfume." And when they brought the ten flasks,
he gave them to his servant--brimful of perfume. "That's
where your good fortune ends" he said. "If you had really
made an effort, and kept on giving me flasksfor three
months, they would all have been in the same condition
as these are." That's all.

SULTAN ALIYU (I/LXII)

Here's a tale I've heard of the days of Sultan Aliyu.
One day he gave out five hundred horses, a hundred
suits of chain mail, two hundred shields and a thousand
spears, and ordered everyone to prepare for war, for he
was about to mount. Then he wrote a letter and sent it
to the King of the Gobir pagans, telling him to make
ready, so that they might meet next day within the space
of a single farm. Then Aliyu rode forth and found the
King of Gobir, fully prepared to fight him. Then Aliyu
defeated them and drove them away. From there he went
on to Kotorkoshi, and in one day conquered ninety cities.
Then he made for Argungu, but the men of Gwandu stopped
him going on and he returned home.

SULTAN UMARU AND THE MEN OF
AZBEN (TUAREGS) (I/LXI)

This is a tale told of Sultan Umaru, the men of Azben and their serfs. They all used to gather in front of his compound, every countryman who came into Wurno to visit the market, and he would have them fed. From the market they would go on to the Sultan's compound, eat the tuwo, and then go off home. But I have heard that when Umaru died, no one else gave them tuwo, and ever since then the men of Azben have not come here so frequently, because tuwo is no longer so freely handed out--they have to buy it for themselves.

HOW DAMRI AND SABON GARI AND RUWAN
'BORE WERE CAPTURED (I/LV)

After this Sultan Umaru rode out from Wurno to war and came and stayed at Kaura. He spent seventy days there, and all the eastern area came to him. Then, on a Wednesday, he died.

The same day Abdu was made Sultan, and dismissing the kings of the east, he set out for home, spending nights at 'Boko, Faru and Gora.

Then the King of Mafara, Buzu, sent his greetings to him, but Abdu refused to receive them, saying that he should come in person. But by the time he reached Wurno, Buzu still hadn't come. Then he sent his Galadima to take his greetings, and this time they were received, but Abdu added "On condition you give up the town of Birnin Tudu." This Buzu, King of Mafara, refused to do. Then the Sultan threatened that, if he continued to refuse, he would declare him an enemy. He continued to refuse.

Then the Sultan declared him an enemy, but excluded Anka and Damri from the declaration. He put the declaration down on paper and sent it everywhere, so that the King of Mafara found himself in difficult straits. And then he expressed contrition, and gave

up Birnin Tudu. Then the Sultan told him to ride in so
that they could have a discussion and he could declare
him a friend once more, but Buzu refused to come.

Then the King of Mafara sent to the King of Gobir,
Almu, asking him to send reinforcements, to avoid his
being conquered. And Almu and his army rode and reached
Mafara. He spent two nights there, and going to Tureta,
conquered it. Then the King of Zamfara at Anka sent to
greet the King of Gobir and also Ibo, King of Katsina
at Maradi, and having sent his greetings, set out himself and, stopping at Dan Kadu, came across a party of
the Sultan's men, and fought with them till sunset.
Then he set out and went to Mafara. From there, mounting
again, he returned to Chibiri together with the King of
Katsina from Maradi. Then the Sultan became angry and
collected his army. And riding from Wurno he came and
stopped at Gamji with a large force.

He stopped again at Ruwan Bore, and mounting again
after the first prayer of the afternoon, he attacked
the Vizier and the Galadima and their party. He routed
them after a hard fight, and returned to his camp. Then
he announced that he would go forward and burn every
place from there to Anka, for he was very angry. But
his Vizier and the other kings soothed him, begging him
to forbear. Then he answered "I will forbear, on condition that my son, Marafa Muhammadu, takes a force and
attacks Sabon Gari and Babban Baki." And they all con-
curred.

So he sent off Marafa, with Laje, King of Mafara
and the King of Danko, Alin-na-Bara, and they went and
conquered Sabon Gari and Babban Baki. Then the Sultan
mounted and returned to Wurno, where he made a proclamation, ordering raiders in small parties to go to
Mafara and Anka and Damri and bring back slaves*.

Then the other side sent Galadima to declare their
contrition and to seek peace. But the Sultan said
"Buzu, King of Mafara must come here." But the King
of Mafara said that he was afraid and would not come.
Then said the Sultan "Let him give me back what I gave

---

*Emending sun kama to su kama.

him--Birnin Tudu." But he refused to do that, and the Sultan again became angry, and ordered that they should be raided. They returned home but soon again found themselves in straits, and sent in their submission asking for peace. But he refused them peace, till they had expelled Buzu. So they expelled Buzu, and then the Sultan ordered all of them to come to him--which they did.

Then he appointed Ali to be King of Mafara and imposed a tribute of a thousand slaves on them. They accepted and chose to give mares and donkeys, at the rate of a beast for a slave, and they paid in full.

Then Ibo too found himself in difficulties, and sent his submission to the Sultan and sought peace. But this was refused unless he came in person, which he refused to do. But soon he was again in difficult straits and again sent to seek peace. But the Sultan again insisted that he should come himself, and again he refused. Again the same situation arose, and still the Sultan refused him peace unless he came. At last he was really reduced, with all access to the outside cut off, and mounting, he went to the Sultan himself to sue for peace. But the Sultan saw that even if he granted him peace, he was not to be trusted, and he killed him. And then he gave Damri and Sabon Gari and Babban Baki and Ruwan Bore to Na-Abu, King of Burmi.

Then Hasan, King of Zamfara, at Anka sent in his submission to the Sultan and sued for peace. He was told to come in. So he mounted and went in, and was granted peace. Then the Sultan gave him a present of clothes and sent him home, and, mounting, he made his way home.

THE KING OF TAMBAWEL WHO USED TO
WALK OUT AT NIGHT (I/XXXV)

It is said that once the King of Tambawel took a cloth and covered himself with it and walked out through the town late one night. And he came to a compound with a cornstalk fence right on the road. Then he hid against

the fence and listened, and he heard a woman talking
with her husband, and she said "The way things are with
this King of Tambawel--may God make them less difficult
for us!" and her husband said "Amen." And then the
King went back to his compound.

Next morning he came out to his assembled courtiers
and had the woman and her husband summoned. They came
before him and, both kneeling, said "May God prolong
your life!" But the King of Tambawel said to her "Woman!
What did you say last night when you were in bed with
your husband?" Then she answered "May God prolong your
life, I said nothing." But he said "Do you swear before
God that last night you didn't say that you wished that
God would make the present state of things less difficult
for you, and that your husband didn't say 'Amen'?" Then
she bowed her head, and he said "Very well! You can pay
a hundred thousand cowries." And they paid a hundred
thousand cowries, but with great difficulty for they
were poor people, with barely a cowrie.

From that day to this no one in Tambawel speaks
ill of another behind his back.

HOW UMARU NAGWAMATSE CAME TO
LEAVE SOKOTO (I/XXX)

Umaru Nagwamatse was a son of Atiku, who was the son
of Shehu Usumanu, son of Fodio. "Son of Fodio" means,
in Filani, "son of a cow". Nagwamatse's mother was a
concubine of Atiku, a Kwararafa girl. When he was
born, Atiku's relatives advised him to get rid of her
as she had borne a very devil of a boy. But he refused
and kept her. In fact, he trusted her so much that he
would leave his things with her: all his weapons were
with her. Atiku died when Ahmadu Rufa'i was Sultan.

Umaru Nagwamatse left Sokoto on the day of the
Greater Festival. The prayers had been said outside
the town, and the people had returned and reached the
Taramniya Gate. Then he spurred his horse to a gallop,
and his black straw hat* fell off. His _zagi_ picked

---

*Worn loosely over the turban.

it up for him, but he said "Put it back on the ground!
No one else picks up what I drop for me." So the _zagi_
put it back, and he spurred his horse up to it, made
him kneel and then stretch out full length. Then he
put out his hand and picked up his straw hat, and so
they re-entered the town.

But in the afternoon, leaving the town by the
Taramniya Gate for the usual celebrations of the Festival, he spent the night at Shuni. Then, leaving
there, he went to Tureta, from there to Dimasa, from
there to Bakura, Jandamo's town. After that he spent
a night at Gora, and then Faru, and then Kaura. From
Kaura he went to Zurmi, from there to Kamane, and into the land of Katsina. Then into the land of Kano.
At that time Ahmadu Rufa'i son of Umaru was Emir of
Katsina and Usumanu, Maje Ningi*, Emir of Kano. On
he went to Zazzau, whose Emir then was Abdu. From
there to Kafi, and then Nupe.

·He found them involved in a war with Umar, a
Kanuri in origin, who had come there to trade, when
Masaba was Emir of Nupe. Masaba trusted him and made
him his war leader, giving him his warriors to go out
and conquer other towns. But when he had become powerful, he set up his own rebel camp, and began to war
with the Nupes, leaving as a ruin any town he captured
throughout the land. Umar's opponent was Umaru Majigi
who strove to subdue him.

Umaru took to sending many presents to Umar's
wife, all without Umar knowing. When she had received
many of these, she asked him "What do you want from
me?" and Umaru replied "I want your husband's cap--get
that for me." "Very well" said she and, getting it,
she sent it to him. And still Umar knew nothing of it.
Then one day he saw the host of Umaru Majigi, son of
Masaba, Emir of Nupe, appear and said to his wife "Give
me my cap!" But she complained of pains in her stomach
and refused to get up, in spite of all the efforts made
to persuade her to do so.

---

*I.e. he who died in Ningi.

Then he mounted, went out and set forth. And the
battle was fought and Umar's men were routed and some
of them killed. And he too left them and went off,
travelling till he reached the water of Chanchaga. Dis-
mounting there, he performed his ablutions and jumping
into the water, died.

At that time Umaru Nagwamatse had but few people.
But Umar's people came over and joined him, and fought
on his side, till there came a day when they conquered
a town called Lalle. There his son Abdu was killed.
Then said Nagwamatse to his people ."We've conquered
Lalle, and the fame of it has reached even to Sokoto.
Where shall we conquer next, so that they may be astonished at that too?" And they said to him "Let us go and
conquer the great city of Yauri." So they went and conquered the city of Yauri.

After that Umaru Nagwamatse had their bukkas set up
at Kwantagora, and later a city built there, from where
he attacked the towns of the Yauri people and of the
land of Zazzau, and the districts of Nupe, the land of
Katsina, Birnin Gwari (the city of the Gwari), and lastly
Kogo. And when Umaru Nagwamatse died, his son succeeded
to the title, and after him Ibrahimu--and he is still
emir today.

THE CHARACTER OF SULTAN ABDU (I/XII)
(Abdurrahman, 1891-1902)

Here's a story of Sultan Abdu--"Unbaked Pot"--in the time
when he killed people so freely. Anyone convicted of
any offence against him he would have killed. Forbearance and mercy were unknown to him. If any man begged
him to forbear, he would himself rush at the man and
kill him. In the days just before the European occupation, if he saw anyone wearing shorts and a singlet, he
would have him seized and killed*.

Then one day, at this time, an upright man committed
some offence and was brought before the Sultan. "Is this

---

*? because such garb indicated traffic with Europeans?

the fellow?" said he and was told that it was. "Cursed hypocrite" said the Sultan, "I'll kill you right away." But the man said "May God prolong your days! For the honor of Shehu Dan Fodio, spare me!" But he answered "You go off to the place where Shehu Dan Fodio is!" and his throat was cut like a beast. And the courtiers said to themselves "May God preserve us from the nature of this ruler! May God part us and him without further ill!"

SULTAN ABDU, "UNBAKED POT" (II/XVIII)

Another account of something from Sokoto. Sambo, Sultan Abdu's son, had a horse, which broke free and entered someone's compound. There it attacked the householder's horse. He came out and struck the horse of the Sultan's son. Well, the blow that he gave it, by ill-chance, brought about the horse's death. And word of it was brought to Sultan Abdu, "Unbaked Pot", how someone had struck the horse of his son.

Then Sultan Abdu ordered "Go and arrest the man-- him and his horse, and take them to the market and kill the horse. And kill the man too, and take him and put him on top of the horse, for everyone, for all the people of Sokoto to see. Then they won't do that again in future." So they went and arrested the man, and brought him along, together with his horse. "Take them to the market" said the Sultan.

Then they were taken to the market--at Dajin Malleri here--and the horse and its owner were both put to death. And the man's body was left on top of the horse, for everyone to see.

Now this was something that Sultan Abdu caused to be done here, in Sokoto. It is not a rumor, or a mere report; this was done, here, in Sokoto, and everyone knows it. That's all. This with peace.

SULTAN ABDU AND HIS CONCUBINES
AND WIVES (II/XIV)

During his reign, Sultan Abdu--"Unbaked Pot"--forbade
the practice of sapphism with an artificial penis, both
in the town and in his own compound.

One day, however, he went into his compound very
quietly, and caught his concubines at it. He had them
seized, and ordered that the Yari should be sent for.
And when the Yari arrived, he said to him "Take these
concubines and go and cut their throats." So he had
the Yari kill them. Then he had the plaits on the heads
of each knotted together; and a pole brought and erected.
And there he hung them.

Then said he "Fetch here my wives, my concubines
and the slave-girls who are not secluded." "Come here
and look" he told them. And they went, and looked--and
then ran quickly away. "By God above" he said to them,
"So will I treat every one of you that I find doing this
thing." That's all.

MORE ABOUT SULTAN ABDU, THE
"UNBAKED POT" (II/XV)

During the reign of Sultan Abdu, "Unbaked Pot," he made
a law; he summoned the keepers of the Sokoto gates and
said to them "You're not to allow any man that you don't
know come into my city--wherever he may come from. You're
to come first and tell me." Thus whenever he saw a
travelling trader, he would put him to death; so too
with Yoruba people, on the grounds that they were
Christians.

Well, the men of Argungu were harassing the people
of Gande continually with their attacks; and one day
thirty of the chief men of Gande set out from Gande and
made their way to Sokoto. And they arrived at the Kadê
gate. Now the keeper of that gate had gone off to market, but had left someone in charge, and he it was that
they found there when they arrived. Says he "Hey! Where

are you from?" "We're from Gande" they said, "We're
going to the Sultan." "Then pass" said he, and they
passed in.

They made their way to the gate of the Sultan's
compound and word was brought to him. "Tell them to
come in" said he. When they reached him, he asked them
"Where are you from?" "We're Gande men" they answered.
"Which gate did you enter by?" "The Kade gate." And
the Sultan ordered that the keeper of the Kade gate be
summoned. They fetched him, and Sultan Abdu said to
him "What about the orders that I gave you? Why did
you let these men in, without sending to tell me?" "May
God give you the victory" said the keeper of the gate,
"I wasn't there. I had gone to market, but I left someone in charge. And it was he, when they arrived, who
told them to pass in." "Yari" said the Sultan, "Seize
him!" And the Yari seized the keeper of the gate. Then
the Vizier, Buhari, rose and came before him; and the
Galadima of the town; and the Magajin Gari; and the
Majidadi; and the Sarkin Rafi; and his own younger sister, Modi's wife too. All the leading men of Sokoto
came to the Sultan and pleaded with him. They besought
him in the name of God, and of His Messenger, and of
Shehu Dan Fodio that he would spare the keeper of the
gate, and not kill him. And the Sultan said "All right.
I see. Let it be." But then he called the Yari over
and said to him "Go now and take the keeper of the gate
by night, and go with him outside the Wurno gate*, and
there behead him. Tomorrow morning I shall be going for
a ride. When I pass under the Wurno gate*--let me see
the keeper of the gate's head close by that gate." Says
the Yari "Consider it done," and he took the keeper of
the gate away, and went and cut off his head.

Next morning the Sultan went riding, and came to
the Wurno gate, and there he saw the head of the keeper
of the gate on the ground. "Praise be to God!" said he,

*I.e. the gate of the city through which passes the
 road to Wurno, a few miles N.E. of Sokoto, where the
 Sultan had a residence.

"Blasted infidel!" But when he entered the town he was
taken ill, and he never left Wurno again, but died there.
And people said "Good! God has rid us of an evil ruler."

And they went on "Of all the rulers we have had at
Sokoto, we have never had one as evil as this. See the
calamity that has overtaken him, for refusing to listen,
although he was appealed to in the name of God and His
Messenger. And now God has exacted the penalty for his
crime against the gate-keeper. May God preserve us from
such a wicked Sultan! But since He has rid us of him,
we thank Him and we thank His Messenger. Now we shall
get food to eat, traders will again come in and the town
will revive." This with peace.

YARIMA DURBAL* AND THE MALAM (II/XXVIII)

When Abdu, "Unbaked Pot", was Sultan, his son Yarima
Durbal* went out of the city riding, and reaching
another town, stopped there. His eye fell on the
daughter of a malam there, a beautiful maiden, of age
to marry. Said Yarima Durbal to his servants "See
that girl there? Go and get her for me." And they
went over and brought her.

But the girl's father--who was a malam--followed
her. Says he "For shame, Yarima Durbal!" and again
"In the name of God and His Prophet, let my daughter
go, and don't dishonor her!" But Yarima Durbal answered "You--you damned bastard! I'll have you thrashed
here and now." "Very well" said the malam, "I understand. Go ahead--but by God's help, and that of His
Messenger, she's the last woman you'll ever enjoy."

And the malam returned home, washed himself, performed his ablutions, and going into his hut, prayed
to God. And so Yarima Durbal became impotent.

The news reached Sultan Abdu, "Unbaked Pot", and
he had the malam summoned. Says he "I hear that you
have made Yarima Durbal impotent." "Sultan" said the
malam, "Thus it was. And I did it." Then Sultan Abdu

---

*Yarima being his title, and Durbal his fief. See
J. p. 139.

"Unbaked Pot", said "I'll give you money, if you will only, for God's sake, undo the magic that you have performed." But the malam answered "May your life be prolonged--but the pen nib is dry now. The only thing that will enable me to undo this magic is the restoration of my daughter's virginity." Says Sultan Abdu "I'll give you a thousand bags of cowries*." But the malam said "No, no. Sultan, you heard what I told you. I said that my daughter's virginity must be restored."

Now, at this period Sultan Abdu was having people killed very freely. If anyone committed some slight offence, he would order him taken out and killed. But the malam rose and made his way home unharmed--before the eyes of everyone. Nor did Sultan Abdu ever say another word to him, as long as he lived.

But as for Yarima Durbal, he's still alive, but he has been impotent ever since. That's all.

SULTAN ABDU, "UNBAKED POT" (II/XXXIII)

Once when Abdu, "Unbaked Pot", was Sultan, he went to Wurno and was in residence in his compound there. The sun was setting one day, when a young slave-lad from the compound of the judge of Daji**, went to the market that was just by the entrance of the Sultan's compound. Along comes a girl, selling bean-flour dumplings. The slave-lad went up to the girl and seized her, intending to drag her off and rape her, very much against her will. Now, he didn't know it, but it chanced that the Sultan had come to the entrance of his compound, and with one hand on the doorway was standing there watching what was going on in the market by the entrance to his compound. Then he saw the slave-lad from the compound of the judge of Daji** dragging the girl away against her will.

---

*I.e. one million, or say $60-$70 at the 1900 rate of
   exchange from cowries to sterling.
**Or, perhaps, "rural judge".

Then said Sultan Abdu, "Unbaked Pot" "Hey! Arrest
that fellow!" And he was seized and brought over. Then
the slave-lad expressed his contrition and promised
never to do it again. But the Sultan said "I--I'll have
you put to death instantly."

But word reached the judge, his master, that the
Sultan had had the boy arrested, and he came along and
said to the Sultan "In the name of God, in the name of
His Messenger, by Bello's tomb and by Shehu Dan Fodio's
tomb, spare my slave-lad; I'll ransom him with two
slaves, which I'll bring you." But Sultan Abdu, "Unbaked Pot", said "Judge of Daji, spare us your joking!
I'm having your slave-lad put to death at once."

And so the Sultan had the boy from the judge's
household slaughtered--just like a ram. That's all,
that's the end of that account.

THE EASTERN EMIRS AND SULTAN ABDU,
"UNBAKED POT" (II/XXIII)

The Emir of Misau, who was called "Mai-Manga" went and
bought a brown ram and a white ram. Says he "The white
ram is Abdu "Unbaked Pot", the Sultan, and the brown
ram is me, Emir of Misau, Mai-Manga. Now if the Lord
God has destined me to conquer the Sultan, the brown
ram will knock down the white ram." And he put them
to fight each other.

For he was refusing to visit Sokoto to pay homage
to Sultan Abdu, "Unbaked Pot". Well, the two rams set
to, fighting, and the white one butted the brown one,
and the front legs of the brown one gave way and he
knelt. Then said Mai-Manga "So the Sultan is stronger
than I. Then, even if I don't go in person, I'll send
a representative."

So that year he wouldn't go, nor would he for
several years after. Nor was he the only one. For
Aliyu, Emir of Kano, and Abubakar, Emir of Katsina,
and Kwasau, Emir of Zazzau, and Mai-Gardo, Emir of
Daura, and the Emirs of Kazaure and Hadeja, and Umaru,
Emir of Bauchi, and the Emirs of Katagum and Adamawa--
all these refused to go to Sokoto and pay homage during

the reign of Sultan Abdu, "Unbaked Pot". For he was an evil man, and that was why they refused.

But when Attahiru, son of Amadu became Sultan--he was the one driven out by the Europeans and who went to Bima where they pursued and fought him--during his reign Aliyu Mai-Sango, Emir of Kano, hearing that Attahiru had become Sultan, said "Good! Come, men of Kano and let us go to Sokoto, that I may do homage to Sultan Attahiru, son of Amadu." He continued "When Abdu became Sultan, he treated us as enemies--and not only me, but all the emirs on this side of the bush."

So they set off for Sokoto, but when he reached the bush, word was brought him that the Europeans had reached his town. "I see" said he, "Then I must hasten and get to the Sultan to pay him my homage. Then I'll come back." When he arrived at Sokoto, the Sultan heard of it and said "Excellent! God bless you, Aliyu" and repeated his words. And Sokoto was filled with horses to overflowing.

The day came when the Sultan gave Aliyu leave to depart, and he set out and took the road for Kano. He sent his people ahead, but himself turned back, taking a northerly course. As for his people, they reached Kotorkoshi and passed it, and there clashed and fought a battle with the soldiers of the Europeans. The Vizier of Kano was quickly killed, and the rest fled.

Meanwhile the Emir of Kano continued on his way, till he reached Chibiri (Tsibiri). News of him reached Magaji Karnanne Babba, son of Tamashaya, and he set off and came up with the Emir in the middle of the bush. But--though Emir Aliyu didn't know it--the Europeans and their soldiers were following him. They caught up with him there, in the district of Gobir, arrested him and took him away. Then they appointed Abashe (or Abbas) Emir of Kano--and he is still emir. That's all.

SULTAN ABDU, "UNBAKED POT" AND MALAM MASALLACHI (II/CIII)

Malam Masallachi of Katami was living here at Katami, an ally of Isma'ila, King of Kebbi. And once Sultan

Abdu, "Unbaked Pot", brought an army to attack Argungu.
Whereupon the King of Kebbi, Isma'ila, sent to Katami,
to Malam Masallachi, saying "Whenever you get news that
Sultan Abdu, 'Unbaked Pot', has set out from Sokoto to
come and attack Argungu, let me know of it, Malam
Masallachi." And Malam Masallachi agreed.

Presently Abdu "Unbaked Pot" reached Katami and
dismounted by the gawasa* trees on the river bank, over
there to the north of Katami on the light-soiled higher
ground. Now he had sworn that when he got to Katami he
would seize Malam Masallachi and kill him.

So Sultan Abdu sent his guards with orders to go to
Malam Masallachi's compound and put up there**. As for
Malam Masallachi, he watched the road for signs of a
messenger from the King of Kebbi. But Isma'ila, King
of Kebbi, sent no messenger to Malam Masallachi. So
Malam Masallachi wrote on three arrows, and saddling
his mare called his eldest son (whose name was Abdul
Mumuni). Says the malam "Come here and mount the mare,
and hasten to Argungu, to Isma'ila, King of Kebbi, and
say to him that he told me that if Sultan Abdu, 'Unbaked
Pot' came here, he would send me a messenger to summon
me to join him in Argungu. Tell him that I have watched
the road for his messenger, but haven't seen him. Ask
him how this can be, and tell him that these three arrows are to be fired off first, when Sultan Abdu, 'Unbaked Pot' begins to attack; after that he may, if he
wishes, begin the battle." And off went his son and
brought the arrows to the King of Kebbi, Isma'ila.

Then Malam Masallachi saw the guards in his compound. Now it happened that the king of the town, Samna,
had gone out to pay his respects to the Sultan, leaving
Malam Masallachi alone with his servant and his younger
son, Malam Abubakar, who was then quite small.

Malam Masallachi sent off his servant, telling him
to go to Samna, the head of the town, and suggest to him
that they should go and pay their respects together.
And the servant went along to Samna's compound to do so,

---

*Parinarium macrophyllum.
**Or, possibly just "dismount there".

but when he got there he found that they had all already
gone off to the Sultan's camp to pay their respects.
And the servant returned to his master, Malam Masallachi,
and said "Oh, malam--there is no one left in the whole
town, except us."

Now it was between nine and ten in the morning,
and Malam Masallachi rose and performed the prayers
appropriate to that time*, first duly carrying out the
ritual ablutions and putting on his white gown and white
cloth. And he went on to perform the prayers appropriate
to the early afternoon and those of the evening too. Then
said he "Good! God be praised that I have done the afternoon prayers and the evening prayers. If my head is
still on my shoulders at sunset, I'll perform the sunset prayers."

At that time Malam Masallachi's mother was still
alive. He rose and went to her. "Mother" says he, "Give
me your forgiveness and may God cause us to meet again!"
And his mother answered and said "My boy, go your way,
you have my forgiveness in this world and the next."
"Praise be to God" said he, "Since you have forgiven
me, mother, I, Malam Masallachi, thank God."

And rising, he took the road and set off. But his
mother came along, all bent as she was, and caught him
up. Says she "But you're not to show any cowardice,
even if you're going to be killed. If you show cowardice, then I don't forgive you." Then indeed he lamented
bitterly.

But he went on till he came near to the Sultan.
He approached no one to be an intermediary to request
permission for him to approach the Sultan with his
respects, but went right up to Abdu, the Sultan, walking
with a swagger. And so Malam Masallachi came, tossing
the sleeves of his gown carelessly, right up to the
Sultan.

The Sultan was lying on his side on a mat under a
gawasa tree, together with his imam, and he was reading
from Dala'ilu**. Says the imam "Here's that infidel

---

*Not one of the normal five.
**A well-known book of prayers, Dalā'ilul Khairāti.

puppy come. Sultan, if you don't kill this Malam
Masallachi, but spare him--then neither will you kill
Sama, King of Kebbi. Kill Malam Masallachi, this in-
fidel here, and then we can go on and kill Sama."

But for the whole morning Sultan Abdu, "Unbaked
Pot", said not a word to Malam Masallachi. The sun
passed its zenith, and the Sultan said "Imam, I don't
see the judge, where is he?" So a servant was sent to
tell the judge that Sultan required his presence. The
judge mounted and rode over, and when he got there dismounted and approached the Sultan. Says "Unbaked Pot"
"Is that you, judge?" "Yes" says the other.

Then said the Sultan's _imam_ "Judge, why did you
let this infidel come here--this enemy of almighty God?
Why have you spared him?"--three times he asked him.
And the judge answered the Sultan's _imam_ "Where is the
infidel you speak of?" The _imam_ pointed to Malam
Masallachi, and the judge said "But--this man is no
infidel, for since coming here you have enjoyed the
benefit of his virtue." "What!?" said the other, "Why
do you say that, judge?" "Well" answered the judge,
"I say it because some men in this army of yours were
without food, but when they reached this town, they
obtained food. Well, this good fortune was all due to
God and to his Messenger--that you were able to obtain
food. If this malam hadn't been in this town, there
would be no one here now, in Katami, except birds.
God forbids that this town be ravaged; so does the
Prophet of God; and so too does Malam Masallachi."
Whereupon the judge was given leave to depart and he
went home.

But Malam Masallachi spent the whole day just sitting there, in the full sun; sitting in front of Sultan
Abdu, "Unbaked Pot". At one point he crossed his legs,
and the Sultan looked at him, but Malam Masallachi
avoided his gaze.

The Sultan made a sign with his hand, and every
one in the camp leapt up and came running. Then someone said "All right, all right--it's nothing." But
they galloped over to where the judge was, intending
to kill him. And presently the Sultan's mat was taken

up and carried into the little fenced compound there.
But Malam Masallachi just went on sitting there, until
all this hubbub was over.

A little later the Sultan's official, 'Yan Ruwa,
sent to Malam Masallachi. By then Malam Masallachi was
covered in dust and dirt--even his face. And two servants took his hands and helped him to his feet.

And he walked over to where 'Yan Ruwa was. When
he got there, he found the chief man of his village,
Samna. "Is that you, Malam Masallachi?" asked 'Yan
Ruwa. "Yes" said he. "And so you're still up to your
old tricks, are you?" says 'Yan Ruwa, and went on "Malam
Masallachi, why have you not come with your respects*
to the Sultan this year?" "Who says so?" answered Malam
Masallachi, "Who accuses me of not going and paying my
respects to the Sultan?" and he went on "Look, 'Yan Ruwa,
I on my own from my compound--leaving aside any of my
family--gave thirty bundles of corn and a ram worth
seventeen thousand cowries; and members of my family gave
a hundred bundles of corn." "Oh" said 'Yan Ruwa, "But
when Samna came, he said that the presents were his
gift and that you had given nothing." "Very well, 'Yan
Ruwa" said Malam Masallachi, "Seeing that he says that
I gave nothing--very well, now I haven't yet paid for
that ram that I bought for seventeen thousand. And now
I won't pay for it, and I am declaring as much in front
of you, 'Yan Ruwa. But Samna--he can pay the price of
the ram. But lend me one of your servants to come with
me to my compound, and I'll give him two rams--one for
you and one for the Sultan." And Malam Masallachi rose,
returned to his compound and gave them two rams. And
these were taken out to the camp.

Then Samna said "Malam Masallachi--in front of
'Yan Ruwa--I ask you to get up and come home with me."
But Malam answered "Oh, no! I'm not coming with you!
For if we go together now, when you get back into the
town, you'll start saying that it was you rescued me
from the Sultan." And the people there laughed. And
another man said "Come on, Samna, let us go. Leave

*In tangible form.

Malam Masallachi to his own devices; for if he refuses
to do something, in this whole world there is no one
can make him do what he doesn't want to." And so Samna
got to his feet and went off home on his own.

Then Malam Masallachi too rose, walked a little
way back along the path, and then stopped to say the
prayers appropriate to the time between sunset and the
last prayer at night*. From there he went on, reached
his compound and going in, settled down again.

His mother rose and came to him "My boy" said she,
"I thought that you were killed. But now I find you
still alive!" "Yes, I'm still alive, mother" he said.
And so the night passed.

Next morning, before it was light, the drums started
up to mark the Sultan's advance to Argungu. And some of
the footmen came into Katami, right here, into the compound of Malam Masallachi, shooting their arrows. And
the malam took his satchel. Now** one of his wives,
whose name was Ige, had not long before had a child,
and had the girl fastened on to her back. To her Malam
Masallachi said "Be off with you, Ige! Get up and go
into the town and take the boy, Abubakar, with you!"
But she answered that she wasn't going anywhere. One
of his servants said to her "Ige, do you want to have
Malam Masallachi killed before your eyes?" As he said
these words, someone fired an arrow, which passed behind Ige's back, and hit the nose of the little girl
she was carrying--and carried the nose clean away.

And Malam Masallachi's servant again said "There,
Ige--do you see what I meant? I was just saying that
you should go off out into the town." But Ige answered
"Not likely! All the others who've gone out into the
town, are being driven away (into slavery)."

---

*As at note above--Malam M. seems to have been char-
  acterized by supererogation.
**The apparent zeugma after dauki seems improbable H.
  I therefore postulate a full stop after tasa, and
  take da = akwai (which is common).

But when news reached the Sultan that the footmen
had entered Katami and were fighting there, he sent his
horsemen with orders, saying "Go and reprimand the footmen and tell them to come out of Katami." And so they
were duly driven out. But, as for Malam Masallachi, he
too left Katami and made his way to Argungu.

And when Sultan Abdu, "Unbaked Pot", attacked
Argungu, he was routed by Sama'ila, and fled home,
passing Katami, to which he never returned. When he
got home, he said to his imam "I can tell you now that
that obstinate fellow at Katami--Malam Masallachi was
his name--when he sat there that time caused me some
fear. For there--I seemed to see him lifted up on
stilts*."

And to his dying day, Abdu never returned to Katami.
And it was Malam Masallachi himself who, on the 13th
of the month of Muharram, told me what happened between
Sultan Abdu and himself.

He told me too that Abdu "Unbaked Pot" had on a
check-pattern cap, and that he was surprised to see that
he was a good-looking man, light-skinned. Also he had
the scars of smallpox, his eyes were red and his hair
grey, with side-whiskers.

And Malam Masallachi went on to say, that even when
he was old, he could still see Abdu "Unbaked Pot" and
grow frightened at the sight. For never, he affirmed,
had he seen a man the like of Abdu "Unbaked Pot".

The people of Sokoto marveled for a long time at
this incident. Previously, if Abdu "Unbaked Pot" had
said that he was going to kill a man, he would kill him.
But this time, although he had sworn before leaving
Sokoto that when he reached Katami he would kill Malam
Masallachi, when Malam Masallachi came and sat down in
the same place as the Sultan, Abdu "Unbaked Pot" failed
to kill him.

As for Malam Masallachi, he is still here, living
in Argungu, and if a thief steals something from him,
and they come and tell him what has happened, saying
"Malam, you've had a theft," he will answer "Oh--I sup-

---

*I.e. miraculous recognition of the malam's piety.

pose it's cornstalks from the farm*?", and he will go
on "Stay where you are--don't leave the compound. It'll
be brought back." And that is just what happens. The
man who took it, comes and says "Malam, here, I've
brought your property back to you," and the other says
"Good, put it down there." And the thief does so and
goes his way.

That's all for that account, which I got about
Malam Masallachi, father of Abdul Mumuni, father of
Malam Abubakar. They are all here, in Argungu. (For
more on Sultan Abdu, see Kano Traditions.)

HOW ATTAHIRU, SON OF AHMADU
BECAME SULTAN (III/VIII)

On the death of Sultan Abdu, "Unbaked Pot"--when he
died at Wurno--the Sultan's sons**, all of them, gathered, and having considered the matter, declared that
the office would go to Attahiru, son of Aliyu--that is
the present Sultan, whom the Europeans confirmed when
they took Sokoto.

Then Attahiru, son of Ahmadu, went to Marafa and
said "See here now, Marafa--don't make me suffer double
shame⁺; for the office of Sultan, I surely wish to hold
it." And Marafa answered "For myself, Attahiru, what
I am fearful of is that, when you are Sultan, you take
away what little wealth I have collected." But Attahiru
said "What, Marafa!! I--look, if it is God's will that
you do this for me⁺⁺, I shall let you be. Whatever
you do, I'll not say anything to you; but leave you to
the judgment of God." And then Marafa said "For you see,

---

*I am not certain of the exact significance of this
   remark, but imagine that the point is that this is
   the sort of theft that is easiest to get away with
   and unlikely to be pinned down, in normal circumstances.
**Or perhaps, vaguer, "males of the ruling families".
⁺? i.e. miss the selection twice?
⁺⁺I.e. help me become Sultan.

Attahiru, when our father died, I only had the one
horse." He went on "Well, now, if you were to become
Sultan and take away all the wealth I possess--I couldn't
agree to this." And Attahiru, son of Ahmadu, again assured him that he would touch nothing of his.

Then Marafa summoned allies. This was the day before the morning when Attahiru, son of Aliyu, was to
have the office of Sultan confirmed to him (that is the
present Sultan). Along comes Marafa, Mai-turare, with
Tuaregs and guns of French make; and they go into the
mosque, where the new Sultan was to be made, by Vizier
Buhari and the others.

And Marafa said to the Tuaregs and the men with
the guns "When you hear the royal drum beaten to announce that a new Sultan has been made, if it is not
Attahiru, son of Ahmadu, then everyone who comes out
of the mosque--kill them, and don't pick and choose,
and that includes Attahiru, son of Ahmadu."

Then they heard the royal wooden trumpets blown
and the drums beaten, announcing that God had given
Attahiru, son of Ahmadu, the office, and then Marafa,
Mai-turare said "God be praised."

That was the origin of the enmity between Marafa,
Mai-turare and the present Sultan, though a European
officer did reconcile them. For the present Sultan
wanted the Europeans to arrest Marafa, Mai-turare.

But, as for Mai-turare, if the Europeans demanded
corn for the horse-soldiers, Mai-turare would busy himself for fourteen days bringing in corn, saying "I've
saved you the trouble, Sultan." And again he would
say "Anything the Europeans ask for, Sultan, send word
to me, and I'll give you my aid." And even now, Marafa,
Mai-turare still acts thus. So their relations became
very slightly more amicable.

Still in the time of his elder brother's sultanate,
the Emir of Kano, Aliyu Mai-sango, made a visit here to
Sokoto for the purpose of doing homage. The Sultan,
Attahiru, expressed his pleasure and thanked him and
prayed God's blessing on him. And Sultan Attahiru, son
of Ahmadu, in addition, bestowed his own daughter on
him in marriage. Then the Emir of Kano said "My thanks.
May God's help be with you! May God give you length of
days."

Then, one day Aliyu, Emir of Kano, made his preparations and set out to return to Kano. And as he travelled, he met with a man who told him that Kano had been
taken. Then the Emir of Kano, Aliyu, ordered him to be
seized and tied up. And it was done.

They set off again, and presently as they travelled,
met with two more men, who also reported that the Europeans
had taken Kano. "Seize them and tie them up" ordered the
Emir of Kano. And it was done.

But presently as they travelled along they met the
senior wife of Aliyu, Emir of Kano, and then he said
"So this thing is true after all." They reached their
lodgings at night. That night the Emir of Kano rose and
fled.

Next morning when it was light, the Vizier of Kano
mounted and came to the entrance of the Emir's compound,
saw no one, then dismounted and went into the compound.
When he found no one there, he came out again, put foot
to stirrup and mounted. And all the men of Kano followed
after him.

They had passed Kotorkoshi, when they fell in with
the soldiers with the Europeans. Battle was joined,
and on that day the Vizier of Kano was killed. But
Aliyu, Emir of Kano, had fled and made his escape to
the North.

After Sokoto had been taken, a European officer
was sent North to Chibiri in the land of Gobir. There
he took Aliyu, Emir of Kano.

They brought him down through Sokoto and Argungu
and took him away. He is still away, he has not returned
to his home in Kano. That's all. That's the end of what
I know about that.

HOW THE FIGHTING WITH THE MEN OF SATIRU
CAME ABOUT* (III/IX)

This is the origin of the Satiru fighting. There was a
malam called Malam Mai-ƙaho**, who lived there and prac-

*See J. p. 162.
**"with the horn".

ticed conjuring. Once he called some strong fellows
and told them to try and lift the horn, saying that if
they could get it off the ground, then they would be
defeated if they made a rebellion. "But if you can't
lift it, then we shall defeat them. We shall defeat
anyone who comes against us."

Eventually word of this reached the people of
Sokoto and put them in fear of the men of Satiru.
Then the Europeans came and conquered Sokoto.

Well, Sultan Attahiru, son of Aliyu (that is, the
present Sultan) one day said "Majidadi*, when you reach
him, tell the European that there is a certain malam
at Satiru, of whom we are apprehensive; that, even before
the Europeans came, he was claiming that he was the
Mahdi." The Sultan went on "We don't want you to think,
if Malam Mai-kaho proceeds to start a rebellion, that it
is with our knowledge. This is why we are telling you--
that you may know of his existence. Even before you
came and conquered us, we were apprehensive of him."
He repeated that he was warning them now, so that if
Malam Mai-kaho started a rebellion, they would not think
that it was with the Sultan's knowledge.

Then the European said "Where is this malam now?
Let him be called here." So the Sultan had a messenger
sent to Satiru and Malam Mai-kaho called. The latter,
as he was setting off, did not take the horn with him,
but left it at home.

When he reached the Sultan, he was taken to the
Government station (fort) to the European. The European
said to him "Malam Mai-kaho, I hear a report that you
claim to be the Mahdi." "Lion" answered Malam Mai-kaho,
"I have said that I am the Mahdi, but not a Mahdi of
war, but of farming." Three times the European questioned him, and he said "Yes, but I am a Mahdi of
farming." Then the European ordered that he be taken
back to the Sultan and made to take the oath, "Majidadi,
you are to tell the Sultan that it is my order that
Malam Mai-kaho be given the oath."

---

*The holder of this title was the daily messenger
 from Sultan to Resident, to the end of British rule.

Then Majidadî took Malam Mai-ƙaho to the Sultan
and he was given the oath, which he took. After he had
taken the oath thus, he remained in the city of Sokoto,
but after only three days, he died.

Then his son took over (?lifted) the horn, and he
too began conjuring in the same way as his father had
done. He would come and point to a place and say "Let
this place be struck." And when the place was struck,
it would ring like metal that has been struck.

About this time, another malam, a Zabarma man, in
French territory, also caused people to start a rebellion.
The French brought a force and went and burnt down the
town. That malam was a blind man, he couldn't see. He
fled, and going round by the land of Gwandu and Jega,
and on to Gumi and thence to Tureta, from there went
down to Satiru, and there, when he arrived, he found
the son of Malam Mai-ƙaho. So the two of them, Malam
Mai-ƙaho's son and ᗡan Makaho* began living together.

Then one day Malam Mai-ƙaho's son set off and went
to another town, where he had some relations. And when
he got among them, he killed twelve of them. And that
was how the Satiru revolt began. But the European had
just left to go home.

So another "judge**" set off with a European officer and a doctor, and Majidadî and Mai-nasara and
some horse-soldiers and a machine-gun. The "judge"
went to the town to try to persuade them to calm down
and not fight. But, as it happened, the men of Satiru
had prepared, all of them, and were ready for war.

So when the "judge" arrived, with the other Europeans,
they dismounted, and the men of Satiru promptly attacked
them with arrows; beat them with clubs and with axes,
killing immediately the Europeans of the horse-soldiers.
But the "judge" went into a hut with his little gun
(?revolver).

The doctor fell, wounded, but a soldier, Mamman
Zaria came and picked up the doctor, put him on a horse,
assisted by another soldier, called Mamman Wurku. Then

*Lit. "the little blind chap" or, possibly, "son-of-
the-blind man".
**Assistant Resident.

the doctor galloped and galloped, nor did he stop at
any place until Uku-uku (?). There he was shown the
way to the Government station.

Meanwhile the "judge" fired his little gun till
the bullets were finished. Then the men of Satiru captured him, tied him up and killed him.

Next they took the machine-gun, dug a hole and
buried it in the ground. They killed a large number
of the horse-soldiers.

They reached Majidadi and caught hold of his gown,
but he put spurs to his horse and escaped. As for
Mai-nasara, they caught him and he fell, but used a
charm of invisibility so that they couldn't see him--
but they got his horse.

As for Dan Makaho, he told them to come and strike
his head. And when they did so, his head kept making
the sounds "Ma-di-di-di" and so the people of Satiru
believed firmly in his cause.

The rest of the soldiers returned home. Now the
European (i.e. the Resident) had already set off for
Europe, but the note reached him at Tureta, reporting
that Satiru had rebelled. At this, he returned, but
he didn't come back by Dengi, for the people of Satiru
had stopped people using that road. He had to go round
by the Zamfara area, and then made his way back to
Sokoto.

Then the soldier Europeans and the "town" ones all
collected in the fort that had been built here in Sokoto--
like a city it was*. And some of the soldiers' wives
were sent into the town.

Next the European said to Majidadi "Majidadi, I
want you to tell the Sultan that the town called Satiru
has rebelled." "Very well" said Majidadi and went and
did so.

"Right" said the Sultan, "But let me first summon
my younger brothers, and we will take counsel about this
war."

_____

*I.e. had mud walls.

And the Sultan sent to Marafa, Mai-turare, at
Gwadabawa, he sent to the King of Raba, he sent to
Shehu of Tambawel, he sent to the King of Zamfara--all
these the Sultan, Attahiru, son of Aliyu, sent to, and
they all came and gathered.

Then he said "Now, look--Satiru has rebelled, and
the Europeans say that we should go and subdue them."
Then Marafa, Mai-turare of Gwadabawa said "Sultan, if
now we go and subdue Satiru, the Europeans will say
that it was with our knowledge--that we knew before-
hand and that we permitted them to revolt. No, it will
be better, Sultan, if we go and keep them in check, until such time as the Europeans have finished their prep-
arations--then they can go and subdue them, themselves."
And the Sultan agreed.

Then Marafa mounted and went and held the people in
Satiru in check--the town he stopped at is there on the
road. If you leave Shuni on your way to Sokoto, there
is a little town there called Kwannawa--that's where
Marafa stayed.

Twenty-seven days passed, and on the twenty-ninth
day a force left the Government station and made for
Satiru.

The European said "People of Sokoto, let everyone
follow the soldiers, to watch the war."

The horse-soldiers were sent to go ahead and they
went firing their guns, but without bullets. But the
men of Satiru were out of their minds, saying that the
guns would not fire, and they followed close to the
horse-soldiers.

But the horse-soldiers, when the people reached
them, divided, leaving (them exposed to) the soldiers
on the other side. And as soon as they reached them,
they were killed, not one man escaping. Next the town
was attacked and firing continued, no order being given
to cease. And the men of Satiru were killed as they
were found; and even the wall of the town, and the huts
and the store-bins--all were flattened to the ground.
Then the European said "Not even a bird is to be permitted to live in Satiru." And presently that European
departed, went home, and another "judge" came to live
at Sokoto.

When they brought the men of Satiru that they had
arrested to the Sultan, he said "Take them to the
Government station, to the European, and bring me back
word what the European says, Majidadi." But the European said that they were to be taken back again, for
he had no wish to see the people of Satiru. So they
were taken back into the city of Sokoto, and Majidadi
went and told the Sultan.

Then the Sultan said "Those Satiru people that
have been brought here, let them be taken to the prison
(lit. "the Yari's* compound") and tied up." This was
done. All of them died, except for two, who spent a
year imprisoned. Then they were taken before another
European, and he said "Release them, but they are not
to return to Satiru." He went on "Every month the horse-
soldiers must visit Satiru to see if anyone has made a
farm or set up a bukka, and to arrest anyone who has."

These visits were made regularly, and one day they
found two men who had set up bukkas in the ruins of
Satiru. They were arrested and imprisoned and spent
a year there, before being released to settle here, in
Sokoto.

But Malam Siba** ran away. Search was made for
him, but it was four years before he was discovered
away in the land of Dandi, where he was thought to be
a pious scholar, when in fact he was a scoundrel. Word
of this was brought to the Emir of Gwandu and to the
Europeans there, and then guards were sent to arrest
him. He was taken to Sokoto, to the European there.
They tried him and asked him if he was Malam Siba, and
he said that he was. Next they asked him if he had
incited Satiru to rebel, and he answered that he had
had nothing to do with it, denying it. Then witnesses
were obtained.

Then the European at Sokoto said "You can go now.
You are imprisoned with labor for five years." Again
he said "Take him to the Sultan. I leave him in his
care. Let him look after him for me, until I ask for
him, and then let him give him back to me."

---

*Being the title of the chief warder.
**? = Dan Makaho.

As for the Sultan, when he was brought to him, he said "Where's the Yari? Where's the Gebe?", and again "Bring the guards. Here you see Malam Siba. I want you to guard him well for me. But if you're not able to, I'll do the police work myself." Then the Yari said "Gebe, bring some ropes," and Gebe put his hand in his pocket and brought out five ropes. Then he put them back and said "Yari, have twelve guards guard Malam Siba, while I go and get some rope."

Ropes were duly brought by him, Gebe, and Malam Siba was tied up. Then said the Sultan "That is excellent, Gebe." And he was taken to the prison and tied by his feet; and a post was brought and set up behind. When night came, a chain was brought, he was tied with it and it was passed behind (the post); and he spent the night sitting, until next day when it was light. Malam Siba is still there in the prison. That's all. This with peace.

ANOTHER ACCOUNT OF THE SAME* (I/LIII)

This occurred after the European occupation of Sokoto, in the time of Sultan Attahiru, son of Aliyu, on a Wednesday, the 19th of the month of Dhu'l Hijja, that is on the seventeenth day of the twelfth month of the 1323rd year after the emigration of Muhammad, Prophet of God.

On the Monday, Major Burdon (lit. "the white-headed-one") had set out from Sokoto for Zunguru, accompanied by Kyari and the Vizier's Dangaladima, also Na-Malam, son of Majidadi. Then, on the Tuesday that Major Burdon reached Dabagin-Lafiya, Babawala brought him a message to say that on Wednesday three Europeans

---

*The original of this is one of those in the Kaduna Archives. It is a pencilled letter from Malam Bako to Malam Ja'afaru of Argungu, written in 1906. There is also a copy in ink made by Malam Ja'afaru in 1910. Presumably it was this latter that Edgar transcribed.

had gone to Satiru with Mai-nasara and some of the horse-
soldiers. They had gone to investigate the disturbances
caused by the people of Satiru in which they had killed
thirteen men and a woman of the people of Tsomau.

When the Europeans reached Satiru, the people of
Satiru tricked them, and eventually, fell upon them.
They killed three of them, and the doctor was wounded
with an arrow in his right hand, but escaped, lost his
way and with difficulty reached home.

It was night by then and we were sitting there*.
In the evening we* had been studying with Major Burdon
and Kyari, when Major Burdon received news that in one
of the Sokoto villages, called Satiru, between Bodinga
and Dange, a seditious, heretical malam had appeared,
Malam Isa his name, son of another malam, Malam Mai-kaho.
He had gathered the people and they had rebelled, burning
to death the people of a nearby village, Tsomau--thirteen
men and one woman. When the news reached Major Burdon,
he wrote a letter and sent it to the European whom he
had left to do justice at Sokoto. But before that letter reached him, three other Europeans had set off--two
of them from those concerned with justice, and one of
the horse-soldiers--together with Mai-nasara and Majidadi,
to find out what was happening. Then the people of
Satiru killed the three Europeans and captured a machine-
gun. But while Mai-nasara was galloping along--on a
black horse with light-colored stirrups and an orna-
mented saddle--he fell into a well and broke his arm.
As for Majidadi, he narrowly escaped being taken. Thereupon a report was sent to Major Burdon of what the people
of Satiru had done.

So, on the Friday, Major Burdon set out from Dabagin-
Lafiya and met Marafa who was on his way to the scene.
They exchanged greetings and Marafa said to Major Burdon

---

*The introduction of the 1st person, the duplicated
account of the attack and the jumping backwards and
forwards of the time sequence suggest corruption in
the MS--perhaps due to the extra stage it went through
before transcription.

"If you leave them to me, I'll crush them by myself.
For, you know, this isn't the first time this has happened with them--it goes back twelve years." "Very
well" said Major Burdon, "Off you go and finish your
journey!" So Marafa, with his people, went on to
Kwannawa, and stopped there.

And as Major Burdon went ahead and reached the
outskirts of the Government station, he met the doctor
and Majidadi, who had come out to meet him. Says Kyari
"Congratulations on your lucky escape, Majidadi--I hear
they tried to kill you." Then, coming into the Government station, they found it empty, for everyone had
collected in the fort--policemen, interpreters and messengers--all gathered in the one place, men and womenfolk, a terrible sight. Then the Sultan came out to
the Government station to pay his respects to Major
Burdon, and the Major greeted him with his people; then
the Sultan took his leave and returned home.

Meanwhile all Marafa's force had gathered--the King
of Raba, the King of Kabi from Yabo, the King of the
West from Kware, the Ardo of Shuni--they were all there.

Then, on the Saturday, the 20th of the month of
the Greater Festival, Major Burdon sent another European,
together with Kyari and Majidadi and Sulaimanu Dogonyaro, messenger, and two horse-soldiers; and these went
off intending to see the battle that was to be fought
with the men of Satiru. Of horsemen alone there were
more than two thousand, not counting footmen.

So they all went forward, until they came close
to the town, when Kyari said to Majidadi "Let us make
way for Marafa so that he may go by." So Marafa passed
in front, and the European said to him "Let me have a
horseman to take a letter to Major Burdon." So Aliyu
of the house of Nagwamatse was picked out, a letter was
written and given to him and off he went--like a slave
who has been sent back to his own town! Then said
Kyari "Let us press closer to that locust-bean tree
over there."

Soon after this the followers of the King of Kabi
from Yabo entered the town and began to seize people--
when we noticed the horsemen scatter. "How's that?"

exclaimed Kyari in surprise, and Majidadi said "Perhaps
they are trying to draw them out of the town." Presently
he added "Hey, Kyari, looks like it's time to be moving!
You don't understand the Hausa character!" For Marafa
had retreated and the pagans, the men of Satiru, were
following them, shooting arrows. Then said Kyari to the
European "This way."

As they went, they came to a stretch of low-lying
land, and Kyari said to Majidadi "Now, Majidadi--won't
any of us stand?* Let's give them a hand and kill a
few of those who are pursuing Marafa!" And Majidadi
said to his servant, Jari "Stay with the European and
go ahead slowly." Then Kyari and Majidadi both drew
their swords; and Haliru, messenger, also drew his, that
Kyari had given him. Dogon-yaro had a gun slung on his
shoulder. Then one of the soldiers who was riding with
the European--one of the horse-soldiers--fired his gun,
but it misfired, and he realized that it was useless!
And with the men of Satiru close upon us! So he put his
horse into a canter and went over to Kyari and said to
him "Devil take it! Give me a gun, give me a gun!" And
Kyari said "Haven't you already got your own, eh?" "I
have" he replied. "Then be off!" said Kyari.

Meanwhile Jari, Majidadi's servant, and the European moved on a little way, and Jari kept saying to him
"Take care, sir! Oh my, let's get on!" Then the Ardo
cantered up and said to Majidadi and Kyari "Don't fail
to protect the European, keeping him out of the way!"
All this time the pagans were pressing close behind
them, firing their arrows, even killing the younger
brother of the Sarkin Fada (Chief Chamberlain), who was
close to Marafa. But Marafa didn't even turn his head.

That day also the King of Dutsi and the Kofa of
Rini were killed, and others too. And the Sultan's son,
Mai-gandi, was taken, and all his _zagis_ killed. Mai-
gandi himself managed with great difficulty to escape,
but his horses were cut down. Then God helped him, for
in spite of his wounds he fell in with a charger, and
escaped. And the Marafa of Gwadabawa also was within

---

*Reading ? for ﹐ after tsayawa.

an inch of being taken, and if Dan Aljanna and Dodo Mai
Tabshi hadn't helped him, he would have been killed.

When the news was brought to the Sultan, Attahiru,
son of Aliyu, he was extremely troubled and could not
remain seated. They tried to soothe him, but he kept
saying that they should saddle a horse for him to be
off. He kept getting up, in spite of the attempts to
calm him down, and finally vomited. Then he calmed
down.

Then Majidadi took a gun from Kyari and went back
and aimed it at one of the Satiru pagans, wearing dark-
blue trousers, a shirt and a fez, holding a piece of
paper in his hand--or it may have been a piece of cloth,
I'm not sure.

On we went and ascended a hill. When we got to the
top, Hasan, Kyari's _zagi_, could go no further and he gave
someone else his blanket, sword, turban, leading rope
and hobbles, and metal water-jug, and sat down. But
Kyari didn't know of this until someone came up and said
to him "One of your servants is behind there and can go
no further, and he has given me what he was carrying.
See, here they are!" Then said Kyari "Where is he?" and
the other answered "He's back a bit, sitting down." And
then Kyari returned, with Malam Bako and his servant,
Haliru. They cantered for some two miles till they came
across the _zagi_. Malam Ahmadu, a Nupe, had picked him
up and was bringing him along on his horse. So they
got him home.

Well, that Saturday had seen a noteworthy event:
the likes of Marafa, and the King of Raba, and the King
of Kabi from Yabo, who were used to sending others out
to conquer large towns and bring back slaves to them,
themselves routed by eighteen people.

But it was also a shameful thing, and the people of
Sokoto began to say "This is too much. They conquer us,
they impose tax on us, they impose cattle-tax on us--they
impose everything, and we do it! And now they are making
us fight for them, while they go off about their own
business."

Then all the kings of Sokoto were collected, the
King of Tambawel, of Talata Mafara, the King of Danko

from Bukkuyum, the King of Burmi from Bakura, and others
too. But the King of the West from Dogon-Daji didn't
come--perhaps he thought better of it, I don't know.
The King of Gobir from Isa and all the other Kings from
Zamfara were set to watch the edge of the bush near the
Satiru lake.

It was a Thursday that a great force collected,
with many soldiers and many Europeans, all come to
reinforce the fight against Satiru. The Sultan sent
Dan Galadima Ambo, with Majidadi and the King of
Tambawel and a host of other people, to meet them.
The reinforcements arrived and encamped.

But while the people of Satiru had been chasing
Marafa and shooting arrows at him, on that day I saw
a funny incident. Majidadi rode in amongst Marafa's
horsemen, and said to them angrily "For all your numbers now, just eighteen men have routed you, you cursed
cowards!" But they answered Majidadi "We've heard your
comments, now get along! In circumstances like this
abuse means nothing!"

So we got back to Sokoto, but it was <u>sauve qui
peut</u>*. After that no one ventured back to Satiru till
military reinforcements had arrived from Kano, Kontagora,
Zunguru, Lokoja--from all these towns--Europeans with
their soldiers.

When the force had gathered, it was a Saturday,
the fourteenth of the month of Muharram, and the Europeans set off at 3 a.m. for Satiru. When the people
of Satiru saw the Europeans, they rushed towards them
with the weapons they had seized, with drums and oboes.
For a while the Europeans merely watched them.

But when they got near to them, then the soldiers
knelt, and killed them with one volley. Others came
to the attack, and they were destroyed. Then the pursuit made for the town, killing them as they went. The
man Majidadi had aimed at was one of the first to be
killed.

On the Sunday the town was taken, and some thousand people killed, with about eight hundred wounded--

*I have tried to match an Arabic phrase in the H.

apart from those who died of thirst. About a hundred
women made their way to the Europeans, it is said.
Believe me, Malam, in all my life I have never seen so
many corpses as that.

Major Burdon entered the town, where he dismounted
and rested for a while. Then he left it again, and they
set fire to the town. Then Major Burdon returned home,
but the horse-soldier officer didn't do so, for he had
kept after the fugitives, right after the fight. He
followed them till it was dark, and when morning came
still they had not returned.

Believe me, Malam, the people of Satiru have done
a terrible thing to themselves, and God has exacted
retribution. On Sunday, Major Burdon had the kings
destroy the town, and he told the Sultan to announce
to the people that no one was to farm that land ever
again.

That's not all the news, but my paper has finished
and I am fatigued with writing. Otherwise you would
have heard some more news.

But from beginning to end, the whole affair took
only twenty-six days. That finished it and we all
relaxed again.

May God keep us from the revelation of our hidden
secrets, and give us health and happiness. May God give
us fulfillment and faith. May God deliver us from two-
tongued men and make our enemies ashamed. May God
strengthen the religion of the Prophet Muhammad, upon
whom be the blessing and peace of God.

But if I hear anything else, or call to mind anything, I'll send it to you--if God will. That's all.
This with peace.

III
Zamfara Traditions

THE ORIGIN OF THE PEOPLE
OF ZAMFARA (I/XXXIV)

The first of the mighty kings of Zamfara was Bakururuwa,
and after him Bakara, Gimshiki, Argoje, Karfau, Gatama
Kudamdam, Bardau, Gobirau, Tasgarinburum Durkusa, Muwashi,
Kiganna, Tabarau, Daudaufanu, Burum, Fitifiti, Tareto,
Zartai, Dakatasau Zaudan, Aliyu, Hamitu, Karma, Abdu-na-
ba-wanka-Sulaimanu, Muhammadu-na-Makake, Abdu-atamani-
maliki, Babba, Yakubu, Jimira, Babba, Gigamma, Malugado,
Maroki, Dan Bawa, Abarshi, Fari, Dan Bako, Dan Gado,
Takudu, Abdu, Abubakar Muhammadu-dan-gigala, Alhasan,
Muhammadu-farin-gani, Abdullahi, Gado, Abdu; forty-four
in all.

And as for their leaving the city of Zamfara, when
Malu was King of Zamfara, there was hostility between
him and Yunfa, King of Gobir. The King of Gobir's mother
said "I want to see that monkey completely and humili-
atingly destroyed (lit. holding his excrement in his
hand)."

Time passed and the hostilities didn't cease or
show any sign of doing so. Then the King of Zamfara
went into his hut and tying his turban to the beam of
the roof, made a noose, and climbing on to a mortar,
put his neck in it, and began to swing by it. Then the
turban snapped, but the noose end choked him and he
died.

Presently the King of Gobir heard of it and sent
about a hundred horsemen, saying "Go and cut off the
King of Zamfara's head and bring it to me." But before
they could get the head, they had to fight for some
twenty days, and when the fighting became very fierce,
then the Ubandawaki of Zamfara cut off his king's head,
put it in a wooden bowl, covered it with a mat and sent
it to Alḱalawa. This was Friday and it was brought to
the gate of the King of Gobir's compound. It was uncovered and the King of Gobir looked in, saw the head
of the King of Zamfara in the wooden bowl and said
"Praise be to God! Thus ends that fire in the south!"

But just then Gozo, Emir of Katsina, was on a
tour of the towns there. Every town he came to, he
would say "Look at me now, I'm ninety-seven years old.
I get no pleasure from riding, or food or women. So I
travel around just to see the world, and for the world
to see me." Thus he went on till he came to Alḱalawa,
where he found the King of Gobir rejoicing over the
death of the King of Zamfara. Then said he to the King
of Gobir "That fire's out, but there is another fire
going to start up close to you. And when it starts,
you can pour the water of a whole river on to it, but
it won't go out." And the King of Gobir replied "Just
so, for there is a holy man here who is seeking to cause
me vexation." Then Gozo, Emir of Katsina, departed. And
not long after his departure, Shehu's movement really
began to be felt.

And this is how the leading men of the City of
Zamfara came to gather and take counsel. Then they said
to the people "It is best for us to move from this place,
lest worse than this befall us and bring us suffering."
And the common people understood and agreed to their
proposal. Then they set out from there and moved to
Anka where they settled.

UMARU, SON OF MAMUDU, KING OF ZAMFARA AND THE OLD WOMAN (I/IX)

It is said there was once a time when Umaru, King of Zamfara, was troubling his people by the number that he killed. All the people of the town were abusing him and in all the town there was not one who liked him. Then he, knowing his own unpopularity, put on a dark cloth over his gown, and began to wander through the town to listen for any that spoke ill of him.

This continued for some time, and one day he left his compound at night and went walking through the town, and came to the compound of an old woman who was frying groundnuts. Coming up to her he said "Peace be upon you." "And upon you peace" said she. "Do you sell groundnuts here?" says he. "Yes" said she. "Here's my money--let me have some!" "Right" said she, "Come on into the hut."

So he went in, and before she could count out his groundnuts for him, he asked her "Old woman, I want to ask you something." "What is it?" said she. "I'm a stranger here" said he, "And I want to find out about the king of this town--is he good or bad?" "Wha-at!" said the old woman in surprise, "You surely are a stranger. May God preserve us from our king! As for me--well, I tell you straight, I shouldn't be sorry if our king died. If you're a stranger here, get away out of here tonight. I wouldn't want even an enemy of mine to come and settle in this town. For the king spends his time killing people without rhyme or reason."

Next morning the King came forth to the gathering of his courtiers and took his seat as usual on his couch before all his people. He sent off his guards, saying "Fetch here the old woman who fries groundnuts." And they went off to her compound and said to her "The King wants you." "What have I done?" said she and, her body all a-tremble, she came before the king and prostrated herself. "May God lengthen your days!" said she, "Here I am."

"Old woman" said the king. "Yes" said she. "Did a man come to your house wearing a dark cloth?" "He did." "And when he inquired of you, what did you reply to him?" But the old woman just bowed her head, and the king went on "I see. Well, it was me you abused yesterday. Now you can pay a hundred thousand cowries-- otherwise, in spite of your age, I'll have you killed at once." And she replied "I haven't got a hundred thousand--let me then be killed." "Very well! Kill her" said he, and she was killed. May God preserve us from evil men, amen!

UMARU, SON OF MAMUDU, KING
OF KAURA (II/XCIX)

When Umaru, son of Mamudu, was king of Kaura, he used to send money to Bawa Jan-Gwarzo, King of Gobir; and also to Dan Balkore, King of Maradi, inviting them into his country to help him make war. And when they had come and had done so, they would divide the booty in two parts, and give him half of the people of his own country, who had been taken as slaves. And the king of Kaura would take his share, and proceed to sell them--for all that they were his own subjects! Thus the King of Zamfara, Umaru, son of Mamudu, would regu- larly join forces with the men of Gobir, killing the people.
But the day came when disagreement arose between him and the kings of Gobir and Maradi. Then said the King of Gobir to the King of Maradi "Come let us go to the land of Umaru, son of Mamudu, and attack it." "Very well" said the King of Maradi. And he set out and went and joined the King of Gobir, and the two of them pro- ceeded to the land of the King of Zamfara, Umaru, son of Mamudu, and attacked it. And five of the men of Gobir were taken prisoner and brought to Umaru, son of Mamudu. "Put them to death" said he, and they were taken away to be killed. Four were killed, and one remained. Says he "I want you to take me to the king, Umaru, son of Mamudu, for I have something to say to

him." So they took him before Umaru Mamudu, king of
Kaura. Then said the young Gobir man "May your life
be prolonged, King of Zamfara, Umaru, son of Mamudu."
"Amen, man of Gobir" said the king. "Are you Umaru,
son of Mamudu?" asked the captive, "Are you Tino's
suckling*?" "Yes" said the king. "You damned bastard"
said the captive and went on "Your mother*! Umaru,
son of Mamudu, Tino's suckling," and again "Mamudu had
testicles as big as a pitcher. Your mother*!" Then
the Gobir man went on "For, you see, I want you to kill
me. That's why I abused you so shamelessly." Then
said Umaru, son of Mamudu, king of Kaura "Yari**, it's
not this Gobir man who had abused me, but you--you
abused me," and again "Untie the Gobir fellow." And
they loosed his bonds.

Next he ordered them to go into the compound and
fetch one of the kitbags, and they did so. Then he
clothed the Gobir man in gowns, trousers and turban,
and, turning one of his chief slaves out of his compound, had the Gobir man brought in, in his place. Then
he said to him again "Man of Gobir, see--I give you this
compound. If you want to go riding, come to my stable
and choose the horse that you want, and have him saddled
for you to ride. And here--here's my own daughter: take
her as your wife. If you want to stay, stay; but if
you prefer to go home, then go home." And the young
fellow stayed. And the girl was brought to him in his
compound and the two of them were married.

Time passed, and there came a day when the men of
Maradi again attacked the land of the King of Zamfara,
Umaru, son of Mamudu, Tino's suckling. And the young
Gobir fellow rose and mounted and galloped out--and
passed right through the men of Maradi! For the horse
would not respond to the bit, giving him no chance to
fight them. He returned to the King of Zamfara, who
said "Catch hold of the Gobir man's horse and take that
bit off it and put another one on." And they took it
off and fetching another put that on. Then he drew his

---

*Reference to a man's mother, especially by name, is
   very insulting.
**The gaoler.

sword and going amongst the men of Maradi, quickly cut
down four men, horsemen. And then he led their horses
back, and brought them to the King of Zamfara, Umaru,
son of Mamudu. And so they continued together.

Again one day one of Umaru, son of Mamudu's, wives
erred and offended him. And she left the compound and
went to his mother and supplicated her help. News of
this was brought to him. "Hm" said he, "She's not really
serious!" and again "Tell Tino to come here." So they
summoned her and he said to her "Why have you hidden my
wife?" "Umaru" said his mother, "You know she has done
you wrong, and she ran away and came to me, supplicating
my help, in the hope that you would spare her." "For
shame, Tino" said he, "Do you really think, just because
you're my mother--very well, I'll have you put to death
at once." And he seized his own mother, Tino, and
slaughtered her.

And such was the evil of his character, that if
Umaru, son of Mamudu, took a ride, no one would stay to
watch him. No native of the city of Kaura would allow
his eye to meet that of Umaru, son of Mamudu, King of
Kaura. For as he took his ride, he would strike people,
and if he saw a man standing and watching him, he would
order him seized. And the man would be arrested and
put to death.

There was the woman who sold corn, here in Kaura
market, measuring it out--but she made it very dear.
This was reported to the King of Kaura, Umaru Mamudu,
who said "Someone go into the bush and cut down a stout
tree, a straight one. Trim its head, sharpen it and
bring it along." So they went to the bush and felled a
tree and trimmed it. Next he ordered "Seize that woman
who sells corn, and impale her through the arse*, so
that the wood goes right through and comes out at her
neck. Then take her to the booth, where they are selling
the corn, and set up the post there, with her on it.
And so all the cornsellers there will see it. So anyone
else who puts up the price of corn--I'll kill him and
treat him as I've treated her. And anything else for

_____
*He used a vulgar H. word.

sale too--not necessarily corn--any merchandise--let no
one in Kaura demand an excessive price for it." And
while Umaru, son of Mamudu, was king, a visitor to Kaura,
wherever he might come from, would find things there
cheaper than any other town.

That's all I have to relate about Umaru, son of
Mamudu, King of Zamfara. Finish.

THE KING OF ZAMFARA AND THE
SNAKE-CHARMERS* (I/XVI)

Here's a story that a Zamfara man told us about Umaru,
son of Mamudu, King of Zamfara.

One day some snake-charmers--the sort that dress
their hair like women--who were travelling from town to
town, came to the town of the King of Zamfara. And they
came to the entrance of the King's compound with the
snakes that they had caught, and began their begging
very early, when the King was not yet out of bed. The
noise they made woke him up. "Hey" said he, "Who are
those, disturbing people with their noise so early?"
"They are snake-charmers" said his jekadiya. "Is that
so?" said he. "Yes" said she. "Hm" said he, "Let me
go out and wish them godspeed!"

So he went out to where his courtiers were gathered
and sat down. "Call their leader here" said he. He was
called, and coming in he made his greetings. "Are you
their leader?" asked the King of Zamfara. "Yes" he
answered, "I am the chief snake-charmer."

Whereupon the King of Zamfara sent his jekadiya
into the compound to fetch a large, wooden bowl. She
brought it out to the assembled courtiers, and the chief
snake-charmer's head was cut off and put in the bowl.
Then the bowl was covered and put in a corner. Then the
King of Zamfara ordered "Call the others in, to eat, so
that they may enjoy their sport the more afterwards."
Then the King retired into the compound, and all the
other people went away.

---

*See J. p. 141.

When the other snake-charmers came to that corner,
they saw the big bowl and thought there was <u>tuwo</u> in it.
So they uncovered it. But when they saw the head of
their chief in the bowl, they scattered, each one going
his own way, nor did they speak of it to one another.
And never after that year have snake-charmers returned
to Zamfara, for they are too frightened.

A VARIANT ON THE LAST,
WITH ADDITIONS (II/XXIV)

There was once a king in the Zamfara region, at a town
called Kaura Namoda, and his name was Umaru, son of
Mamudu. Every year the snake-charmers would visit his
town, execute their performance, and then go off home--
until the next year came round, when they would return.
But once, they had come into the town and were noisily
soliciting support, when the king asked "What's that?"
He was told it was the snake-charmers. "Call them here"
said he. They were fetched to him, and "Which is your
leader?" he asked. "This one--may the King's life be
prolonged" they answered. Says the king "I'm delighted
with you. Let your chief come on in here." And the
chief snake-charmer went into the compound with Umaru
Mamudu, King of Kaura. But when they were in, the King
of Zamfara* had the chief snake-charmer's head chopped
off. Then he ordered "Go on into the compound and get
a wooden bowl, a good one, and a good mat for covering
it and bring them." This was duly done, and the head
of the chief snake-charmer taken and put into the bowl
and the bowl covered with the mat.

Then said Umaru Mamudu, King of Kaura "Here, take
this bowl to the snake-charmers, something for them to
take home and eat. Afterwards they can come back and
give their performance. I like them very much. Let
them take the bowl and get along; their leader will be
along presently."

So the bowl was taken to the snake-charmers. They
received it and were given the King's message. So they

------

*Same man. This was his title.

returned to their lodging and sat down to wait for their leader to come, that they might eat their _tuwo_, and then return to give their performance.

Presently one of them said "Let me look in the bowl to see what sort of food the King of Kaura has given us. You know, we're lucky to find a king like that!" So he uncovered the bowl--and saw the head of their leader. Next moment they were tumbling over each other in their eagerness to get out of the city of Kaura, for fear Umaru should send to arrest the remainder. And so they left the city and ran and ran. And never went back to Kaura Namoda, so long as Umaru Mamudu remained king.

For this King of Kaura would have a pregnant woman seized and slaughtered, saying that he wished to see how the child lay in her belly. Another of his habits was to have a man seized and put alive into a mortar and pounded*. He would have a baby taken, put into a mortar and pounded, and the flesh dried. Or else he would have people taken and their hands tied behind their backs and a fire lit by them: the heat would reach them and they would start screaming, but no one would dare go and rescue them.

And on the day he died, his grave was dug and he was put into it--but the earth pushed him out! Another was dug, again he was put into it and the earth filled in--but the earth pushed him out again. So they put a building up, and buried him there.

No other king in the whole world did such evil as this one. During his rule, people wouldn't go to Kaura, and it is only since his death, that people started to visit the town again, and have continued since.

For Umaru Mamudu would have a man seized and rocks brought and his arms broken by pounding, from the fingers all the way up to the shoulders. Then he would take the right hand and fix it to the left shoulder, and the left hand to the right shoulder and say to the man "Get up

---

*It must have been a big mortar! The next sentence is more easily credible. Perhaps it is meant as an explanation of this one.

and be off! I've spared you. I haven't killed you,
only got you ready to play langa*."

May God preserve us from an evil ruler! Umaru
Mamudu was king right here, here in Kaura Namoda. What
I have said is not rumor, or hearsay or gossip. Everyone knew that king, Umaru, son of Mamudu--"Coals of fire
that no one will cram their mouths with! Son of Mamudu,
no pocket-sized king! Red-hot bath water that few will
toss into their mouths**!" That's all. This with peace.

UMARU, SON OF MAMUDU, KING OF ZAMFARA (II/XXV)

Umaru Mamudu, King of Kaura Namoda, was walking through
his compound when he saw a slave-girl carrying a wooden
bowl full of tuwo, just near a back entrance to the compound. "Hey, where are you going?" he asked. The girl
began to tremble. Says she "I'm going--er--I've been
sent..." Says he "If you don't tell me, I'll kill you
now with this sword"--and he had it in his hand. Then
she said "Nana has sent me." "Which Nana?" he asked.
"Shafurji's daughter. She has sent me to the judge's
son and told me to take the tuwo to him." "Right" he
said, "Go on. Go and take it to him--but don't tell
anyone that I spotted you." She acknowledged his order
and went on out.

Next day when it was light, he had the judge's
son summoned; and seizing him, he had his penis and
testicles cut off. Then says "And now for Nana,
Shafurji's daughter--go and tell her to come here."
They called her and she came. "Put a rope around her
neck" said he. They did so and throttled her to death.
Then he said "Bring three fine cloths from in the compound, and go and cover her with them; but don't dig a

---

*Tentative translation, taking lagye = lago, "holding
  right foot with left hand or vice-versa in game
  langa" (Abr.).
**This must be Umaru's kirari. The untranslatable
  compression and mixing of metaphors is normal in
  such.

grave for her." And the body was picked up and taken
and thrown out. And three fine cloths were brought and
she was covered with them. And the townspeople saw the
cloths, but no one would go and lift them, for fear.

Her corpse lay outside the town for seven days. No
hyena touched it, nor vulture, nor Ruppell's griffon.
Then at length Umaru Mamudu had it carried away and
taken and buried. As for the testicles of the judge's
son, he had a post cut and brought to the entrance of
his compound and there set up; and there they were hung
for everyone to see.

And this is something that actually happened in
Kaura Namoda. That's all. This with peace.

THE KING OF ZAMFARA, UMARU, SON OF MAMUDU, AND KWASAU, EMIR OF ZAZZAU (I/II)

Once the King of Zamfara, Umaru, son of Mamudu, sent
some horses to Kwasau, Emir of Zazzau.

The Emir of Zazzau bought the horses, but refused
to pay. Then the King of Zamfara sent to the Emir
saying "If you won't pay, give me back my horses." But
the Emir said "Tell the King of Zamfara to come and collect them with an army."

Then the King of Zamfara told Sultan Abdu "A Filani
has taken my cattle and gone off to the banks of the
Kaduna." And Sultan Abdu made answer "Then go and get
back your cattle." But he didn't realize that the King
of Zamfara was speaking of the Emir of Zazzau.

So the King of Zamfara sent for Kaura Hasau, and
the son of Waire, and Jinfi, son of Malam Hasan, and the
men of Azben. And the host gathered. Then the King of
Zamfara set out and coming to the land of Zazzau, divided
up his horsemen. And they spread throughout the land
taking cattle and people, from Fatika to Galadimawa; to
Morai, to Riyoka, whence they crossed the bush and came
to Tami, and took many people at night. Then, coming
back to Nasarawa, near Kazagi, they burnt the town.

When the Emir heard that the King of Zamfara had
invaded his land, he gathered all the people together

from both city and village. And when they had gathered,
the Emir said to them "I have called you together, people,
for you will have heard that the King of Zamfara has
sent an expedition and invaded our land. Now let us go
forth and meet them and take back what they have stolen
from us." And all the people shouted agreement. They
mounted that very night and set off by way of Fatika.

By this time the King of Zamfara was on his way
home, going by way of Kazagi. The Emir had reached
Dogon Daji, and they were like to meet soon, when one
of the Emir's men came and said to him "If you allow
yourself to clash with the King of Zamfara, he has with
him men like Kaura Hasau, and the son of Waire, and Jinfi,
son of Malam Hasan, and they will bring disgrace upon
you. For you are the greatest king in the world. And
they--for you should know it--are mighty horsemen."
Whereupon the Emir returned home exceedingly quickly,
saying to himself "All right, the King of Zamfara has
done this to me. Now I must have my revenge."

Then, when the Muslim festival came, the Emir of
Zazzau said to the people of Zazzau "Let everyone make
ready. For I'm going right up to the gate of Kaura,
and I'll dismount and defeat the King of Zamfara."
Then he sent a messenger to Sokoto, saying "Tell the
Sultan that the King of Zamfara has made war on one of
his flag-bearers."

So the Sultan sent to the King of Zamfara, saying
"Tell the King of Zamfara, every man he has taken from
the land of Zazzau by war he must return and also the
people of Tami." And the King of Zamfara answered
"Tell the Sultan that because it is his wish I will
return the men of Zazzau; if it weren't for that, the
Emir of Zazzau could come by himself and get them back.
For he said that he would come and attack Kaura." And
the Sultan said "Let all their people be returned to
them."

Then the King of Zamfara had all the Zazzau people
who had been taken in war collected and sent back. But
when Kaura Hasau and the son of Waire were told to
bring back the men they had captured, they didn't bring
them all back. So they were collected together and the
Sultan had them taken back to their towns. .

Moreover in that year the Emir of Zazzau had little
leisure to rest still. With the hot season came the
Emir of the Sudan (i.e. Nagwamatse), driven out by the
Europeans, who made his way into Zazzau and settled down
at the gate of Fatika. Then the Emir of Zazzau said to
his people "You know that the Emir of the Sudan has come
and settled in our land, driven here by the Europeans.
What do you advise?" Then some said "Let us go and drive
him out." Others said "Ignore him. He's a fugitive,
he can't do any harm."

But then the Emir of the Sudan began raiding in the
land of Zazzau, and blocked the roads leading to the
city from the villages.

Then the King of Fatika sent word to the Emir of
Zazzau saying "Tell the Emir of Zazzau 'The Emir of the
Sudan is ruining your whole land; and you remain silent'."
When the Emir of Zaria heard this, he sent fifty horse-
men to Fatika, with fifty men with guns too. And these
remained at Fatika ready to fight.

But after that the camp of the Emir of the Sudan
was attacked by a fatal epidemic, and the Emir moved
from there to Kaya, where he settled. There the Emir
of Kano, Aliyu, sent him supplies and money. The Emir
of the Sudan then began raiding the people of Kaya.
During the rains his Vizier moved to Rogo and remained
there.

Then, when it was time for harvest, the Vizier set
off and went to Kano. Then, leaving Kano he came to
Zazzau to find out what was happening in the land of
Zazzau. But when he had been two days in Zaria city,
the Europeans arrived and camped at the gate of the
city. Whereupon the Vizier said to the Emir of Zazzau
"Since it seems that you are now with the Europeans, I
must be going" and he departed by night. And the Emir
of Zazzau sent his son with him to escort him and to
escape from the Europeans, who were now settled near
to the Emir, Kwasau.

Next Captain Abadie (lit. "the one with the ostrich")
went to Kaya and arresting the Emir of the Sudan, brought
him to Zaria. And the Emir of Zazzau came out and saw
the Emir of the Sudan. And he said "So it's you, Emir

of the Sudan! God has brought about your capture, you breaker of faith." And the Emir of the Sudan answered "Emir of Zazzau, have you no shame? For I am a greater one than your father or your grandfather." And the European, Captain Abadie, interrupted "Cease this talk, for it is evil!"

Then the Emir of the Sudan was taken away, and his camp dispersed. And the people of Zazzau said to the Emir of Zazzau "Congratulations on your good fortune!"

ORIGINS OF TOWNS (I/XXVIII)

The people of Burmi were originally blacksmiths from Alkalawa. It began when a malam came to a hill just east of Bakura, called Mai Gaba (? = "with an eagle"), and said that there would be a big town there one day. Then two brothers, Korau, the elder, and Ango went to consult another malam, called Atagala, and he told them "You'll not be lucky until you go to a hill with an eagle (?), east of Bakura, and settle there." They accepted his advice.

And presently they set out and came here and made their home by the hill, in the time of Bawa, King of Gobir and Uban-Abarshi, King of Zamfara. Soon the town grew and Ango became its king. And he appointed his younger brother Dan Galadima. And it was Dan Galadima who cleared the site for Tureta--or some say it was Magajin Gari who built Tureta. When Ango died, his son, Jan-Damo succeeded to the title; and after him, his son, Dan-Kwai. When he died, his younger brother, Na-abu, became king. But Sultan Attahiru, son of Aliyu, deposed him and he died at Gwiwa. In his place he appointed his nephew, Ahmadu, son of Dan-Kwai, and he is the present king of Bakura.

But of all the kings there have ever been here in Bakura, only two of them ever died here. As for Rini-- that was where the Chief Farmer lived. Gora too is very old, while Bazai, also an old town, dates from when Gobir was powerful. It was Bawa-jan-gwarzo, King of Gobir, who appointed the king of Bazai, and the district of Bazai under him stretched as far as Isa. On this side it marched with Gobir; to the west, the Gundumi Bush and the district of Mafara, also Gidan Goga. Its other neighboring districts were Zurmi and Kware.

Time passed and there was a Filani nomad who used to come regularly to pay his respects to Uban-Badambo, King of Bazai. Until one day the King said to him "I give you Shinkafi. You can start a town and have farming land there." "Very well" said he and went off and built a compound and made a town. He also founded Shanawa, and it grew to be a big town. And they chose a king, who was subordinate to the King of Bazai.

Time passed and he (? the king of Shinkafi) gave his allegiance to the Sultan, who appointed (him) Magaji of Shinkafi. As for Isa, Aliyu, son of Bello, entered it and took it be force. Mu'allaidi was with him, and he was appointed king. But the Sultan appointed his son, Abdurahmani, to be king of Isa. (He held the title of) King of Gobir of Isa, and when he died, his younger brother Shehu of Isa, succeeded him. And after his death, his younger brother Umaru succeeded. When Sultan Abdu died, Umaru came to seek confirmation of his appointment, which was not given him. Instead the Sultan appointed his own son. Then Umaru's younger brother, Halidu, and Shefu, 'Dan Bafada, went to Gangara, to Balarabe, King of Gobir*, who restored them and drove out the Sultan's son, and made Halidu, the elder, king.

Meanwhile Umaru heard what had happened, and saw how the Sultan's son came and then set off, so he went off too with the Sultan's son and his family. Then Sultan Attahiru sent out to all his districts, to forbid anyone to allow Umaru to enter their town. But Atto** told him to enter Chibirin Kwairanga and settle there, and he did so.

There he remained for some time, till the day came when he set out to go and turn his younger brother, Halidu, out. The latter mounted and came out to meet him with war, but Umaru's sons cut him down with their

---

*Several kings held this title.
**See I/XXVII.

swords, and then they all entered the town, one Sunday.
Then there was a long period of settled obedience to
Umaru's rule. After which Umaru appointed his son king.
Then Umaru died. His son, Shefu, is the present ruler.

There was another Filani who used to come and pay
his respects to the King of Bazai, and he went on doing
this regularly till one day the king said to him "I
give you Moriki, so that you may build a compound there
and have a place for pasture." He accepted and went
and built a compound, and the place grew into a town.
Mud buildings were set up, and he was appointed King of
Burmi, of Moriki. While he was king and Ahmadu was
Sultan, the latter made him independent of Bazai.

As for the origin of Gidan Goga, this was when a
malam came to the bank of the river there and said
"One day there'll be a great town here." And after
that a man called Goga came and settled, built himself
a compound, cleared a farm, and before long there were
a lot of people there. And it grew to a city which
was called "Goga's Home" (Gidan Goga).

THE ORIGIN OF THE PEOPLE
OF BANAGA (I/XX)

The people of Banaga came originally from Anka. The
reason they moved was a fraternal dispute, for they
were not driven out by war. At that time Dan Kwara
was king. After him came Dan Zangina, then Mai-Yaki,
then Bako, then Dan Jai, then Maigizo, then Buwai,
then Abubakar na Buntsulu. The King of Zamfara was
their enemy.

Their land was a large one--from Sabon Birni to
Akare was formerly all theirs, and eastwards as far
as Maska too. All this came into their power together
with Mashi by means of Banaga of Morai.

When Dan Bature was Banaga, the men of Zamfara
agreed together and made him king. But he was only a
boy and the other sons of his father made trouble for
him. So he left and moved to Sabon Birni, meaning to
go to Wamba. But after only three months, before he
had made any more preparations, he died.

Banaga-Moru, on the other hand, owes its origin
to some Filani from Sabon Birni, who decided to create
a chieftainship like that of their brothers, to preserve the family, but they are subordinate to Sabon
Birni. And when Sultan Bello attacked the land of
Burmi, Banaga Dan Bature went to the help of Burmi,
and that was why the Filani were worsted and lost
drums and quilted armor. From Sabon Birni Banaga would
carry war to the banks of the Damari and of the Kaduna.
But Banaga himself would not ride out in person, sending
others to conquer towns for him.

"Banaga" is the title of the office. Whoever is
made king is called Banaga--and that is what they have
always done. They have famous and very learned malams
in their town. It is now eighty-eight years and eight
months since the founding of Sabon Birni.

It was left to Sultan Aliyu Babba to invade them
in a war that was called the "surrounding war". For he
didn't conquer them until he had allied himself with
the pagans of the area. They all came and surrounded
the place and then it was taken. That is why it was
called the "surrounding war".

In the days of Banaga Dan Zangina, a Sullube picked
out a fine horse, meaning to take it and sell it to
Banaga. But when he was only one day's journey from
the town, the horse died. Then, taking the halter from
the horse's head, he came on and reached Banaga and
said to him "I set out to come to you with a fine, big
horse, but he died at the town where I spent last night.
So I came on to tell you of it, and ask you for something to feed me on my way home." Then the king said
"Good. Where's the horse's halter?" "Here it is" and
the king took it and gave it to his chief _zagi_, saying
"Go to the stables, to the horses, and try this halter
on all their heads. Then come and tell me which one it
fits." "Right" said the _zagi_.

He went to the stables, and began trying the halter
on the heads of the horses there, one after the other,
until he reached a horse that had been bought for twelve
slaves, and it fitted him. Then the _zagi_ returned to
the king with the halter and said "The halter fits that

horse that was bought for twelve slaves." Then the
king turned to the Sullube and said "Since you were
counting on me to buy the horse, even though you couldn't
bring it to me because it died, I'll pay you. Here are
twelve slaves; go and get another one and pay for it
and bring it me, so that I can buy it." And the people
said "Only a king can afford the loss of a horse." And
many such were the manifestations of power at Banaga,
there were a hundred others which cannot be reckoned,
and others again have been forgotten.

IV
Gobir Traditions

THE KINGS OF GOBIR (II/LVI)

The first was Bataram--at the time that Gobir was
founded. After him, Majigi; Barnatuta (Baznuta);
Banazawa; Bartakaskus; Surtaka Sa Gilme; Barnakumra;
Dagumi; Zabarma; Bayamusu; Gome Chiroma; Miajijjir;
Kasumi; Chidagoje-Jelayataje; Gintsarana; Bachiri Babba
Dalla (Dana) Chiroma; Munzaka; Chiroma Muhammadu*; Dalla
(Dana) Gungume; Dalla (Dana) Karma; Chiroma Muzaka; Dalla
(Dana) Mai-Kashewa Karanbi; Dalla (Dana) Nan Makatsufa;
Dalla (Dana) Gungume Muhammadu; Nan Makasufa Muhammadu
Maje; Gumasara Umi; Bachiri Babba; Dalla (Dana) Chiroma
Munzaka; Muhammadu Ubandoma; Bachiri Ubandoma Yakul;
Uban Isa Yarima; Akala; Babari Dan Adiya; Bawa; Yakubu;
Nafata; Yunfa Salihu; Gwamki Aliyu; Jibirila Bachiri;
Mai-Yaki; Bawa.

I obtained this account from the hand of Malam
Masallachi** of Argungu.

---

*The first Muslim name.
**Cf. II/CIII.

73

THE WARRIOR, THE HUNTER AND THE
HUNTER'S WIFE (III/V)

In the days when Bawa Dan Gwanki ("son-of roan antelope")
was king of Gobir, there was a warrior, of whom it used
to be said "Kuturun-kusu (= leprous rat?), fouling the
winnowing with blood.*"

Bawa mounted to set off to war, and they invaded
the land of the Fulani. Kuturun-kusu seized a woman,
and she said "Oh, were my husband but here, I shouldn't
now be enslaved!"

And as they went along, again she said "Oh, were
my husband but here, I shouldn't now be enslaved!"--
three times in all. Then said Kuturun-kusu "Here, you--
come on back. We'll go back to your home, and wait for
your husband to come, so that I may see if he prevents
me taking you away." And the woman said to Kuturun-kusu
"That's what I think--if he's here, you won't be taking
me away." "Let's go along to your home" said he again.

So they went home--the woman's home, and Kuturun-
kusu said to her "Go and get on with your work. I'm
going to dismount and wait till your husband comes."
"Right" said she, and went and got on with her work.
And he went and dismounted, took off his horse's bridle,
so that it might graze. And Kuturun-kusu lay down close
to his horse.

Now it happened that this woman was the wife of a
hunter, and presently he returned from the bush. Says
the hunter to his wife "What a surprising thing, wife**!
However did you get involved in the battle without them
seeing you?" But his wife replied "Oh, I was involved
all right, for I am a slave." And the hunter asked
"Where's the man who took you prisoner?" "Look" she
said, "Do you see the horse there? And there's its
master, lying down there? It was he who took me, I'm
his slave." And the hunter said "Hey, you with the
horse, here I am--I've arrived."

---

*His kirari.
**Inserting mamaki after abin, whose -n seems to indi-
cate a lacuna.

Then Kuturun-kusu got up, caught his horse and put
its bridle back on; tightened its girths, took his cudgel
of baushe wood, put foot to stirrup and mounted; then
he spurred his horse into a gallop, and reined him suddenly back to a halt--three times in all.

The hunter drew out an arrow and fired at Kuturun-
kusu, but the arrow lodged in the ground and burst into
flames. Kuturun-kusu came for the hunter without checking,
and the hunter drew out another arrow and fired at
Kuturun-kusu. But that one too lodged in the earth and
caught fire.

Then Kuturun-kusu unfastened his waistband and
tossed it towards the other, saying "Tie him up"--and
the thing tied the hunter up. Then said Kuturun-kusu
"Go on ahead, and your wife can follow." And he set
them in front of him.

Next Kuturun-kusu said "Hunter, stop. Let your
wife go ahead, and you follow her." And the hunter did
so, and his wife passed ahead.

They travelled for a while. Then Kuturun-kusu said
"Hey, you, hunter--you had a charm, but a real man's
charm was worth more than yours. But come back, for
I'll let you--you and your wife--go home. But, you must
leave this place, and go and live among other men, where
there are many of them. You must live there." That's
all. This with peace.

BAWA, KING OF GOBIR AND THE
BORI-MEN (II/LXIX)

One day Bawa, King of Gobir, heard some of the bori-men
speaking of how they practiced their cult. Says he
"Magaji Karnene, I want Magajiya* and the chief bori-
man summoned. For I hear that they boast of practicing
bori. Well, I want to see this bori; I want them to
show it me, so that I see it with my own eyes. And if
they don't show it me--I'll kill them all, Magaji
Karnene." "May the King's life be prolonged" said
Magaji, "I'll call them to you at once."

---
*See Glossary.

So Magaji Karnene got up and made his way to Magajiya.
Says he "Magajiya, the king sends for you." "Very well"
said she. Then Magaji Karnene went on and to the compound of the chief <u>bori</u>-man. "Chief <u>bori</u>-man" said he,
"The king sends for you." "Right" said the other, "May
the King's life be prolonged! Let me go and hear what
it is about."

He rose and went off to the king, who said to him
"Chief <u>bori</u>-man, this is why I have sent for you, you
and Magajiya: it is my wish to see this <u>bori</u> that you
practice. I want you to show it to me. And if you
don't show it to me, tomorrow, I'll put you all to death."
"King" said Magajiya, "Was that really all you sent for
us to tell us?" "Yes" said he. "Right" said she, "Then
tomorrow, if God spares us--what time do you want us to
come?" "I'm easy" he replied, "If tennish is too soon,
let it be when I come out to join my gathered courtiers."
"No" she answered, "Let it be the afternoon, towards the
early evening. We'll be along." And they agreed on that.

The two of them departed, the chief <u>bori</u>-man so
shaking with fear that he couldn't speak. When he got
home, he made preparations to run away. So when Magajiya
sent to the chief <u>bori</u>-man, they found him packing up
his things for flight. Says Magajiya "For shame! Chief
<u>bori</u>-man, how could you think of making us all lose face?
No--when we go before the king tomorrow, you just leave
the talking to me." "Really, Magajiya?" asked the chief
<u>bori</u>-man. "Yes." "But" said he, "Bawa, King of Gobir,
is going to k-k-kill us." "No" said Magajiya, "Not
when he has heard what I have to say. Unless of course
you start contradicting me. Then the King of Gobir
<u>will</u> kill us. But if you don't contradict me, he won't
<u>kill</u> us." "Oh no" said the chief <u>bori</u>-man, "We won't
contradict you, Magajiya." "Good" said she. Then she
ordered that all the followers of the <u>bori</u> cult in the
town, men and women, should gather together at her
summons. They gathered in her compound. "Now" said
she, "Followers of <u>bori</u>, this is why I have sent for
you. Tomorrow Bawa, <u>King</u> of Gobir, has ordered that
we are to go and show him <u>bori</u>. Well, tomorrow, when

we get there, just leave it to me, don't interfere, and
I'll show him bori." "Very well, Magajiya" they said,
"May God spare us to see tomorrow." "Amen" said she,
and sent them all home.

Next day, in the early afternoon, she again collected them all, and went with them to the entrance of
the compound of Bawa, King of Gobir. She sent in to tell
the king that they had arrived. And it was reported to
him that Magajiya and the chief bori-man had come. Then
he had them carry his couch out to the entrance to the
compound. "Ah, you've come, Magajiya" says he. "Yes,
we've come" she replied. "Very well, Magajiya. Show
me your bori." Now Magajiya had had them bring along
some red guinea-corn and some white; some bulrush-millet,
some beans and some acca.

Then said Bawa, King of Gobir "Magajiya, conjure up
Doguwa for me." And Magajiya called forward the girl,
to whom she had given the red guinea-corn to hold, on a
mat-cover. "May the king's life be prolonged" said
Magajiya, "You behold Doguwa." And the King of Gobir
saw guinea-corn, red guinea-corn. Says he "Is that really
Doguwa, Magajiya?" "Yes" she answered. And the King of
Gobir said "What you say is true, Magajiya."

"Good" said he, "Now conjure up Malam Alhaji." And
Magajiya called forward the girl carrying the white guinea-
corn, on a mat-cover. Says she "May the king's life be
prolonged. You behold Malam Alhaji." And the King of
Gobir said "And is that really Malam Alhaji, Magajiya?"
"Yes" she answered. And again the King of Gobir said
"Your words are true, Magajiya."

Again he asked her "Magajiya, conjure up for me the
one that I have heard speak of as a crazy spirit, the
one they call Janzari." And she made them bring forward
the beans, and showed them to the King of Gobir. "Is
that really Janzari, Magajiya?" he asked. "Yes, that's
him--may the king's life be prolonged" she answered.
Then Bawa, King of Gobir, said "But, Magajiya, what is
your reason for saying that this is Janzari?" "Well"
she said, "If you have the beans cooked now, and give
them to someone and he eats them; and then you don't

allow him any water to drink--won't he quickly go mad?"
"Yes, Magajiya. What you say is true" said the King.

And he went on to say "Magajiya, conjure up Dangaladima for me." And Magajiya called forward the other
girl, and the one carrying the mat with bulrush-millet
said "King, you behold Dangaladima." And then the king
said "So, Magajiya, bori is true after all. When I sent
for you and the chief bori-man today, I meant, if you
didn't show me your bori, all of it, to put you to death.
But now--well, it seems that bori is true after all."
Then he had cloths brought, and gowns and money and cola-
nuts, and he said "Well, Magajiya--you and your followers--
you may go now. And here's something to divide among
them." "Thank-you" said she. Then she and the chief
bori-man rose and went home. That's all. All this happened in Chibiri, in the district of Gobir. End.

V

Kano Traditions

ALWALLI, EMIR OF KANO AND THE OLD MAN WHO GAVE HIM SOME NEWS (I/L)

Here's a very old tale that our fathers told us.

One day Alwalli, Emir of Kano, was out riding when he overtook an old man on the road. He had him called, so that he might inquire the news from him.

He was called and came before the Emir and the Emir asked him, saying "Good sir, what news of the rains this year?" "The rains are good" he answered, "--for the neighbors." Again he asked him "How's distance?" "Distance has come close" the old man replied. "What news of the meeting?" "The meeting has dispersed." Then the Emir of Kano made him a present and dismissing him, sent him home. But he didn't ask him the meaning of what he had said.

It wasn't till next day that the Emir said "Where's the Galadima of Kano?" "Here I am" said the Galadima. "I want you" said the Emir, "To tell me what that man

yesterday meant when he said to us that the rains were
good--for the neighbors; that distance had come close;
and that the meeting had dispersed."

Said the Galadima to the Emir "The reason he said
to you that the rains had been good--but for the neighbors, was that he had had children, but they were all
girls, and he would not be having them in his own home.
That's why he said that to you. Why he said the meeting
had dispersed, that was because he had only two teeth
left in his mouth. And when he told you that distance
had come close, he meant that the matter was one he had
formerly seen far off but that now it had come close.
That is the meaning of distance having come close."
That's that story.

ABDULLAHI, EMIR OF KANO, AND
THE SULTAN (I/X)

Once when Abdullahi was Emir of Kano, he came to Sokoto
to make his formal visit when all the other emirs were
gathered there.

While he was there, the Sultan left Sokoto and
moved to Kaura Namoda, and all the emirs with him. But
while they were travelling in the bush, the Sultan's
horse was attacked by an illness in its stomach, and in
all that whole party of travellers there was no one with
a cure for it.

Then an old Filani came before the Sultan and said
"May God prolong your days! I have a cure for stomach
illness in a horse, but we need some used indigo-dye."
"I see" said the Sultan, "But where shall we get that,
travelling as we are?" And one of his guards said "The
only place you'll find used indigo-dye in this column
is with the Emir of Kano, for his people are dyers."

So a horseman was sent off at a gallop, and reaching
the Emir of Kano he greeted him, and said "The Sultan
says that you must give him some used indigo-dye, to
prepare medicine for a horse sick in the stomach." "That'
very easy" said the Emir and, to his own people, "Tell
the chief dyer to produce some used indigo-dye, ten
pitchers full and have it taken along!"

The message was taken to the chief dyer. "Right"
said he, "Where are the men to carry it?" Then ten
big fellows came forward and taking up the pitchers
went off with them and took them to the Sultan.

The Sultan was astonished, but the Emir of Kano's
messenger said "Indeed there is nothing here for aston-
ishment, so far as the Emir of Kano is concerned. He
has thousands of things more remarkable than this."
Then the Sultan gave the Emir a horse fully accoutred,
and, when it was brought him, the Emir sent his thanks.

ABDULLÁHI, EMIR OF KANO, AND
THE MALAM* (I/LVI)

This is the tale of a judgment that Abdullahi, Emir of
Kano, once gave. And because he based it on mere sup-
position, afterwards he spent thirty days lamenting it.
For a wise man does not rely on supposition.

For it happened that a girl came into her mother's
hut, and, not finding her mother there, took some cloths
and went out. No one saw her and she went off to amuse
herself. Then her mother came back to the hut, and not
seeing the cloths there began to scream. People gathered
and asked her "What's the matter with you?" And she
replied that someone had stolen her cloths.

Then some people close to her compound said that
they had seen a malam go into the compound. He was
summoned and asked if he had gone into So-and-So's compound. "Yes" said he, "I went in, but as I didn't find
the people home, I came out again."

Then the Emir of Kano asked him "Where are the
cloths that you stole from the compound?" And he said
that he hadn't stolen anything. "You are guilty of
theft" said the Emir, and again "Cut off his hand."
And his hand was cut off before the afternoon was well
advanced.

In the evening, the girl returned home, bringing
the cloths. Then the Emir began to lament, crying and

*See J. p. 137.

bewailing what he had done. And getting up he retired
into his compound--and remained there for thirty days.

When at last he again came forth, on that very day
he sent for the malam whose hand he had had cut off,
and said to him "I give you ten horses, ten cattle, ten
gowns, ten burnouses, ten rams, ten camels, ten young
male slaves, ten slave-girls, ten towns, and a hundred
thousand cowries, as compensation for the hand that I
have cut off." And the malam answered "This is a matter
for Muhammad the Prophet of God alone, may the blessing
and peace of God be upon him."

Then the Emir of Kano again retired into his compound and was there for thirty days. On the day that
he again came forth, there were crowds of people waiting
for him with their complaints. And the Emir of Kano
said to them "Fourteen days must be allowed for each,
single case, before the truth can be reached" (and he
maintained that rule) till he died.

A VARIANT OF THE LAST (II/CI)

When Abdullahi was Emir of Kano, there was a certain
malam living in the city of Kano. Now this malam had
no other occupation than writing out Korans. These he
would sell and so earn money to buy food. Now there
was a woman, an old woman, just close by the compound
of the Emir of Kano, Abdullahi; and this malam was in
the habit of visiting this woman to exchange compliments,
and she would give him alms in the shape of cola-nuts.
And she had a slave-girl.

Well, one day the woman had gone out about her
business, and the slave-girl too was out, in the compound of her mistress' daughter. Along comes the malam
to pay his usual call on the woman, but finding her out,
he returned home, and, getting there, remained there.

Meanwhile the girl, the slave, left the compound
of her mistress' daughter. Now there happened to be a
party on, and the girl, going into her mistress' compound, borrowed some of her cloths, and so off to the
party. Presently her mistress returned.

Well, it chanced that some people had observed when the malam went into the woman's compound; but they subsequently failed to observe the girl come back, go into her compound and take the cloths. All they saw was the malam go in and come out again.

So, when they heard her screaming, the neighbors asked her "Hey, what's the matter with you?" "My cloths have been stolen" she answered. "Well!!" they said, "But we saw that malam who is always coming--you know, the one you give cola-nuts to--he was the only one that we saw go in." "Really?" says she, and they confirmed that it was so.

So she went off and took her complaint to the Emir of Kano, Abdullahi. He ordered that the malam should be summoned. And when he had been fetched, the Emir of Kano said to him "Here, malam! Where are the cloths that you stole?" And the other replied that he had not stolen any cloths. "Did you enter her compound?" asked the Emir. "Yes, I entered her compound." "Well" said the Emir, "Bring me her cloths, malam." Says the malam "May the Emir's life be prolonged--but I did not take the cloths." "Malam" said the Emir sternly, "Don't prevaricate! If you don't bring back those cloths, I'll have your hand cut off this instant." But the malam insisted that he had not taken the cloths. So the Emir ordered that the malam's hand should be cut off, and it was done. Then the malam returned home, very troubled in his mind, that he had had his hand cut off, although he was innocent.

Evening came, and the girl returned from the dancing at the party--and returned the cloths. And her mistress pressed her hands to her breast and ran off as fast as she could to the Emir. Says she "May the Emir's life be prolonged. But I fear that we have taken upon ourselves full responsibility for the malam (at the last day). For we accused him of theft--and indeed he has even had his hand cut off. But it seems that he was innocent of theft." She continued "It was my slave-girl who borrowed the cloths to go to a party, and now she has returned them." "God in heaven!" said the Emir of Kano, "It seems that we have incurred guilt indeed."

And rising, he went into his compound, and for seven days did not emerge. Then at length he came out and ordered the malam summoned. They went and fetched him, and the Emir of Kano said to him "Malam, I give you ten horses, and ten cattle, and ten camels, and ten mules, and ten donkeys, and ten slave-girls, and ten slave-boys, and ten burnouses, and ten gowns of check cloth, and ten turbans, and ten pairs of trousers, and ten towns, and ten mats of cowries*." He concluded "I give you ten of every sort of wealth that this world contains, malam."

Then answered the malam "Oh no, Emir of Kano, Abdullahi for I want none of these things. I leave you to God and to His Messenger. Let God reckon between us, you and I. As for me, my occupation has been writing out Korans for sale. And with this hand, that you have cut off, if I wrote out a Koran and sold it, the buyer was filled with joy, for I had earned great merit in my work. Some of them had spent many years and much money seeking a Koran that was excellent, perfect, without fault--and had not found it. But when they came to me, they found their perfect copy, without a fault, without a wrong vowel-point to be seen. As for you, I leave you to God, who will do justice between you and me. Keep your things-- I don't want them." And the malam rose and made his way home.

The Emir of Kano too rose and entered his compound, and for thirty days lamented that he had incurred guilt in his treatment of the malam. And thereafter if complainants came to him, he would say "Very well. Let them wait for fourteen days." Then** he would say "Take them to the judge's compound." And never again did Abdullahi, Emir of Kano, consent to take a case in his own compound--from the day that he cut off the hand of the malam, who was innocent. If any complainants came, he would order them taken to the judge's compound. And so he continued till the day he died. That is all that I have heard of that account of Abdullahi, Emir of Kano. Finish.

---

*I.e. 200,000.
**Closing the quote after fuɗu, and inserting a full stop.

ABDULLAHI, EMIR OF KANO, AND
THE THIEF (III/XXII)

In the time of Abdullahi, Emir of Kano, a thief went
and stole some donkeys, six of them, and drove them
back home towards Kano city. The donkey-owners followed
the thief. Eventually the thief reached the city and
took the donkeys to the market. He gave them to a
middleman, saying "Here are my donkeys, six of them--
sell them for me. I'm going to settle into my lodging,
but I'll be back presently." "OK" said the other, and
the thief went off to his lodging.

    Presently the donkey-owners reached the market, and
saw their donkeys. But one of them said "Look, you see
our donkeys by that middleman--but let us not say anything. Let us sit here quietly until whoever gave him
the donkeys to sell--until we see him. Then we'll grab
him, that man." And the others agreed.

    But the thief meanwhile said to his host "Look, I
brought some donkeys, six of them, and not wanting to
trouble you with them, I took them to the market and
gave them to a middleman. But now that you've given
me fura, and I have drunk, and water, come, let's go to
the market and I'll point out to you the donkeys that
I brought, six of them." So the two of them went off
to the market, and he pointed out each donkey, one by
one, saying that it was his. He did this for all six
of them.

    At this point the owners rose and arrested the
thief of their donkeys, and the Sankurmi* brought a
chain and fastened it to the thief's neck, and grabbing
him he took him along to the Emir of Kano, Abdullahi.
The latter ordered the guards to seize him. They did
so, lifting him up and letting him fall. At which he
fell to the ground again, saying "Woe and alas! God!
Today I met the angels of God approaching invisibly."
He went on "But now, here they are, fully visible before
me and they have seized me!"

*Official in charge of markets and prisoners.

Whereupon the Emir of Kano, Abdullahi said to the guards "You, there! Stop--let the man be!" They let him be and presently he became calmer. Then the Emir of Kano asked him "Now, you--where can you see the angels of God?" "Here they are, standing just above my head" was the reply. "Where?" he was asked again. "There they are, just above me."

Then said the Emir of Kano "You--are you a thief, or are you a madman? Who on earth are you referring to?" He went on "So you're invoking God upon us humans, bringing us before Him, are you?"

Then said the Emir of Kano, Abdullahi "Where are the donkey-owners? Come here! How many are your donkeys?" "We have six" they answered. "Very well" he said, "Now-- what I want you to do is to tell me what you paid for your donkeys. Then I'll pay it to you." And they told him, and the Emir of Kano took the money and gave it to the men and said "Get up and be on your way." And they did so.

Next the Emir of Kano said "Where's the middleman? Let him come and I'll pay him his commission." The middleman came and the Emir of Kano produced the com- mission and gave it to him. Then he said "And now you too, thief--get up! Go to the market and receive the price of your donkeys."

Says the Emir of Kano "I, Abdullahi, ever since the case of the malam whose hand I cut off, and who said that he left me to the judgment of God--ever since, if anyone else does the same to me, he has me at his mercy."

So that was that, they separated and each went his way. That is a tale that I heard tell of the days when Abdu was Emir of Kano.

THE KANO CIVIL WAR--CAUSED BY SULTAN ABDU, "UNBAKED POT" (III/XI)

Once when Sultan Abdu, "Unbaked Pot", took an army against Argungu, his people refused to fight, except for Tukur, Galadima of Kano--he fought well. But Isma'ila, King of Kebbi, mounted and defeated them.

So when Sultan Abdu, "Unbaked Pot," got home, he
was very angry with his people. He accused the Vizier
of playing a double game, of sending people to tell the
kings on the other side of the bush* not to come and
fight.

And moreover, after they had returned home and
were again settled there, Sultan Abdu, "Unbaked Pot,"
was angry with all the chief men of Sokoto, saying that,
since they had played a double game with him, he would
never again consult them about anything.

Then one day a letter came from Kano, saying "Sultan, Bello, Emir of Kano, has died." And the Sultan
said "Vizier Buhari, go off to Kano and appoint a new
Emir of Kano. But I, the Sultan, will not give the
office to anyone but Tukur, Galadima of Kano--because
he helped me in the war against Argungu. All the other
kings from the other side of the bush gathered, but none
of them fought for me like Galadima Tukur. And it's
him I'm giving the office of Emir of Kano to. When you
get there, you're to turban him." "Very well, I understand, Sultan" said Vizier Buhari.

So Vizier Buhari made his preparations and set off
along the road; reached the city of Kano, and found
there the members of the ruling family ("sons of the
emir") gathered. Vizier Buhari gathered the malams in
the city of Kano and the Emir's slaves. He said "Now,
since Bello, Emir of Kano, is dead, Tukur is the new
emir." But the people said to him "No, Vizier, you
shouldn't give the office like that. For, look now,
if you award Galadima Tukur the office of Emir of Kano,
Yusufu will start a war with the people and many people
will be killed by him." Then Galadima Tukur himself
came along, and all the members of the ruling house
gathered in the mosque.

Vizier Buhari didn't make the appointment, but
wrote a letter and sent it to Sultan Abdu, "Unbaked
Pot," in which he said "Sultan, you said to give Tukur,
Galadima of Kano, the office of Emir of Kano. But,

---

*I.e. most of the Fulani emirs.

consider, if he is given the office, Yusufu will kill
him, and many lives also will be destroyed. For the
people of the place, all of them prefer that Yusufu
should be made Emir of Kano."

But Sultan Abdu, "Unbaked Pot," in his turn, wrote
his letter, saying "Take it to Vizier Buhari. He's to
appoint Galadima Tukur to the office. If he doesn't,
he'd better not return to Sokoto. For if he does return,
I swear by the living God I'll have him slaughtered--for
he is only related to us through a woman. Or has he
perchance ever heard that one of the house of Nana has
ever been Sultan*? Let him stop joking with me."

So the messenger set off, and getting there, found
Vizier Buhari and told him what Sultan Abdu, "Unbaked
Pot," had said. Then Vizier Buhari appointed Galadima
Tukur to the office of Emir of Kano.

And Yusufu rose, went out and went his way. He
went to Takai and stayed there. Then he attacked those
towns that agreed to give allegiance to Tukur, Emir of
Kano. And if he came to a town, and they didn't want
a fight, they would say "Oh, no--we're Yusufu's people.
We'll follow you, Yusufu." And Yusufu would reply
"Good, since you follow me, I won't wage war on you.
Come with me to war." And off they would go with him
to the next town. ·

But if they said that they were Tukur's people,
then Yusufu's men would attack that town, conquer them
and pass on.

That is how things were when Vizier Buhari left the
city of Kano. For he said "I'm not staying here, in
case Yusufu's men should come and kill me."

Then he set off and entered the land of Katsina
and came to a town called Radda. There he stopped and
stayed in Radda for about two and a half months.

Then Vizier Buhari said to his younger brother,
Dangaladima Ambo (who is the present Vizier) "Ambo, go
off to the Sultan and tell him that what I said about

---

*Sarcastically suggesting, I think, that the Vizier
 was taking it upon himself to act as Sultan.

the office of emir of Kano--not to give the royal office
of Kano to Galadima Tukur, and he insisted that he should
be given the office--well, he has been appointed. And
Yusufu has left and gone to the south of Kano City, to
a place called Takai, and he is attacking the people of
Kano, and he'll capture the city of Kano and seize
Tukur, Emir of Kano, and kill him. I say that what I
think is that Yusufu should be given the office, and
then the common people, and the petty kings will have
peace. As it is, the responsibility for the lives of
common people and kings is on us. For now, had Yusufu
been given the office, everyone would be at home peacefully. As it is, one has had a son killed, another a
father, another a younger brother, and another has been
divided from his wives."

The year in which this happened, things were very
bad. Even when the Europeans fought with Kano, Sokoto,
Satiru and Haḍeja, they didn't kill as many people as
were killed when Galadima Tukur was made Emir of Kano.
The men of Kano who disappeared in that period are
beyond number. And many of them have still not returned
to Kano.

Then Sultan Abdu, "Unbaked Pot," said to Dangaladima
Ambo (who holds the office of Vizier now) "Look, Dangaladima Ambo, get up! You go back! You get out of this
town--for it's not your father's* town! You're only
related through women! And Nana never in all her days
held the office of Sultan! Get up--and get back to
your elder brother, the Vizier."

And Dangaladima Ambo rose, and going out went back.
He met Vizier Buhari who had come to Sokoto. Then
Dangaladima Ambo said "Vizier, know that I went to
Sokoto, and to the Sultan, Abdu. I gave him your mes-
sage--and here is what he said: that I should get up
and leave Sokoto, because we (he said) are the offspring
of women, nor has our father ever been Sultan. So he
drove me away, Sultan Abdu did." And Vizier Buhari
said "Yes, Dangaladima Ambo, Sultan Abdu is right. A
ram is mightier than a ewe."

---

*He insulted him by mentioning his father (ubanku).

But Dangaladima Ambo began to lament. And so did Vizier Buhari, lamented for a day and a night. And this was the cause of Vizier Buhari's becoming blind. He continued blind till he died--for the vexation that Sultan Abdu's words to them had caused him. His heart was very sore, and he became blind.

For he, Sultan Abdu, "Unbaked Pot," would say to all the chiefly men of the city of Sokoto, if one of the people of Sokoto had done something wrong and Sultan Abdu had arrested him, and the leading men of Sokoto-- Vizier Buhari and his younger brother, Dangaladima Ambo, and the Judge of Sokoto and the Magajin Gari and the Sarkin Rafi and Ubandoma, all of them in fact--when Sultan Abdu was angry, if they went to beg him to show forbearance, he would say to them "Get out of here, out of my sight! For you play me false. If you don't get up and get out of my sight, I'll make it the worse for you." So they would leave, having no chance to speak.

But he had a son, of whom he was fond, and he would come and persuade him to be patient. That son of his is still here, he's called Mai-gari of Jabo. But he was the only one who could do it.

When wealth* was brought to him across the Rubu bush, he would say "Where are my sons? Let them come." They would be called, and he would take the wealth, all of it, and give it to them. And people began to say "Sultan Abdu likes no one but his own sons."

Well, one day his court was gathered and he said "Good people, I hear that you are saying that I like no one but my own sons. Well, now, if I don't like my own sons, whom am I to like? But, in fact, the only reason that you are saying this is because you despise me. For if anyone says to you that you are too fond of your son, he despises you; if anyone says that you are too fond of women, he despises you; if anyone says that you are fond of money, he despises you. Well, these three things, in this world of God--I've never seen a man who disliked them." And the courtiers said "Yes, that's so, may your life be prolonged, Sultan. What you say is quite right."

---

*Usually slaves.

Time passed and one day Sultan Abdu, "Unbaked Pot,"
conceived a dislike for Attahiru, son of Ahmadu, the
elder brother of Mai-turare at Gwadabawa. Attahiru was
then living at Chimmola. So Sultan Abdu, "Unbaked Pot,"
announced that he was at war with him. People heard of
it and said to Attahiru, son of Ahmadu, that he ought
to come and see Sultan Abdu, "Unbaked Pot," for they had
heard that he was going to take an army against him.
So Attahiru sent to tell his younger brother, Marafa,
who was in charge of the town of Gwadabawa, "Look, Sultan Abdu, "Unbaked Pot," has declared enmity against me,
but people say that I should go to him. And I'm going."
Then Attahiru, son of Ahmadu, set off from Chimmola, and
eventually reached the Kware Gate. But then he said
"No! Good people, I'm not going to Sultan Abdu for him
to abuse me. I know he is my father*, but if I go now,
he will abuse me, and as for me, since Ahmadu's death,
no honest and respectable man is permitted to abuse me."
Again he said "I'm not going. For if I go, and he
abuses me, I shall kill Abdu. I'm going home." And he
went back there and then from the Kware Gate, and went
back to live at Chimmola.

But Abdu, "Unbaked Pot," rose and mounted, saying
that he was going to make war on Attahiru, son of Ahmadu.
But when he was already mounted, Sultan Abdu's son got
news of it--that his father was going to attack Attahiru,
son of Ahmadu. Whereupon the son, who was called Mai-gari
of Jabo, went to Sultan Abdu and said "Sultan, what is
the reason that you are riding forth now to make war on
your son**? Is he the holder of the title of Sultan
now? Of course not, for you know that in all Sokoto
at present there is no Sultan except you. Now, just
thank God that you have ascended your father's throne,
and as for this journey you are making, make it to some
other place, and don't let us become a byword; for you
know it was once prophesied that the house of Atiku would

*I.e. "of my father's generation," classificatory
    father.
**Classificatory son; in fact, nephew.

fall from internal squabbles (?)." And Abdu, "Unbaked
Pot," said "Very well, Mai-gari. I understand and I
agree. I accept what you say."

And then Sultan Abdu turned and made his way to
Argungu, but he just took a look at them and didn't
attack them; and then went home.

The tales about Abdu, "Unbaked Pot," are many--but
that's all that I have. This with peace.

A VARIANT OF THE LAST (I/I)

When Abdu had been Sultan of Sokoto for three years,
Bello, Emir of Kano, died, and this concerns what followed. On the Thursday that Bello died, the Vizier of
Sokoto, Buhari, was in Kano city. The people collected
and informed the Vizier "Today the Emir has died." And
he answered "Very well. Now, you people of Kano, which
do you prefer--Tukur or Yusufu?" And the people answered the Vizier "We should prefer Yusufu."

Then the Vizier sent a letter to the Sultan, in
which he said "Greetings to the Sultan. After greetings,
the people of Kano say that they would prefer the emirate
to go to Yusufu." But the Sultan replied "Tell the Vizier
to appoint Tukur emir."

The messenger returned and said to the Vizier "The
Sultan says to appoint Tukur emir." And the Vizier answered "Tell the Sultan again--the people of Kano have
gathered together and said that if Yusufu is not made
emir, there will be great dissension among them." But
the Sultan replied "Tell the Vizier that if Tukur is not
appointed emir, the Vizier will no longer be my friend."

So the Vizier rose one night and put the turban of
emirate on Tukur, saying "The Sultan has bidden me
appoint you emir, for the help you gave him in the war
with Argungu." And Tukur thanked the Vizier.

But though Tukur had been appointed, the people
knew nothing of it, until they heard the beating of the
emir's drum. "Where is that coming from?" they asked.
And others said "Tukur has been made emir."

Then the chief slaves and members of the emir's family gathered and said to Yusufu "Since you have not been made emir, let us move completely from this town, and let us take the emirate by force, by war."

Whereupon Yusufu mounted, the people following him, and left the town. And he went to a village called Maimakawa and there he settled. And with him was the Vizier of Kano. And they sent word to the Emir of Hadeja that he should come to Maimakawa. And when the Vizier had brought the two of them together, Yusufu said to the Emir of Hadeja "This is why I have sent for you. As you know, the Sultan refuses to give me the emirate, which he has given to Tukur, on the grounds that he helped him in the war with Argungu. You must help me to return and drive out Tukur, for you see that the leading men are on my side." But the Emir of Hadeja's slaves said "That's not the way we do things." So the Vizier departed, and then the Emir of Hadeja, and then Yusufu went off with all his people, leaving Maimakawa, and going on to Takai. There they settled, at war with Tukur, gathering their forces at Takai.

Then one of his slaves and Musa, his Chiroma, said to Yusufu "Let us set out now and drive out Tukur, and you can then return to your home in Kano and become emir." So Yusufu set off for Kano, and joined battle with Tukur. And Tukur came out and routed them, taking many of those with Yusufu and bringing them home prisoner. And afterwards Yusufu returned to Takai.

Tukur selected a hundred and thirty men and had them taken to the market and executed; and to each of the city gates ten more men, and they too were killed. And then Tukur said "I shall kill any man who goes to Takai and returns here." And from that time, if any man arrived from the south of Kano and entered the city, Tukur would kill him. But if any of Tukur's people went over to Yusufu, he would be given a horse and honored.

Thus things continued, nor was there peace in Kano that year, or indeed so long as Tukur continued there. Yusufu and his party won a victory over the men of Kano, and then moved to Garko. There Yusufu died.

When he was dead his people collected and said
"Today our pride, the people's choice, is dead." Then
Kwairanga, the Madawaki of Kano, and Ahmadu, the Vizier,
and the chief slaves of the Emir spoke out and said
"Aliyu is our king. Let us accompany him and drive out
Tukur, and let us put Aliyu in the palace at Kano." And
the rest of the people expressed agreement.

But while they were still at Garko, Musa, the
Chiroma, said "I should be given the emirate, for I am
the elder. Moreover if it is not given to me, I shall
return to Takai; and I shall make war on whomever you
choose." And the people answered "Then go, by yourself!
For us, since Yusufu is dead, Aliyu is the man." And
then Chiroma Musa accepted the decision of the people.

They continued at Garko, forging harpoons and
collecting weapons against their attack on Kano. And
they kept sending Tukur evil charms to harm him. Then
one Tuesday when they had drawn near to the city, Tukur
came out and a battle was fought early in the morning.
Then they retired to Fage and paused there. On the
Wednesday they attacked again, by the Kuri Gate. This
time Tukur got the worst of it, and gathering those
people that were with him, he said to them "Good people,
I have called you together, for, as you see, Yusufu's
men are coming to bring disgrace upon me. But now know
that I am departing to the Vizier in Katsina." And he
set out and went to Katsina.

Then the men of Yusufu came from Garko and began
entering Kano, saying "Here is the emir whom God has
appointed, Aliyu of the Harpoon." And they entered
the city and took away the goods of those who had been
with Tukur. Then they collected in the city, and said
to Aliyu "Honor those who went to Takai in Yusufu's
time. As for those who went to Kamri, and then returned
to you, do not kill them, but neither should you honor
them."

Then Aliyu sent after Tukur one of his slaves, Garba
Gagare, with the warriors of Kano and many people. And,
as they went they came up with Tukur at Tafashiya. At
that time the Vizier was still at Musawa. Then the
slaves that had been sent killed Tukur there, at Tafashiya,
and returned home.

But Aliyu, Emir of Kano, asked them "Why did you
do that? For you know that I did not tell you to kill
Tukur. I told you to capture him and bring him here."
And they answered "But he was at large, disturbing the
land. That's why we did what we did."

These events of Tukur's reign lasted for one year
and three months, and the people of Kano did not enjoy
peace until Aliyu became emir. Then at last they had
peace--but it was not the Sultan who appointed Aliyu.
It was the people of Kano who appointed him, and it was
said of him "Here's the Emir God appointed, the Kano-
Wednesday one, son of Abdu."

And among the slaves that had killed Tukur, there
was one, Garba Gagare, who had a drummer, who sang and
composed panegyrics to Garba.

It is now twelve years since this happened, all
but three months; and it is eleven years and three
months since Aliyu's appointment. And that is how
these events happened.

THE WOMAN, HER SLAVE-GIRL AND THE
KING OF DURUMAWA (I/IV)

This is the story of a law case in Kano in the time of
Aliyu. There was a rich woman who left the city one
day, accompanied by her slave-girl, on their way to
the country to get some shea-butter.

They had travelled till they were close to the
town of Durumawa, when the slave-girl said "Look there's
a dinya tree with fruit. I'll go and get some for us to
eat." "Very well" said the lady, "Go and get some for
me." So she left the path to go and pick the dinya
plums, but losing her sense of direction, missed the
way and couldn't find the path or her mistress again.

She went on and came to a large farm where men
were harvesting the bulrush-millet. "Where are you
from?" said they. And she answered "We came from the
city to get shea-butter, my mistress and I. And I left
the path to pick some dinya plums, but I became confused
and got lost. And my mistress is there waiting for me

to come so that we can go on." Then the man in charge
there said "Come along, I'll take you to the gate of
the town, and if you see her there, you can go on with
her."

Well, it happened that he was the king of the town,
who had decided to trick her and collect her on the
cheap, meaning to keep her. And he put her in his household and locked her up. And for seven years she was
there in his compound, in the time of Aliyu, Emir of
Kano.

Meanwhile her mistress looked for her, and not
finding her where she had left the path to pick the
dinya plums, returned home. Nor did she leave the city
again for seven years.

Then once again she set out into the country and
went by way of the very town near which her slave-girl
had got lost. Entering the town she walked along and
reached the gate of the king's compound, selling antimony* and the like. Whereupon she was called from
inside the king's compound, and going in she saw her
slave-girl that had got lost. She had had two children.
When her mistress saw her, she said "How did you get
here, girl?" And she replied "Ever since that year we
came here, and I left the path to pick dinya plums and
got lost--the king of this town took me and kept me
here in his household--seven years I've been here. Ever
since the troubles** I've been here, in this town."

When she had seen her, she stopped selling her
wares, and returned to the city of Kano. There she
took her complaint to the Emir, Aliyu. The Emir asked
her "What is your trouble?" And she answered "I have
come to you to complain of the King of Durumawa. I
lost my slave-girl just outside his town. And the girl
says that the King took her--it's seven years ago now--
and kept her, and now she has had two children by him."
"Go and wait" said the Emir and ordered the king to be
sent for.

---

*Primarily used as a cosmetic.
**The civil war of Yusufu and Tukur, see previous
   accounts.

So a messenger was sent to summon the King of
Durumawa, and the messenger returned with him. But
before he left home, he procured three people to bear
false witness for him, giving them a hundred thousand
cowries each, and saying to them "You bear witness on
my behalf when we go before the Emir." So they went
to the city and found the Emir at Nasarawa*.

The woman who was seeking her slave-girl back was
sent for, and there she found the King of Durumawa.
Then the Emir asked him "What is there between you and
this woman?" And he answered "May the Emir's days be
lengthened--ask her!"

Then the Emir asked her "Well, woman, say what it
is that is between you and the King of Durumawa." And
she answered "This girl is my slave-girl. We set out
together to buy shea-butter. And as we travelled, we
came near to the gate of Durumawa, and the girl said
'Look, there's a dinya ripe over there, I'll go and
pick some fruit for us to eat.' And I said to her
'Very well--off you go!' But when she had left the
path to go and pick the dinya fruit, she lost her sense
of direction and missed her way. Then I didn't see her
again for seven years, in fact since the troubles. But
then I returned to the town in the course of a journey
and coming to the gate of the king's compound, was
selling my wares. I was called from inside the compound,
and when I went in, I saw her. And when I had seen her,
I said nothing, but collecting my things together, I
came home. This is my reason for bringing this complaint."

Then the Emir said to the King of Durumawa "Now
let us hear what you have to say" and the King of
Durumawa said "Well, I've had that slave-girl since
before the troubles, and she has borne me two children."
"Where are your witnesses?" said the Emir. And the
king called in the witnesses that he had paid money to
to give false evidence for him. They came in.

And the Emir said to one of them "You, there, witness! When did the King of Durumawa get this slave-girl?"

---

*A residence a mile outside the walls.

And he answered "He bought her before the days of the
troubles." "That's all, get up! I've heard your
evidence" said the Emir, and to the next one "You, there!
Come nearer, let's hear what you have to say." And the
second witness said "Well, I knew he had the slave-girl,
but I don't know where he got her." "That's all, get
up! I've heard your evidence" said the Emir, "Let the
next one come and give his evidence." And he came and
sat before the Emir of Kano. The Emir said to him
"You--where did the King of Durumawa get this slave-
girl?" And he answered "I don't know where he got her."

Then the Emir asked the King of Durumawa "When you
got the slave-girl, did you have a search for her owner?"
"No" said he. "Then" said the Emir, "You have committed
robbery. Let the woman be given back her slave-girl,
and the children she has had by you, to be her slaves,
unless you ransom them." Then they took the slave-girl
and her children and gave them to the woman.

ALIYU, EMIR OF KANO (III/XXV)

It was a European officer who captured Aliyu Babba,
Emir of Kano, when he went away near Kyara, towards the
land of Gobir. He captured him there and brought him
back. And they came to the bank of the river at Sokoto,
having followed the road from Kware, and arrived near
the entrance of the city.

Then Aliyu, Emir of Kano, said "Praise be to God!
I, Aliyu, thank God, I thank His Messenger." And he
had them draw some water for him, and he made his ablutions and performed the after-midday prayer. Then
he said "Now, European! I thank God and I thank His
Messenger that I have reached the tomb of my grandfather. Now if you take a gun and shoot and kill me,
I accept; and if you spare me, I also accept. You may
choose--but I won't enter Sokoto, nor will I go anywhere
else. Kill me if you will--even if you kill me, I still
won't go anywhere else."

Then the European came over to Aliyu, Emir of Kano,
and said "Emir, let us have no trouble. Just get up

and let us be going." "No" said the Emir of Kano, "I've
told you--I'm not coming. Nor will I enter Sokoto in
your company. Here I sit and here I stay." Whereupon
the European said "Emir of Kano, let there be no trouble.
Get up and let us be going." But the Emir of Kano
repeated his insistence on staying there.

So the European walked three times round Aliyu,
Emir of Kano, and stood right over him; and stretched
his arm above the head* of the Emir of Kano. And there
sat the Emir, facing east, holding his rosary, shrouded
in a white burnous, over his dark turban.

The European waited for some time, standing right
over Aliyu, Emir of Kano, stretching his hand out and
actually putting it on the Emir's head. Then he said
"Emir of Kano, get up! Get on your horse and let's go."
Then the Emir of Kano rose and mounted his horse, and so,
with a soldier leading the halter of the Emir of Kano's
horse, they entered Sokoto, passed through and came to
the Government Station, and there spent the night.

Next morning, when it was light, they set off in
this direction and came down here, to Argungu, skirted
it, and so to Yelwa, to Kontagora, and from there to
Zunguru. And that was the departure of Aliyu, Emir of
Kano, and he still has not come back to this country.
That's all--that's all I know of that account. This
with peace.

HOW THE PEOPLE OF KIBIYA REBELLED (I/XL)

In the year of the Satiru fighting, it is said that at
a town called Kibiya in the land of Kano some of the
people gathered to plan rebellion, saying that they
would make wings and fly away. Young and old collected
and made themselves little shirts, with short sleeves,
and put them on. Then, as they gathered, they exhorted
each other saying that they were going to fly away for
the hour was at hand. But while they were doing this,
no one else in the land of Kano knew about it.

_____
*Felt to be a great indignity.

Presently there came a day and their leader said
"You must all prepare to fly away, for the hour has
come." Then one of them rose to make the test, so that
they could see if the hour had come. Getting up, he
climbed a tree and stretching out his arms like a bird
when it begins to fly, he jumped off and falling down,
broke his back. Then the rest of them, when they saw
this, said "Now, all of you! Let's keep this to ourselves! So that it doesn't reach the ears of our rulers--
otherwise they might treat us like they treated the people
of Satiru in the land of Sokoto. To see something happen
to another is enough to cause fear!"

VI
Zazzau Traditions

ABDULKARIM, EMIR OF ZAZZAU, AND HIS SLAVE, DAN KADA (I/XVII)

Once, when Abdul Karim was Emir of Zazzau, he mounted and went off to war in the land of Piti. There they lived in a camp and each day went off to fight. Sometimes they would take a town, sometimes the town would be too strong and they would leave it.

Time passed thus till there came a day when the Emir rode off to attack a large town. But as they were preparing for the fight, one of his warriors, called Dan Kada galloped up to the Emir and said "May God prolong the days of the Emir." "Amen" said the Emir. "I've just broken something" said Dan Kada. "I'm sorry about that" said the Emir, "Go and get a bone-setter to fix it for you." But the other said "May your days be prolonged—it's not bone-setting that's needed; for it isn't a limb that I have broken." "Then what have you

broken?" asked the Emir. "It's my nerve that's broken"
said Dan Kada, and the Emir answered "Devil take that
sort of a break, Dan Kada! Get off home! Otherwise you
might die at the mere prospect of fighting!" So Dan
Kada went off home.

SIDI, EMIR OF ZAZZAU (I/XIV)

Here's a story of Sidi, Emir of Zazzau, father of Aliyu.
It is said that never since Zazzau existed as an emirate
has there been an emir who slaughtered people like Sidi
did. Crimes that merited death, and crimes that didn't--
all of them he punished by death.

At that time anklets and armlets made of copper and
other metals were popular with women, and if a woman
was caught committing an offence and brought to the Emir,
he would have one of these fitted on her! But if it was
a man who was arrested, he would be killed.

Well, one day a woman was arrested along with her
husband, and the Emir ordered "Fit armlets and anklets
to the woman and kill the man!" But the woman said "I
don't want them, since you're killing my husband. I
don't like you and I don't like your rule." And the
Emir said "Well, well! This is a woman who deserves to
be spared shame. Let her husband go!" And everyone
said "That was a fine effort of that woman!"

And a song was made up about him, which ran "You
kill the men and you fix bangles on the women!"

SAMBO, EMIR OF ZAZZAU, AND THE GIRL WITH
THE RAGGED CLOTH (I/XXII)

It is said that Sambo, Emir of Zazzau, once mounted and
went out of the town for a ride, and came to a threshing
place where there were women gathered. There he saw a
girl, who was threshing for hire. She had just one
ragged cloth, and nothing else.

Then he sent someone to fetch her and take her back
to his compound. There he had the women wash her, and
she was given several fine, large cloths which she put
on. After that he married her, but he kept her rags
and rolled them up and hid them.

Time passed, and she went on living in his compound. But she was always doing something wrong. He,
however, never ceased to show forbearance. But there
came a day when she did him even greater wrong and said
"You've never done anything for me." He called her over
and said to her "What you've just done--that's just too
much for me. None of your fellow-wives dare act like
that. Just because I was sorry for you, seeing that
you had nothing, you were working for hire to get something to eat; and I brought you here, into my own home,
because I was fond of you. And you--you must needs
choose me to abuse." Then he added "And now bring back
here all the things that I have given you. The rags
you had when I first met you are here; I hid them," and
picking them up he threw them to her.

Then said she to the Emir of Zazzau "Devil take
you, you're not a worthy son of your father. But I
take after my mother." "How do you mean?" said he,
"In what way am I not a worthy son of my father, and
how do you take after your mother?" "Like this" said
she, "We women, since we were first created, have never
inherited the quality of gratitude. Whatever we have
had done for us, we are never thankful. But you men,
ever since you were created, you've inherited the quality
of forbearance. Whatever was done to you, you have shown
forbearance. Now, since you can't show forbearance to
the wrongs that I do you continually, and keep me here--
you're not a worthy son of your father. And that is why
I said as much to you."

Then the Emir of Zazzau was silent and pondered for
a long while, before speaking. Then he said "I suppose
that is so--that women are never grateful, whatever is
done for them." And he continued "Return to your hut.
You may stay. I'll show you forbearance, and whatever
you do, good or evil, shall be your own affair."

KWASAU, EMIR OF ZAZZAU (I/V)

This is a tale of the days when Yaro, son of Abdu, was
Emir of Zazzau. He was grandson of Hammada and his
nickname was "Manga's damp that ruins strong walls*".
These are the events of a year of his reign.

He set off to war one Friday, after he had returned
from mosque. He began the campaign at a village called
Gwazatoka, as was the custom of all the emirs of Zazzau.
From there he moved to Farakwai.

He slept at Farakwai, and there a malam said "You
see the Emir there--he won't return." And when people
asked him about this, he answered "If you doubt what I
say, you will see before long."

Then they invaded the pagans of Amana and imposed
tribute of three hundred slaves on them, which they accepted. Then they came to another town, also of the
Amana, and collected two hundred slaves from them. On
they went without pause and without opposition, collecting tribute in every district.

But then the Emir was smitten by fatal illness,
and he said to his people "This illness is not one that
I shall recover from." So they stopped there and waited
for what God would ordain. But he rose and moved on to
Riri, and there he died.

And the people asked "Who will be our leader, to
take us home?" Some said "Let us make Madawaki Lauwal
leader," while others preferred Madawaki Kwasau. Others
again wanted Galadima Salmanu for their leader, but
several said "No. Galadima Salmanu has no right to the
emirate. He was a servant of Sambo, Emir of Zazzau.
When he had lost all his cattle and was in straits, he
came into the city from Basawa or one of the other villages near and began to earn his living by plaiting and
selling kabidos**. Then he came to the Emir and became
his servant; and later his zagi. Then he was given a

---

*Edgar notes that Manga was the younger brother of
   Yaro's father; also that Yaro had a wife called
   Manga.
**See Glossary.

horse. Then as time went on and he prospered, he was
given people too, to be with him and follow his leader-
ship. And finally he was appointed Galadima. He has
held this post both under Emir Sambo and Emir Yaro.
And he has had control of the town--but now, now that
Yaro is dead, you say that we should follow Salmanu as
emir! If you must follow someone, let it be Madawaki
Kwasau, and he will lead us home; for he is Yaro's son."

So the people rose and made Kwasau their leader,
and they returned home in peace. When they got home,
the Fast month was nearly over, and the Festival came,
and they celebrated it without an Emir being appointed.
It was only afterwards that the Vizier came from Sokoto
to appoint the Emir of Zazzau.

But before he left Sokoto, the Sultan had said to
the Vizier "You must appoint Iya Usuman to the emirate."

Meanwhile, when Aliyu, Emir of Kano, heard that
Yaro was dead, he ordered one of his chief slaves,
Shatima, to take five hundred horsemen and go to Zaria.
And when they were setting out the Emir of Kano told
them "You must be clear that I am sending you to Zazzau
to help Kwasau and to prevent the Vizier from depriving
him of the emirate; for I have heard that he intends
to give it to someone else. If you find they have given
the emirate to any other of the family, whoever he may
be, kill him! And appoint Kwasau emir, for we have been
friendly since the days of his father, Yaro." So Shatima
set out from Kano and came to Zazzau secretly. And he
paused, without revealing himself, in a town of Zazzau,
Likoro, for a while.

Meanwhile, in the city of Zaria, it was not known
that they were near, and the Vizier gathered together
the sons of the Emir of Zazzau. And when they had collected, he said to them "I have called you together to
tell you that the Sultan has bidden me appoint Iya
Usumanu to be emir." Then a slave, Tagwai Dutsi, jumped
up and said to the Vizier "Don't attempt the impossible!
For if Kwasau isn't appointed emir, there will be an up-
roar in this town." Then he drew his sword, and the
people gathered in the mosque, with more of them outside.

So the Vizier told Kwasau to stand and come forward, and he did so followed by his people, and they
came before the Vizier. "Kwasau" said he, "You see
that the people here prefer you. Their leaders too
are with you. You are therefore emir, and may God
support you in the office!" "Very well" said Kwasau,
"And I am thankful." So they dispersed and everyone
went home. Then, seven days later everyone came to do
homage to the new emir, from the city and from the
country. And everyone rejoiced at the appointment.

But from the time that Kwasau became emir, he began killing people. Whether a man's crime was punishable by death or was a lesser crime, still Kwasau would
have him killed. Until his malams said to him "Emir,
this is not right. You should abstain from killing
those whose crimes are not punishable by death. If a
man commits a crime that is punishable by the loss of
a hand, have his hand cut off; but if it is a capital
offence, then kill him." And he accepted their advice.
That is how things were in the days of Kwasau.

If a man stole and was caught, he had his right
hand cut off. In Yaro's day, when a thief had had his
hand cut, they heated oil and dipped the stump in it
before releasing him. But when Kwasau became emir, if
a thief had had his hand cut off, they didn't use oil,
but pounded pepper and potash and soot and pouring them
into a potsherd, stirred it up and thrust the stump deep
into it, before letting him go. And then boys would be
sent to pelt him. Others would hit him with sticks and
drive him from the city. But before he was clear of the
town the severe beating would kill him. This is what
happened in the days when Kwasau was Emir of Zazzau.

And the people of Zazzau would say of him "Muhamman,
Emir of pepper and potash."

One year he made a campaign against the town of
some pagans called Rimawa. When he and his men got to
the town they found that the pagans had gone fishing,
leaving the women in the town. So about the middle of
the morning, they took the town by surprise and set
about seizing the women, which they did very thoroughly--
and small girls too.

From the time that Kwasau became Emir of Zazzau
he fought nine wars and sent out six raiding parties.
Then came the European occupation.

KWASAU, EMIR OF ZAZZAU AND THE GAMBLERS (I/XV)

A Zazzau man told us how Kwasau, Emir of Zazzau, dealt
with gamblers. He sent his guards into the town and
arrested numbers of gamblers. When they had all been
brought to the Emir's court, he came forth. "Where are
the gamblers?" he asked the chief guard. They were
pointed out to him and he asked one of them "What have
you got to say?" And he answered "Oh, I'm the banker,
I don't throw dice." Then the Emir said to the chief
guard "Get the leaders together and take them to one
side." And then "Go along to the market and kill these
ones who are the leaders. Thus you'll leave the younger
ones without anyone to follow." The young ones were
then whipped and released. And ever since then no one
gambles in Zazzau--except secretly.

KWASAU, EMIR OF ZAZZAU, AND ABUBAKAR, EMIR OF NUPE (I/VI)

Once, in the days of Kwasau, a caravan-leader in the
city of Zaria, whose nickname was Mai-Lasolaso, collected a large body of people, merchants, and itinerant
traders, and they all gathered together in the city,
among them Ubandawaki na Raga, Sharif Dogo, Madugu a
Dafa Dawa, and others.
    They set off and as the caravan left the city, so
large was it that you would say they weren't leaving a
single Kano man in Zaria. So they left Zaria, and their
first stop was at Kasuwar Ganye. From there they went
to Igabi and from there to Rikoka, but this town wasn't
able to provide for such a large party of traders.
Those who were up with the leaders were able to buy
food in the town, but the ones behind couldn't get any

food, even to take as medicine, for it was the hot
season. So they had to pick a leaf called k̇ahon badi,
which they soaked in hot water and boiled, and then
they ate it. This leaf grows on old farmland.

When they left that town, they stayed next at
Ribako, and from there to Karji. From there to Yalwa
and then to Akuro, across the Kaduna.

Leaving there they entered the bush, and travelled
for a whole day until sunset when they stopped at Rafin
Dinya. From there to Kachiya to Koturu, from Koturu to
Kurmin Dangana. Then Arbi, a town of naked pagans, the
Kwaro tribe. Then from Arbi to Kukui, which is a big,
rocky hill. From Kukui to Fanda, from Fanda to Gitata,
from Gitata to Jama'ar Bararo, and from Jama'ar Bararo
to Kafi, a half journey. At Kafi, some of them bought
salt and set off home.

The Adamawa traders--Ubandawaki na Raga, Sharif
Dogo and the others--meanwhile went off to Adamawa,
while Mai-Lasolaso departed for Loko. Thus the whole
caravan split up, each one taking his own way.

Now just then Kwasau, Emir of Zazzau, had arrived
at Dutsin Kwai (sic) expecting that they would fight,
for there was hostility between him and them. But they
came to terms and accepted his conditions, when he imposed on them a tax of two hundred and fifty slaves.

The Emir's party was camped there, when they found
that there were no cola-nuts in the camp, and a swift
messenger was sent out with orders to go quickly to Kafi
and there catch Mai-Lasolaso and buy cola-nuts for them.
The messenger got to Kafi but found no cola-nuts, even
for medicine!

Well, just then a party of traders, who were travelling cross-country from Kagarko, reached the Emir of
Zazzau's camp. There were forty-six of them and their
sole merchandise was cola-nuts! They reached the camp,
and before nightfall they had sold every one of their
cola-nuts. And the prices were high at that camp--five
calabashes of cola-nuts for a slave, ten for a female
slave. And so it was until the traders moved on.

After eight more days, the Emir of Zazzau set off
for home. He reached home, and two days later--before
he had had time to rest from the journey--he received
word from Abubakar, Emir of Nupe, to say that next day
he would be arriving, fleeing from the Europeans. By
then the Emir of Zazzau's people had gone off to their
own compounds.

So in the night the horns and trumpets were blown,
and the people gathered. Then the Emir said to them
"I have called you at this time to tell you that tomorrow, Abubakar, Emir of Nupe, is arriving here, in
flight from the Europeans." And the people were astonished, and some of them laughed, but others said "You
stop laughing--anything that can expel Abubakar, Emir
of Nupe, from his home is something that is to be feared."
And each of them had something different to say about
it.

Then they dispersed, and next morning the Emir
mounted and his people following, set out and left the
town. And so they met Abubakar, Emir of Nupe. He
entered the town, and they brought him to where he was
to stay and he dismounted. Then the Emir of Zazzau
gave him three slaves to cut grass for his horses; and
three slave-girls. And he gave his people gowns and
trousers.

So he stayed for a while in Zazzau. But when the
hot season came, the Emir of Zazzau said to Abubakar,
Emir of Nupe, "I'm sure that you agree that it is not
really possible for you to go on living here in the city.
But I will give you a village, Basawa, and you can move
there and live. I give you the place for your home."
"Very well" said the other, and moved there with all
his people. So they settled at Basawa.

But after a while there, Abubakar, Emir of Nupe,
said to his people "This sort of existence doesn't suit
me. I'm going to Maska, in the land of Katsina. I
hear that the Emir of the Sudan has reached Kaya. I'll
go and call on him and then return here."

And when he had set off for Maska, the Emir of
Zazzau complained to his people "Do you see what Abubakar,
Emir of Nupe, has done to me? He has gone off to the

Emir of the Sudan at Kaya."   "Don't let it concern you"
said the people of Zazzau.

But when the Emir of Nupe got to Maska, he didn't
return to Zazzau, but went on to Kano, to a village near
Karaye, and there he settled.   But after he had been
there for four days, messengers came to him from the
King of Karaye, and said to him "The King of Karaye has
sent us to you, with this message: you must leave here
at once.   For Aliyu, Emir of Kano, has forbidden him to
allow anyone whom the Unbelievers have driven out to
remain here."   "Very well" said Abubakar, Emir of Nupe,
"I understand and I will go.   But tell the King of Karaye
this--just as I have had to leave my home willy-nilly,
the same fate is coming on everyone else who takes pride
in his position!"

Then Abubakar, Emir of Nupe, set off at midday and
went to a village in Katsina, Sabuwar Kasa, and settled
there.   But before he had been there for twenty days,
news arrived that the Europeans had burnt Bebeji and
killed the King of Bebeji.   Then the King of Karaye was
very alarmed and said "Good God!   And the other day we
drove Abubakar, Emir of Nupe, from here!   And now it's
our turn to suffer.   Go and ask the Emir of Nupe to come
back and live here with us*."

But Abubakar, Emir of Nupe, said "Tell the King of
Karaye that since he used such ill words to me, I shall
never return to his town.   And what I suffered--let him
suffer!"

THE KING, THE WOMAN AND
THE MALAM (I/106)

There was once a king in the land of Zazzau called
Maza-Waje-Tukunyar-Gwari**, whom the peasants feared;
if ever there was a rumor that he was mounting and

---

*Presumably as some protection against the invaders.
**Edgar notes that this is a reference to a proverb:
  a Gwari pot won't stand unless a hole is made for
  it--so a bad king oppresses unless expensively
  placated.

setting off, everyone scattered. A king is usually a
popular spectacle--but he wasn't.

Then one day, a woman went to a malam and asked
him to give her medicine which would make her husband
deeply in love with her. Said the malam "Right, I'll
make you some, but you must get me some dust from the
entrance to the king's compound, if you can." "Surely
I can" said she. "Very well" said the malam, "Tomorrow
go and bring some." "Right" said she.

In the morning while it was still dark, she got up
and went to the entrance of the king's compound, and
bending down began to collect some dust. But it happened
that the king had come out of his inner compound and was
squatting in the entrance-hut. He saw her bending down
and collecting dust and shouted angrily at her. Then
the woman was very frightened and spilt the dust. "Come
back here" said he, and she came back and knelt down,
her body a-tremble*. "Very well" said he, "You and your
husband and the malam who told you to come and take dust
from the entrance to my compound, each of you will pay
three hundred thousand cowries. Rascals! You thought
you would make some medicine against me, so that the
Emir of Zaria would dismiss me and appoint another, for
you could find no other way to have me dismissed."

Then the three of them went and collected the money
with difficulty and paid. For that day forward the
woman and her husband never again lived at Fatika. And
the malam made up a song about the town, which went
"Fatika knows no peace, no rest, no security--nothing
but ill."

_____

*There seems something missing here, though the sense
 is clear.

VII
Traditions of Bauchi and Misau

USUMANU, EMIR OF BAUCHI, AND
MALAM HALILU (I/III)

Malam Halilu was well known in Bauchi and he won over
to his side the people, the ordinary people and the
pagan tribes, and they preferred him to the Emir. Malam
Halilu never became emir, though he was the son of an
emir. As for the Emir, Usumanu, nobody liked him, or
just a handful.

So Usumanu sent for Sale, Emir of Bornu*, and said
to him "I have sent to ask you to help me capture Malam
Halilu. For you see how he has won over these people."

Malam Halilu would also say to the people of Bauchi
"Help me to kill Usumanu. If I become Emir of Bauchi,
I won't take your children. If a man commits an offence,
I won't arrest his family--the country will be at peace
and good order will prevail."

So the Emir of Bornu came and they joined battle
with Halilu. And the battle raged for seven days before

---

*A title only. Katagum was his town.

they captured Malam Halilu. Then Usumanu, Emir of
Bauchi, sent word to the Emir of Bornu "Take Malam
Halilu and kill him." But the Emir of Bornu refused
saying "I couldn't kill Malam's son!" And again the
Emir of Bauchi said "Kill him, it will be on my head."
Then the Emir of Bornu said to the Emir of Bauchi "I
came because I hoped to make peace between you and
your brother. But if it is a question of killing and
being killed, I will not kill him. Kill him with your
own hand!" And Usumanu, Emir of Bauchi, took Malam
Halilu into his compound and killed him.

Now three years passed during which he didn't visit
Sokoto. Then he went and found the Sultan, Umaru, at
Gidan Goga. And Sultan Umaru said to Usumanu, Emir of
Bauchi, "You have violated the law! Why did you kill
Malam Halilu? Very well. You are deposed from your
emirate."

So he was deposed and Umaru appointed as Emir of
Bauchi. And Umaru ruled for eleven years till the time
of the Europeans began, and then he was arrested and
taken to Ilorin.

YARIMA SALE, KING OF BORNU* (I/XXXVIII)

One day Yarima Sale collected together all his horsemen, and they came together from the city and the country, for he was to go to Kano to pay his respects to
the Emir.

When he was three days' march short of Kano, he
sent ahead to a butcher, who was a friend of his, called
Danda, asking him to have made for him three hundred
long-sleeved shirts of the best calico, so that he might
give them to his men to put on under their chain-mail,
and not be laughed at by the people of Kano. Now this
was when Aliyu was Emir of Kano.

Then Danda got together twenty tailors and issued
them with bales of calico. And they prepared it and

_____
*See last account.

sewed it all up for him within the three days. And
when the shirts were finished they brought them to him.
Then Danda sent off his messenger to catch Sale and
give him the shirts at a town called Gogyal.

And Yarima Sale collected his finest young men,
and each of them took a shirt and put it on, and then
put his chain-mail on, on top. All three hundred of
them arrayed themselves in this way and ranged themselves round him.

Then, on the day he was to enter Kano, the Emir of
Kano met him, and then the Kano people were amazed,
saying "However did Yarima Sale manage this fine dis-
play?" And it wasn't till he had gone, that the Kano
people said "Oh, you see, he sent to Danda and got him
to have those shirts made for him." And others said
"That must have been what he did."

HASAN, EMIR OF MISAU (III/VII)

There was once an emir of Misau, called Hasan. His
mother's name was Amina. Her pregnancy resulted in
her producing two children, but Hasan's twin was a
lion*. So there were the two of them, but on the day
before they were to be named, the lion died, and the
surviving son was called Hasan.

He grew, and his father said "That son of ours is
an evil boy--he is preparing to be the cause of much
trouble (lit. "to rouse the world")." Then his courtiers
said "May the king's life be prolonged. Why do you say
that?", and he answered "Because Amina does not have
honest, respectable children, but evil ones." He added
"But you'll soon see."

The day came when Hasan went into the emir's compound and began to sleep with his father's wives--until
the emir learnt of it, and then he forbade him to go
into the compound, and had a separate compound built
and a marriage arranged for him.

_____

*He would have been called Husaini, had he been human.

Now, as it happened Hasan had a very large penis, and he would tear* the mouth of the vagina of any woman he slept with.

Well, on another day, his father caught him with one of his favorite concubines, and expelled him from the town.

So he went off into the Tangale** area, and filing his teeth to a point, lived there, in the Tangale area.

Next he went and changed his form, turning into a lion, and began seizing women. If he caught one and she said to him "For shame, Hasan! Of course, I recognize you, you're Hasan"--he would break her neck.

But if he seized a woman who didn't speak to him, then he would bring her home, and when he got there with her, send off his servant to go and sell her, and then bring him back the money to spend.

But the day came when the Emir of Bauchi heard about this--how the Emir of Misau had driven out his son, Hasan. So he mounted and went along, and had Hasan summoned. Then he took him into Misau, and made a reconciliation between him and his father.

Says the Emir of Bauchi to the Emir of Misau "Emir of Misau, don't you know that a man may have a hundred sons, but that each of them will have his own spirit that God has given him, different; each his own character that God has bestowed on him? The hundred sons won't have the same character--everyone will have his own. Be forbearing towards your son, and let him dwell with you." And the Emir of Misau answered "Emir of Bauchi, having heard your words, I accept them and thank you for them." Then the Emir of Bauchi mounted and returned home.

They lived together for a while, and then Hasan put a spell on his father. His father set off to go to war, and travelled for some way and then joined battle with the pagans. Whereupon the Emir of Misau was shot in the thigh.

*saje is, I think, an error for tsage.
**Presuming -e for -i.

Now the Emir of Misau had given one* order to the
people of Misau, saying "If one day you see a snake
coming at me to bite** me, don't kill it--let it be."
And they promised to obey.

Now it happened that Hasan had a small staff in
his hand; and when he saw that his father had been shot,
and carried out and laid at the foot of a tree, then--
as the Emir of Misau lay there--Hasan threw his little
staff on to the ground, and it turned into a snake. It
went for the Emir of Misau where he lay.

One of the Emir's chief slaves got up and struck
the snake, and picking it up, threw it away. They
looked for it, but couldn't find it. And presently
the Emir of Misau died.

Then said Hasan "Well, men of Misau, whether you
like it or not, none but Hasan is going to become king.
As for my uncles and my elder brothers--if one of them
would like to try--well, let me see him try!" And they
went off home.

And presently a man from Sokoto went to Misau, one
from the house of Gidado+, the younger brother of Vizier
Buhari, (himself) younger brother to the present Vizier,
(who was then) Dangaladima Ambo but is now the Vizier.
He was the commissioner (from the Sultan) who turbanned
Hasan as emir of Misau.

Then Hasan went and took up residence in Misau,
and people were in superstitious fear of his power; for
he would tell one of his men to come and grip his foot,
where he sat there in his mud-roofed++ hut. They would
do so and pull it, going outside a long way. Then he
would say "Let go!" And his foot would be seen to
return to its place.

But one day he was taken ill as he sat there. He
seemed to be nodding, but as it happened, it was a fatal

---

*The numeral seems as strange in the H. as in the Eng.
  The style of this whole piece is awkward (? transla-
  tion from Ar.).
**C i s o is an unusual variant for cizo, and almost cer-
  tainly an error.
+Reading capital G, to make it a name.
++I.e. superior to common, thatched one.

illness. He was sitting cross-legged, when he died.
But no one knew of it, until the day was well advanced,
and evening came. Then they realized that he was dead.

They pulled his legs, intending to straighten
them, but they would not straighten. And so it was
with bent legs that they took him to the grave. That's
all. Haza wassalamu.

VIII
Katsina Traditions

KATSINA IN WARTIME (I/XXVII)

There was once a very powerful emir of Katsina. The
number of his own private horses alone was ten thousand,
apart from those of his retainers. For his Galadima
had seventy thousand, his Kaura seventy, or it may be
eighty thousand, his Durbi forty thousand, his Marusa
eighty thousand--all without counting those of the
Emir's sons.

One day, moreover, Durbi went to his town of Mani,
and, returning to the city found that he had forgotten
his pipe. So he turned his head and said that he wanted
his pipe. The word was passed down the line till it
reached Mani where he had set out. The pipe was got
and passed from hand to hand till it reached him. He
smoked it, and entering the city went to his compound--
and the last horse had still not set out, though it was
a day's journey!

Then there was the Emir who never stood up straight, but always went along bent. Until one day his Durbi and some of the princes asked him "Why don't you walk upright, but bent thus?" But he remained silent.

Another day they asked him again. "Bring me four young men" and they were brought. One he ordered to go east, one west, one south, and one north. "All of you" said he, "Travel for thirty days and thirty nights, and on the thirty-first morning turn and come home." "Right" said they and away they went and travelled till the day appointed by the Emir--and on that day the Emir unbent and stood up straight. Then there was a running to and fro in the town and people said "It's war!" Then he again bent himself, and when his messengers returned, they were all asked, and every one answered and said "Where I was thirty days ago, there was a general alarm." So the Emir said to all his leading men "If we stand up straight, then the whole world must be up--that's why we go along bent." Then they were contrite for their presumption, but he told them it was nothing.

Then there was Mu'allaidi, son of Bello, who travelled very widely, before coming back home. Then, setting out again, he quarreled with Sultan Ahmadu Rufa'i. Whereupon, in his anger he left the town and went west till he came to a place called Kaya. There he built a town and settled, an independent king with the title of Sarkin Yaki (War King). After some years there he died.

His son, Alhaji, succeeded him in the title and began taking his neighbors' lands away from them by force. After him came his younger brother Atto, who succeeded to the title. And his younger brother was called "Durumbu". Durumbu went to Katsina to buy a horse, and afterwards often rode to war with the men of Katsina. One day a son of Kaura Isyaku called "Bebeji-dodo" sought leave from the Emir of Katsina, Abubakar son of Ibrahimu, to lead out an expedition. This was granted him--or rather, a raiding party--and Durumbu was one of them. He had become friendly with Kijibta, son of Dabo, but he didn't return from this raid, for he was killed in the course of it. So Atto held the office. But now he has retired in favor of his son.

IBRO (IBRAHIMU), EMIR OF KATSINA, AND THE
YOUNG MAN AND HIS WIFE AND THE
EMIR'S PROCLAMATION (II/XII)

There were once some young men in the city of Katsina
who had acquired some money; and the Emir of Katsina,
Ibro, heard about it. They got themselves married, and
the Emir had them summoned before him.

Then he had a white guinea-fowl caught. And he
held it in his hand and said "Well, you young fellows--
I've heard all about you Tudun 'Yan-Shanu* men" and he
went on "Look, I've a guinea-fowl here--won't you buy
it?" And one of the young men answered "May the king's
life be prolonged, but who am I that I should buy a
guinea-fowl from the Emir himself, to take to my wife
to cook for me?" And another said "May the king's life
be prolonged, if I knew what its price was, I'd buy it
for my wife to cook for me." "Two hundred" answered the
Emir of Katsina. "Cowries or bags?" asked the other.
"Bags" the Emir replied. "May the king's life be prolonged" said the young man, "But who am I to put a
guinea-fowl worth two hundred thousand cowries into a
pot and cook it?" But another of them said "May the
king's life be prolonged--give me the guinea-fowl. I'll
buy it for two hundred and fifty. Give the bird to me,
and I'll take it to my wife to cook for my supper. I'll
buy it for her." Then the Emir of Katsina took the
guinea-fowl and gave it to the young fellow, who said
"Someone go to my compound and bring twelve mat bags
full of money, and open another one and take out ten
thousand cowries; I'm not leaving here till they have
brought the money. And then I shan't bother to go
home; I'll go on to the dye-pit. But if I have any
children, I've left them something to remember me by.
And as for my wife--if I die, it'll be said that I
bought her a guinea-fowl for two hundred and fifty
thousand cowries."

---

*The capitals are my tentative emendation.

Then the Emir had a kitbag fetched, and taking a
gown of black and blue check, put it on him; and a Nupe
gown, and put that on him too. And they went into the
Emir's compound, to his stables, and fetched an Azben
horse, and put a saddle on him, and complete accoutrements and led him in. Says the Emir "Young fellow, get
up into the saddle of that horse, for I've given him
to you, with all his harness. God bless you! For it
is the likes of you that ensure that we escape feeling
shame. And now you may go home." And the young man
went home, and the Emir went into his compound.

But it chanced that the young man's wife had a
paramour, and when she had cooked the guinea-fowl, it
was to him that she took it. He worked at the same
dye-pit as her husband, and when he had dyed a cloth,
he would take it to where the cloths were beaten; and
as he lifted the mallet, he sang "I'm the one who ate
the guinea-fowl worth two hundred and fifty thousand."
Others heard him as he sang thus, and said to him "Hey,
what sort of false boasting is that, to say that you've
eaten a guinea-fowl worth two hundred and fifty thousand?
There's the man who bought it to give to his wife."
"Oho!" he answered, "But when she had cooked it she
gave it to me." And presently the husband began to
hear it being said that the other fellow had eaten his
two hundred and fifty thousand cowrie guinea-fowl. So
he went and asked his wife who blustered and denied it.
But he drove her from his home.

News of this reached the ears of the Emir of Katsina,
and he sent for the young man, and the other--who had
eaten his guinea-fowl--too. The Emir had the latter
beheaded there and then by the drainage-hole in the
wall; and the butchers dragged his body away to a pit
on the west of the city, near the Guga gate. "Right"
said the Emir to the husband, "Young fellow, do you
want your wife?" "May the king's life be prolonged--
I don't want her." "Very well" said the Emir, "If you
don't want her, she can get out and leave my domain."

But her parents came and besought the Emir, saying
that they would pay a thousand, if he would only allow

her to stay at home. All her relatives were Masanawa*
people and they went and raised money and put it together to the amount of a thousand. Then they took it
to the Emir. "Where's that young man?" said the Emir.
"Let him be sent for." So they went and summoned him
and the Emir said to him "Here's the money for the
guinea-fowl, that your wife took and gave to her paramour."

Then he said "Go and beat the drum in the market-
place of the city of Katsina, and make a proclamation,
saying 'With effect from one week from this very day,
whatever woman, whoever her parents or grandparents may
be, comes to the ears of the Emir as having taken something that her husband has brought her and given it to
her paramour--the Emir will put to death her paramour'."
He continued "And add 'As for the woman, and her relatives, and her parents--all of them--I will arrest them
and fasten them together by the necks. I shall then
send them to the Sultan.'" That's the end. That's
all my story.

---

*Reading M for m.

IX
General Traditions and Especially Daura

THE ORIGINS OF THE KINGS AND
EMIRS* (I/XXI)

This is the origin of the rulers of Daura, Kano, Katsina,
Gobir, Zazzau and Nuru**. They originate in a man
called Bayijibda, son of Abdullahi, ruler of Baghdad.
He left Baghdad because of an infidel, by name Zidawa,
who brought a terrible war upon them and shattered
their forces, dividing them into forty parts.

And Bayijibda came with twenty of them to Bornu,
and with his own fighting men. And his people exceeded
those of the ruler of Bornu--whose ancestors came from
Syria. Now Bayijibda knew that his people were stronger
than those of the ruler of Bornu, and those close to him
said to him "Let us kill the ruler, and then you can
succeed him."

---

*Cf. J. p. 111. For a recent assessment of the Baya-
jidda story, see Hallam, W.K.R., J. African History
VII. (1966) pp. 47-60.
**Edgar notes "unknown, probably Rano"--an easy slip in
Arabic script.

This reached the ears of the ruler of Bornu, who
was not to be caught off his guard--much less killed.
"What shall we do about these people?" said he, and
then "Well, my friends, I see nothing for it but to
give him a woman to marry." So he was given the daughter of the ruler of Bornu, Magira her name.

Thus was friendship established between them, and
whenever Bayijibda set off on an expedition, he would
say to the ruler of Bornu "I pray you, give me some of
your people, for I am going against a large town, that
they may assist me in the fighting." And he would be
given two thousand, or even three thousand men. But
when he was returning from the expedition, it would
be without them, for he had given them towns in the
land of the ruler of Bornu.

At last there only remained two of his followers,
and he said to them "My friends, I mean to win for
each of you a place to live." And taking one of them,
he went with him to Kanum and he became king of Kanum.
The other was his son, and he took him to Bagarmi, and
he became king of Bagarmi. That left Bayijibda on his
own, with his wife, daughter of the ruler of Bornu,
and his horse.

But when the people of Bornu saw that Bayijibda
was on his own, they began to make attempts to kill him.
And so he fled, and the flight was a hard one, taking
with him his wife, who was pregnant. But when they got
to a town called Gabas (East), his wife could go no
further; so he left her there and went on. And after
he had gone, she bore a son. The boy was called Birram
and became king of Gabas, which was known as Birram's
Gabas.

When Bayijibda reached Daura, he found a woman
ruling there. Now the first woman to rule Daura had
been Kufunu. After her Gufunu, who had been succeeded
by Yukunu, then Yakunya, then Waizam, then Waiwana.
Next Gidirgidir, then Anagari, and after her Daura.
And she it was who was the ruler when Bayijibda, son
of Abdullahi, arrived.

When he got there he put up at the house of an
old woman called Awaina. He asked her for some water,

but the old woman said "My son, you can't get water in
this town, except on Friday. Then, when all the people
have gathered together, you can drink water." He replied
"I'll get some water. Give me a bucket." So she picked
one up and gave it to him. Now it was night when they
spoke together thus.*

He picked up the bucket and went off to the well,
and let it down into the well. Now this well had a
female snake in it, and when it heard someone throw a
bucket down, it put its head out of the well and made
as if to kill Bayijibda. The snake's name was "Sariki"
(King). Drawing his sword, he cut off its head, and
took the head and hid it. Then he drew water, drank
and gave some to his horse. And the rest of the water
he brought to the old woman, Awaina. Then, entering
his hut, he went to bed.

Next morning the people saw what he had done to
the snake--this stranger Arab from Syria**--and they
were very much astonished at the size of what remained
in the well, so that word of it reached Daura, and
mounting with her host of warriors she came to the
mouth of the well.

Now, when she saw that the snake's head had been
cut off, and the size of what remained in the well,
Daura too was amazed. For she saw the size of what
was in the well and what was out of the well and remembered how it had made the people suffer. Then she
said "If I find the man who killed this snake, I swear
that I will divide the town in two and give half to
him." So one man said "It was I killed it." But when
she asked him for the head, to test whether he lied,
he went away. Then another man came forward and said
"It was I who killed it." "Where's the head?" said she--
but he too was lying. And there were many who made the
claim, but all were proved liars.

---

*This motif occurs several times in the tales, notably
in tales of Auta, the youngest son.
**Not quite accurate--see first paragraph of the story!

Then the old woman came forward and said "Last night a stranger came and lodged in my compound. He had a beast with him, whether a horse or an ox I couldn't say*, and he took a bucket and went to the well, and drawing water, drank some and gave some to his beast to drink, and brought me what was left. Maybe it was he who killed the snake. Send for him and ask him." So he was sent for, and Daura asked him "Was it you who killed the snake?" "It was I" said he. "Where's the head?" said she. "Here you are" he said. Then she said "I swore that I would divide my town in two and give half to whoever has done this deed." "Don't divide your town" said he, "But I will gladly marry you."

So she married him and he came and lived in her hut. Then she gave him a slave-girl and he took her as a concubine. Thereupon, when people were visiting Daura's compound, they stopped using her name, but said "We're going to the compound of the Sariki-killer." So she began to use the name "Sariki (King)".

After a while the concubine became pregnant, but Daura didn't. When the child was born, he sought Daura's approval to its naming. And when she gave it, he called the boy "Makarabgari" (?"Taker-of-Towns").

After this, Daura too became pregnant, and bore a son. And she sought his approval to name him. And when he had given it, she called him "Bawugari". And he was the first of them**.

After that his father, Sariki-killer, died, and he became king in his place. And he had six children: the first, Gazaura became Emir of Daura. Next was Bagauda, of the same mother, and he became Emir of Kano. Then there was Gunguma, who became Emir of Zazzau; Dami who became King of Gobir, of the same mother as Gunguma. Then there was Kumayau, who became Emir of Katsina, and, from the same mother, Zamgugu, who became King of Rano. And that's the story of the kings.

----

*? because horses were then unknown in the country?
    Then how could she put a name to it?
**Of whom? Their children? The kings of Daura?

THE ORIGIN OF ALL THE HAUSAS (I/XXVI)

Here's the origin of the Hausa ruling houses. Daura was a woman who came from Bornu. She settled in the middle of the bush. She remained there for a long time with her slaves, and eventually built a town on the spot. Now she used to wear a gown and trousers like a man; and charms, some hanging on her, some on her head, some on her upper arms.

Later a man came from Bornu, who became angry* and asked her to marry him. But she answered "I'm not a woman to sleep with a man." He accepted this, so she agreed that they should be married.

They were married and she brought a slave-girl, saying "Here is one to sleep with you." He accepted her, and the slave-girl became his concubine, until she became pregnant. And she bore a son and called him "Karaf".

"Is that so?" said her mistress, and took all the charms from her head and put them aside. Then she did her hair and rubbed in indigo, and said to her husband "I'm coming to sleep with you today." Which she did, and so conceived. And she too bore a son, and called him "Bawu"--that is to say "Ba Mu Garinmu" (Give Us Our Town)--"Karaf" stands for "Karɓe Gari" (Take the Town).

Bawu was the father of "Kachi" and "Kanau", and Kachi was the progenitor of the men of Gobir and the Gwaris and nine pagan tribes. From the men of Gobir come the men of Zamfara, of Kabi and Kambara. From the men of Kabi stem the people of Yauri and of Arewa (North). Kanau was the progenitor of the men of Zazzau. But others say that Bawu was the progenitor of the men of Gobir, and these in turn progenitors of the men of Kambara and of Kabi. Thus have I heard.

---

*Why?

THE ORIGIN OF THE HAUSA DYNASTIES (I/LVII)

The Hausa dynasties originated in Daura where the king
was a woman, called Umma, who had no husband.

Then a man came from Bornu. Now his journey from
Bornu arose out of a prize horse that belonged to Maina.
It was never taken out, so no one ever saw it. But
this man's mother heard about it one day and began to
visit the compound and to make herself popular there
with pleasant conversation, until at length she gained
the confidence of the people there. Now she had a mare.

One day she said to them "I want some of the urine
of that horse, to make medicine with." "By all means,
collect some" they answered, and she did so, and taking
it home, inseminated* her mare with it. And the mare
conceived, and bore a male foal. And as he grew, he
grew into the living spit of his father. And she became afraid that the king might take him away. So she
gave him to her son.

And he mounted and rode west on him. He was followed, but they never caught up with him and after
seven days returned. Meanwhile he reached Daura on a
Friday.

There was a stone-lined well in Daura, but no
water was taken from it on Friday, as there was a female
snake in it. And she would come forth and fill the
mouth of the well--that was why no water was drawn on
that day.

Now the name of this fugitive from Bornu was Abba
Kyari. When he got there the snake had come out and
was sunning herself. He made to take the bucket but
was prevented. Then coming up to the snake he killed
her, and gave his horse water to drink.

They brought news of this to Umma, the ruler of
Daura, and she sent for him. When she saw him she named

---

*The word usually means "rectal insertion" but I have
translated it this way to give some verisimilitude
to the operation.

him "Bawu" and married him. And she gave him concubines,
one of whom had four children. But Umma only bore one
son.

When their children had grown, she said to their
father "These boys should be named." Then the eldest
was named Kachi, another Kanau, another Daure, and the
youngest, Yabawu.

Then she said "Allot them towns." And Kachi was
allotted Katsina. Kanau was allotted Kano. And the
youngest, Yabawu, was allotted Rano, in the land of
Kano. As for Daure, Daura was given to him.

Then their father said "Let us give them their
lands." He sent for Kachi and told him to come at sunset when he would give him a gourd-bottle with indigo
seed.

Well, it happened that Kanau was concealed nearby
and heard what his father said to his brother. Then,
at sunset he reached his father before his brother, Kachi,
and said "Here I am, father!" And their father--who
was blind--picked up the gourd-bottle full of indigo
seed, and said "Take this, and take it with you to
your town, and give it to them to sow, that they may
excel every other place in the abundance of their indigo." For he thought it was Kachi, when it wasn't. And
that is how Kano came to have finer indigo than any
other place.

After that Kachi came and said to his father "Here
I am." And his father said "Was it then not you that
I gave the bottle-gourd to?" and he continued "That boy
got here before you--but I'll give you some fire, with
which to fix the boundary of your land and Daura, Kano
and Zazzau." Then, giving him fire, he said "Take it
and when you are a good way from Daura, set the grass
alight and let the fire run through the bush. Where it
dies, there will be the boundary of your land and all
of these."

So Kachi went out from Daura, and when he was a
little way from it, he started the fire, and it caught,
and licked round the lands of Kano and Zazzau. And it
penetrated to Yauri and reached the river Niger before
it died. And that is how the land of Katsina came to
have so many outlying parts.

But Daure* was given corn seed. And that is why Daura came to be a greater corn-growing land than any other.

And when their father died, Katsina acceded to his power, which extended to Bornu and to Zamfara, all the region was under the Emir of Katsina, but not Bornu itself. And there were one hundred and eleven emirs of Katsina; their graves are behind the Gobarau mosque.

This is the mosque which was moved, without falling, to beyond the town where there is low-lying land called "Galangalan", just to the north of the city of Katsina. There there is a lake, also called Galangalan, which has potash in the water, quite near to Takuma.

Also that is where the tomb of the saint, Dan Takun, is, which people visit to seek his blessing. This is north and a little east of the compound of the Emir of Katsina. At the present time the ruins of the Gobarau mosque are still to be seen in Katsina.

And it was said that Katsina was the same distance from Medina and Machina; and that these other two cities were the only ones in the world the equal of Katsina in age!

The men of Gobir and the people of Bedde took their origin from Badar.

As for the men of Azben, they are descended from a jinn--the one that took Solomon's ring. For he went into Solomon's compound where his thousand wives were, and before leaving he made a hundred of them pregnant. Then Solomon expelled them from his compound and they were taken out into the bush, where they were delivered, and their offspring were the men of Azben, called "children of adultery". And as they grew in numbers, they appointed leaders (tambaris) among themselves, and later still a single king for all Azben, like they have now.

As for the origin of Alkalawa, it was land farmed by the judge (alkali) of Zamfara.

---

*Which seems a better reading than Daura in view of the previous reference.

As for the story of how Umaru Nagwamatse went
forth*, and Kwantagora (Kontagora) was built, I don't
have the written tale here with me. If I find it, I'll
write you again, oh ruler of ours who rests not from
doing good day and night!

THE ORIGIN OF THE PEOPLE OF
KWATANKWARO** (I/XVIII)

The people of Kwatankwaro were originally Katsina peo-
ple who lived in a town called Rufa. A man called
Muhamman left Rufa and came and settled at Kwatankwaro.
He himself never became king, but he made his son,
Yabani, king. And Yamusa succeeded him; then Ibiran,
then Yaƙubu. Next came Mamudu, and then Musa-na-biyu,
then Kufagari, then Adan, then Adani. Next was
Masallachi, and after him Usumanu, and after him
Abubakar-ba-mu.

And when he was king they had a war with the
Gwamatsawa⁺. And after he had taken the town, Nagwamatse
killed him. Next Yaƙubu became king, and after him
Muhamman and then Idrisu. He's the present king.

There have been fifteen kings at Kwatankwaro, and
some of them have kept a thousand horses and a thousand
slave-girls in their compound. And even Nagwamatse took
a very long time to take the town, in the days when
Abubakar-ba-mu was king.

It is also said that one day when Mamudu was king
of Kwatankwaro a man committed murder and he was caught
and brought before the king. "Why has he been brought
here?" asked the king, and the courtiers said "He has
done murder." "Very well" said the king, "Is not the
penalty for murder death? Take him and kill him." Then
the fellow burst out crying "Oh, oh, oh! How I shall
suffer!" and everyone burst out laughing. "You--devil

*See I/XXX.
**Kontagora area.
⁺The men of Kontagora--see I/LXV.

take you for a weakling!" said the king, "Didn't you
know about the suffering when you killed the other
fellow?" and he continued "Let him go!"

Certainly the kingship of Kwatankwaro is no petty
one. It has all the appurtenances of the Emir of Kano--
trumpets, ostrich-feather fans, some hundred guards who
precede the king and shout and clear the way for him,
famous malams and wealthy traders. In the old days at
Kwatankwaro there was a man who had six hundred slaves.
Moreover they are Muslims, saying the prayers, fasting,
believing the true doctrine, going on the Pilgrimage,
and having in the town malams devoted to religion. They
omit none of the duties of religion. But those whom
they found already in the town and conquered, they were
pagans, and their tribe is still there--and the origin
of these pagans is lost in antiquity.

THE ORIGINS OF THE PEOPLE OF DARAGA* AND
OF GARACHI AND OF RANKWAI (I/XIX)

The people of Daraga came originally from Garachi; both
they and the people of Rankwai and other towns were
subject to Garachi, until the Filani conquest. It was
then that they left and moved to Daraga.

It was Bachiri, King of Gusau, and Dan Ashafa,
King of the Filani of Bungudu who took Garachi. At
that time Jatau was king of Garachi. After Jatau came
Kikari, then Maikundu; next Inisawa, and after him Dan
Ali, followed by Dan Magaji, followed by Dan Darho.
Next came Bako and then Dan Kada, then Ali, and after
him Dan Kada. He was dismissed, and now lives at
Bena. Next came Idi and he too was dismissed, and now
lives at Morai. After him Dan Turaki, who was also
dismissed, and now lives at Bawa. Next came Dan
Barunje, and then Abdu--he's the present king. It
was Ali whom the Gwamatsawa** killed.

---

*On borders of Zuru area.
**Nagwamatse's men.

Garachi was an old seat of kings, and a thousand horses were kept in the town, and they were never allowed to be fewer.

Once Wake, King of Gwari, attacked them, but he didn't take Garachi itself, contenting himself with raids on the villages. For he would say "I can't take the body of the gown--just the sleeves."

Their reason for moving their capital to Daraga was that the Filani had made the other untenable. But even now they don't let their old town become a ruin. There is a king at Garachi and there is one at Daraga, but the senior king and the senior town is Garachi. Nor is their origin from anywhere else but from Garachi.

They are Muslims but not very strict ones. They are great farmers, and for crafts they have weaving, dyeing and trading. Thus both men and women earn their livings.

Nagwamatse took Daraga and razed it and left it as it now is. Had it not been for him, it would still be a great town. It and Rankwai are the main towns of Garachi.

WAKE, KING OF GWARI, AND THE MALAMS AND THE WIZARDS AND THE BORI-DEVOTEES (I/XLIX)

Wake, King of Gwari, was sitting surrounded by his courtiers one day and the Madawaki of the town asked "All of you, I ask you to tell me--malams, wizards or bori-devotees, which of them is better at telling fortunes?" And one said "But--surely you can't compare anything else with malams?" And another said "Oh, well--scholarship apart--for seeing what is hidden and making it known, give me wizards!" And yet another said "Nonsense! Bori-devotees are the best at telling fortunes." The argument became involved, but the truth remained to seek.

Then the King of Gwari said "Very well--leave it at that for now. Tomorrow I'll settle your argument

for you." Then the King retired to his compound. There
he had a hut built without entrance. In it was put a
black ox, and the hut sealed up*.

Next morning, the King came forth to his assembled
courtiers and said "Send for the malams, the wizards
and the bori-devotees." They were summoned and when
they had gathered, he went into his compound.

Then first he called in the bori-devotees. He
asked them, saying "I want you to use clairvoyance and
tell me what is in this sealed hut." Then their leader,
Ajingi, went into a bori-trance and said "In that hut
there is--a beast, black, with four feet." So the bori-
devotees were told to go and wait on one side now that
they had done their bit.

The wizards were called in, and when they came in
the King said to them "I want you to use clairvoyance
and tell me what is in this sealed hut." So their king
did his mumbo-jumbo, and having looked, said "Oh, there's
a black ox in the hut." And they too were told to go to
one side and wait now they had done their bit. "Tell
the malams to come in" said the King.

But before this, the chief malam had made all his
colleagues perform their ablutions. Then they went
into the mosque and he said to them "Now! What I want
is for us all to pray to God about what we are going to
be asked. Whatever is in that hut, let God turn it into a black horse, so that the wizards and the bori-
devotees may not put us to shame; for if they are more
truthful than we, it will be a terrible blow for us,
and no one will have any more respect for malams."
They agreed and sitting down in the mosque, they began
to pray and besought God and continued till when the
King sent to summon them.

When the malams came before the King of Gwari, he
said to them "I have sent for you, because I want you
to use clairvoyance and say what is in this sealed hut."
Then their leader looked and said "May God prolong your
days--there is nothing in that hut that I can see but
a black horse, without a patch of white on him."

---

*Cf. II/LXVI.

Then the King of Gwari sighed and said "Is that
really what you see?" And the malams answered "It is--
if God so please."

Then the wizards and the <u>bori</u>-devotees formed one
group and each announced to the people what he had seen.
And after that the King ordered the hut to be broken
into--and out stepped a black horse, without a patch
of white on him. And the smiles of the wizards and the
<u>bori</u>-devotees were on the other sides of their faces!

Then said the King of Gwari "Whoever fears not
malams, fears not God!"

THE MEN OF GWASARO (III/XVIII)

The men of Gwasaro once revolted and expelled the King
whom the Europeans had appointed over them. They drove
him out and he went to Kuta and settled there. From
Kuta he set off again and went to Minna, and there, when
he got there he found the Europeans who deal with justice
and the policemen.

Then a European set off from there with about 25
government policemen to whom he issued five rounds a-
piece. They set off from Minna and they reached Kuta
and there they spent the night.

In the morning they set off and took to the road
and travelled for a while until they reached (Gwasaro).
But they hadn't quite got to the town when the men of
Gwasaro came and intercepted them at a place where
there is a little hill among some <u>doka</u> trees on the
edge of a forest.

When they met the "judge" and the policemen, they
began to shoot at them. But the "judge" kept saying
"For shame! Men of Gwasaro, this isn't a fighting matter, forbear!" They quickly shot the "judge", they
also hit the doctor, shooting him, but they didn't inflict a mortal wound and he escaped.

However, they got the doctor's horse and then the
European serjeant came up and said "Doctor, get on my
horse, we'll ride it together," and they both mounted
the horse. They travelled for a little way, and the

serjeant said "Doctor, let me get down, for this horse
won't carry the two of us." And the serjeant went and
jumped into the water.

The men of Gwasaro were advancing, killing the
policemen. One policeman had ten arrows in his body,
another had seven arrows in his body, another had five
arrows in his body. One policeman was hit in the penis.

When they returned home here, to Kuta, a letter
was written and sent to Minna; and another was sent to
Zunguru.

On the day that the letter got there, on that same
day some soldiers set off in the evening. They set off
in the evening and travelled for some time. Next morning
when it was light some artillery men were selected and
they set off. The commander of the force was a European.
The force set off and travelled for some time, and after
a night and a day we reached Kuta, and there we spent
the night.

In the morning we set off and went to the north of
the town. The men of Kuta showed us the place where
the grass was all lying flat. They said to us "Look,
here's the place where the police serjeant-major was
captured, that's Malam Bako, an Argungu man*. They
captured him, they threw him to the ground, and were
just going to cut his throat like a ram, when a carrier
took his gun and catching hold of the barrel began
laying about the men of Gwasaro, who scattered and left
Malam Bako. And then Malam Bako managed to get into
the town."

When we reached the place that was pointed out to
us, the Europeans made the carriers put down their loads
and the gun (? guns). Then the European ordered "Soldiers
Let everyone put eleven rounds in his magazine**." He

---

*One of the scribes who wrote many of Burdon's MSS was
  so called and also hailed from Argungu.
**This story is full of military words and is surely
  the account of an old soldier, perhaps an old
  artilleryman. Most of these words have never become common in Hausa.

ordered the advance guard, and said "Go on ahead leaving
20 feet between you and us. If you see anyone in front,
don't speak to him, but shoot him."

As for the policemen who had been killed, I saw
the corpses of eleven policemen and one groom; and in
addition there was the "judge" who had been killed,
that is, all added up, there were thirteen corpses.
Then there were the horses which had been killed, but
the men of Gwasaro had taken away all the flesh of those
horses and eaten it.

Then the men of Gwasaro, when they saw the Europeans and the soldiers coming in the distance, divided
up the people, some to the right of the road, some to
the left of the road, and some of them were away ahead
in the forest.

The soldiers advanced. The men of Gwasaro let
the advance go some way, let the soldiers of the Niger
Company past, but when they saw the artillery approaching
with their head loads, then they began to move menacingly
towards the artillery. Straight away one of the artillery
Europeans said to the soldiers "Halt! Action right!"

At once, before he could even get down off his horse
the gun had been put together. Immediately after that
the shells were brought, and firing started. On one
side the men of Gwasaro were firing away arrows at the
gun, especially trying to hit a certain corporal. He
had loaded the shell and was just going to fire it when
an arrow landed in the spot that he had just left. The
men of Gwasaro were hit very quickly, scattered and
fled.

When the town was reached, it was found that they
had all fled with their women and their children, and
had crossed the Kaduna. Three days were spent in the
town, and word was sent to the men of Kuta, word was
also sent to the men of Kurmin Gurmuna, telling them
all to come and help themselves to corn.

All the walls of the town were smashed down, and
soldiers were left there, one company. They were told
to arrest anyone that they saw. The rest of the soldiers
and the artillery came back to Kuta.

From Kuta we moved on, the soldiers and the artillery were taken, and we made for another town, that is up on the hill. The king of the town was summoned and was asked "Have the men of Gwasaro come to your town?" They answered "No," and said that he wouldn't allow the people of Gwasaro to come to his town. So we set off again and came back to Kuta and spent the night there. All together we spent seven nights and on the eighth day we got home. This account of what happened at Gwasaro is all that I myself saw.

X
Kebbi Traditions

It seems clear that Burdon and Edgar used mainly an
Argungu scribe or scribes. The names Baƙo and Ja'afaru
occur frequently on the MSS in the Kaduna Archives.
The latter seems definitely to have been an Argungu
man. Hence the quantity of material about Kebbi (with
strong anti-Fulani bias) and the marked dialect, in
which much of it is written.

THE KINGS OF KEBBI (II/LVII)

The first was Baranbaram; then Argoje; Tabari; Zartai;
Gwabrau; Dundunfani; Gitama; Bardau; Kudamdau; Shiriya;
Badauji; Karafau; Durkushi; Kututturu; Tasau; Zaudai;
Muhammadu na Makake; Sulaimanu; Hamir Kurma; Abdu Ɗan
Bawaka; Ali; Atamana; Tasgirin-Burum; Mawanchi; Muhammadu
Ƙarfe; Batamusa; Humi--who introduced the <u>tambari</u> drum
to Kebbi; Kutam--who used* one <u>tambari</u> drum; Gimbe;

*Or perhaps "introduced".

141

Sakai; Murtamu; Marakanta; Ratayag-Giwa; Gudu-da-Masu;
Chi-da-Goro; Ubangari; Marsa-Kebbi; Marsa-Kuka; Lazim;
Giwara; Mashirana; Makata--who used* one <u>tambari</u> drum;
Kanta--who used* three <u>tambaris</u>; Gofe; Dawuda; Hummadu
Ja; Sulaimanu; Malo; Ishaku; Muhammadu na Kawu; Amar;
Muhammadu Kanna; Ibrahimu Kanna; Muhammadu Sifawa;
Hummadu; Tomon Kebbi; Muhammadu Dan Giwa; Sumaila;
Muhammadu Dan Tagande; Toga; Sulaimanu; Muhammadu Hodi;
Sama'ila; Yakubu; Yusufu Mai Nasara; Muhammadu Ba'are;
Abdullahi Toga; Sama'ila.

I obtained this account from the hand of Malam
Masallachi of Argungu.

THE SAME (II/LVIII)

First was Kulalu who reigned for seventy years; next
Sakaye, sixty-seven years; Gimba, forty-nine; Makata,
eight; Kotai, seventeen; Muhammadu Kanta, who was the
first of the Kings of Kebbi to embrace Islam, thirty-
eight years; Ahmadu, Kanta's son, thirty-five; Dawuda,
Ahmadu's son, twenty-three years and eight months;
Ibrahimu, one month and ten days; Sulaimanu, son of
Dawuda, fifteen years; Muhammadu, son of Ahmadu, thirteen; Maliki, son of Ibrahimu, thirteen years and eight
months; Umaru, twelve years; Muhammadu, two years and
one month; Ibrahimu, son of Muhammadu, eight years;
Muhammadu of Sifawa, two years; Ahmadu, son of Umaru,
twenty-five; Tomo, son of Ibrahimu, four years; Muhammadu
Dan Giwa, seven years; Isma'ila, son of Muhammadu of
Sifawa, thirty-three; Muhammadu, son of Isma'ila, son
of Tagandu, four years and eight months; Abdullahi Toga,
ten years; Sulaimanu, son of Abdullahi, nineteen years;
Abubakar Ukara only reigned for four days before being
turned out and his brother killed; Muhammadu, son of
Tarana, ruled for one year in Birnin Kebbi, and twenty-
six years with his capital sometimes at Augi, and sometimes Kimba; Isma'ila, son of Sulaimanu, five years;
Jatau, son of Shehu, three years; Jibrila, ten years;

---

*Or perhaps "introduced".

Jatau Damani, three years; Yaḳubu, five years and five
months; Yusufu Mai Nasara, son of Sama'ila, five years
and five months; Muhammadu, son of Yaḳubu, nicknamed
"Ba'are", one year and four months; Abdullahi, son of
Sama'ila, nicknamed "Toga", twenty years; Sama'ila, son
of Yaḳubu--well, God alone knows the years of his reign*.
I obtained this account from the hand of Na'ibi** of
Argungu.

THE SAME (II/LIX)

First was Kulaye, who ruled for seventy years; next
Sakaye, sixty-seven years; Gimba, forty-nine; Makata,
eight; Kotai, seventeen; Muhammadu Kanta, first of the
Kebbi royal house to accept Islam, thirty-eight; Hummadu,
Kanta's son, thirty-five; Dawuda, Hummadu's son, twenty-
three years and eight months; Ibrahimu, one month and
ten days; Sulaimanu, son of Dawuda, fifteen years;
Muhammadu Nkau (?), son of Hummadu, thirteen years;
Maliki, son of Ibrahimu, thirteen years and eight months;
Umaru, twelve years; Muhammadu Ḳaye, two years and one
month; Ibrahimu, son of Muhammadu, eight years; Muhammadu
of Sifawa, two years; Hummadu, son of Umaru, twenty-five
years; Tomo, son of Ibrahimu, four years; Muhammadu,
nicknamed "Dan Giwa", seven years; Samaila, son of
Muhammadu of Sifawa, thirty-three years; Muhammadu, son
of Samaila, nicknamed "Dan Tagande", four years and
eight months; Abdullahi, nicknamed "Toga", ten years;
Sulaimanu, son of Abdullahi, nineteen years; Abubakar,
nicknamed "Ukara", four days before he was turned out
and his brother killed; after that, Muhamman, nicknamed
"Dan Tarana", ruled for one year in Birnin Kebbi, and
then twenty-six years with his capital sometimes at
Augi, sometimes at Wakara; Samaila, five years; Jatau
Sama'ila, son of Sulaimana, five years; Dan Tsoho +,
three years; Jibrila, ten years; Jatau Damani, three

---

*Presumably because he was still ruling.
**Or, probably, the assistant imam.
+Patently, a nickname.

years; Yakubu, five years and five months; Yusufu, five
years and five months; Muhammadu, one year and two
months; Abdullahi, nicknamed "Toga", eighteen years.
I obtained this account from the Imam of Samna, in
Argungu town, in the year 1329 AH.

THE SAME (II/LX)

Kulayi ruled for seventy years, and then died; Sakayi
ruled for sixty-seven years; Gimba, forty-nine; Makata,
eight; Kutum, twenty-seven; Muhammadu Kanta, thirty-
eight; Ahmadu, son of Kanta, twenty-two years, eight
months and ten days; Sulaimana, son of Dawuda, four
years; Ibrahimu, son of Kanta, twenty years and one
month; Muhammadu, son of Ahmadu, thirteen years; Maliki,
son of Ibrahimu, thirteen years and eight months; Umaru,
son of Muhammadu, twelve years and two months; Muhammadu,
son of Sulaimanu, eleven years and one month; Ibrahimu,
son of Muhammadu, one month; his younger brother, Ahmadu,
son of Umaru (sic), twenty-five years; next the king who
built Kebbi, Tomo, son of Ibrahimu, son of Kanta, three
years; Muhammadu, son of Umaru, twenty-seven years;
Isma'ila, son of Muhammadu Sifawa, twenty years; Muhammadu,
son of Isma'ila, three years; Abdullahi, son of Sama'ila,
Muhammadu's older brother, eleven years; Sulemai, son of
Toga, eighteen years; Muhammadu Hodi, son of Sulaimana,
ruled two years at Birnin Kebbi--and then the Fulani
power became established; Isma'ila, Hodi's younger
brother, son of Sulaimana, five years and five months;
Yakubu Nabami, son of Sama'ila, five years and six
months; Yusufu Mai Nasara, five years and five months;
Muhammadu, son of Nabami, one year; and, lastly,
Abdullahi Toga.
    I obtained this account from the hand of Malam
Masallachi of Argungu, son of Muhammadu, who was head
snake-charmer at Katami; and Muhammadu himself received
the account from his father, Malam Musa of Argungu.
Dated 1329 AH.

THE SAME (II/LXI)

First was Kulaye, who ruled for seventy years; then
Sakaye, sixty-seven years; Gimba, forty-nine; Makata,
eight; Kotai, seventeen; Muhammadu Kanta, who was the
first ruler of Kebbi to embrace Islam, thirty-eight
years; Ahmadu, Kanta's son, thirty-five; Dawuda, Ahmadu's
son, twenty three years and eight months; Ibrahimu, one
month and ten days; Sulaimanu, son of Dawuda, five years;
Muhammadu, son of Ahmadu, thirteen; Maliki, son of
Ibrahimu, thirteen years and eight months; Umaru, twelve;
Muhammadu, two years and one month; Ibrahimu, son of
Muhammadu, eight years; Muhammadu of Sifawa, two years;
Hummadu, son of Umaru, twenty-five; Tomo, son of Ibrahimu,
four years; Muhammadu Dan Giwa, seven years; Isma'ila,
son of Sumaila, son of Muhammadu of Sifawa, thirty-three
years; Muhammadu, son of Sumaila, nicknamed "Dan Tagande",
four years and eight months; Abdullahi Toga, ten years;
Sulaimanu, son of Abdullahi, nineteen years; Abubakar
Ukara, four days--then he was turned out and his brother
killed; Muhammadu Dan Tarana ruled for one year in
Birnin Kebbi and for a further twenty-six years, varying
his capital between Augi and Kimba; Sama'ila, son of
Sulaimanu, five years; Jatau Dan Tsoho, three years;
Jibrila, ten years; Jatau Damani, three years; Yakubu,
five years and five months; Yusufu Mai Nasara, five
years and five months; Muhammadu, son of Yakubu, one
year; Abdullahi, son of Sama'ila Toga, twenty years.

    I obtained this account from the hand of a pious
man* in Argungu. But Isma'ila, King of Kebbi, himself
has added "When the Fulani defeated Muhammadu Dan Tarana,
he retreated from Birnin Kebbi to Gungungye, where he
spent the day; then in the evening he moved on to
Baibaye. From there he went to Wakara, and from Wakara
to Augi. From Augi eventually he reached Kimba and
there fought with the men of Gimbana, who killed him.
The next move was to Kebbi**--but he never got there.

---

*Emending <u>Bawan</u> to <u>bawan</u>.
**Meaning Argungu?

So, to this day, the place where he was killed is
known as "Death-Place of Hodi Dan Tarana".

THE SAME (II/LXII)

They were all sons of Abbas. First was Aliyu Abarwa,
who ruled for a hundred years (!); Antaru, son of Aliu,
fifty years; Sulaimanu, twenty years; Ka'abu, son of
Sulaimanu, eighteen; Aliu, son of Ka'abu, twenty-five;
Kalamu, son of Aliu, seventy years; Sakaye, sixty;
Gimba, fifty; Makata, son of Kotam, twenty years;
Muhammadu Kanta, son of Makata, thirty-eight years;
Ahmadu, son of Kanta, thirty years; Umaru, son of
Ahmadu, ten years; Maliki, son of Umaru, one month and
ten days; Muhammadu, son of Umaru, five years and ten
days; Muhammadu Sifawa, son of Maliki, two years;
Ibrahimu, son of Muhammadu, two months and one day; Tomo,
son of Ibrahimu of Kebbi, son of Kanta--the first to
live at Birnin Kebbi, four years; Ibrahimu, son of Kebbi
(sic), ten years and one month; Umaru, son of Muhammadu,
thirty years and two months; Muhammadu Dan Giwa, seventy
years; Kanna, son of Ibrahimu, sixty years; Hummadu,
son of Kanna, five years; Sumaila, son of Umaru, ten
years; Abdullahi Toga, son of Sumaila, twenty years and
ten days; Sulaimanu, son of Toga, fifteen years; Muhammadu
Hodi, son of Sulaimanu, two years. Then the Fulani took
(the city). Isma'ila, son of Sulaimanu, Hodi's brother,
five years, one month and twenty days; Yakubu Nabame,
son of Sama'ila, five years and six months; Yusufu Mai
Nasara, five years; Muhammadu Ba'are, one year and one
day; Abdullahi Toga, son of Sama'ila, twenty-eight
years; Isma'ila, son of Yakubu--well, the length of
his reign is known to God alone.

I obtained this account from the hand of Malam
Masallachi of Argungu.

But Isma'ila, King of Kebbi, and his courtiers, all
being present together in the king's chamber, said
"Abdullahi Toga, son of Sama'ila, ruled for eighteen
years only."

THE SAME (II/LXIII)

First was Kulaye, who ruled for seventy years; then
Sakaye, sixty-seven years; then Gimba, forty-nine;
Makata, eight; Kotam, twenty-seven; Muhammadu Kanta,
who was the first King of Kebbi to embrace Islam, and
the first of the royal house of Kebbi*, thirty-eight
years; Ahmadu, son of Kanta, thirty-five years; Dawuda,
son of Ahmadu, twenty-three years, eight months and
ten days; Sulaimanu, son of Dawuda, five years;
Ibrahimu, son of Kanta, twenty years and one month;
Muhammadu, son of Ahmadu, thirteen years; Maliki, son
of Ibrahimu, thirteen years and eight months; Amar,
son of Muhammadu, twenlve years and two months; Muhammadu,
son of Sulaimana, two years and one month; Ibrahimu, son
of Muhammadu, eight years; Muhammadu Sifawa, son of
Sulaimanu, two years; Muhammadu Kanna, son of Amar,
one month; Ahmadu, son of Amar, twenty-five years;
Tomo, son of Ibrahimu, four years; Muhammadu, son of
Amar, nineteen years; Sulaimanu, son of Muhammadu
Sifawa, thirty years; Muhammadu, son of Sulaimanu, four
years; Abdullahi, son of Sulaimanu, eleven years;
Sulaimanu Abdullahi, nineteen years; Muhammadu, son of
Sulaimanu, two years--and during his reign God took
away the power from them and gave it to Shehu Usumanu
Dan Fodio, so that he was thirteen years as a subordinate
ruler**.

I obtained this account from the hand of Malam
Sani, nicknamed "Dan Mutuwa" of Zazzagawa.

THE SAME (II/LXIV)

First was Kulaye, who reigned for seventy years; next
Sakaye, sixty-seven years; Gimba, forty-nine; Makata,
eight; Kotai, twenty-seven; Muhammadu Kanta, who was

*Lit. "began the kingship at Kebbi".
**Lit. "without the horns of a king's turban".

the first Kebbi king to embrace Islam, and also the
first of the royal house*, thirty-eight years; Ahmadu,
son of Kanta, thirty-five years; Dawuda, son of Ahmadu,
twenty-three years and eight months; Ibrahimu, one month
and ten days; Sulaimanu, son of Dawuda, fifteen years;
Muhammadu, son of Ahmadu, thirteen years; Maliki, son
of Ibrahimu, thirteen years and eight months; Amar, son
of Ibrahimu, twelve years; Ahmadu, son of Sulaimanu,
thirteen years; Maliki, son of Ahmadu, thirteen years
and eight months; Amar, son of Muhammadu, twelve years
and two months; Muhammadu, son of Sulaimanu, two years;
Ibrahimu, son of Muhammadu, eight years; Muhammadu
Sifawa, son of Sulaimanu, two years; Kanna, son of
Amar, one month; Ahmadu, son of Amar, twenty-five years;
Tomo, son of Ibrahimu, four years; Muhammadu Dan Giwa,
nineteen years; Sumaila, son of Muhammadu Sifawa,
twenty-three years; Muhammadu Dan Tagande, son of
Sumaila, four years and eight months; Muhammadu, son
of Sulaimanu, four years; Abdullahi Toga, son of
Sulaimanu, eleven years; Sulaimanu, son of Abdullahi
Toga, nineteen years; Abubakar, son of Sulaimanu, four
days, after which he was driven out and his brother
killed; Muhammadu Dan Tarana, twenty-six years; Sama'ila,
son of Abubakar, five years; Jatau, son of Shehu, three
years; Jibrila, son of Muhammadu, ten years; Jatau
Damane, three years; Muhammadu Hodi, two years. Then
came the Fulani conquest. Sama'ila, son of Sulaimanu,
five years, one month and twenty days; Yakubu Nabame,
son of Sama'ila, five years and six months; Yusufu
Mai Nasara, five years; Muhammadu Ba'are, son of Yakubu,
one year; Abdullahi, son of Sama'ila, thirty-eight
years; Sama'ila, son of Yakubu, twenty-five years.

I obtained this account from the hand of the Imam
of Lailaba.

_____
*See above.

THE ORIGINS OF ALL THE MEN
OF KEBBI (II/LXV)

Abbas was the ancestor of them all. First was Aliu,
who ruled for a hundred years before he died; then
Antaru, fifty years--he was the son of Aliu; then
Sulaimana, twenty years; Ka'abu, son of Sulaima (sic),
eighteen years; Aliu, son of Ka'abu, twenty-five years;
Kulaye, son of Aliu--it was he who crossed over from
Mecca, and settled in Cairo--seventy years; Sakaye,
sixty years; Gimba, fifty years; Makata, son of Kotam,
twenty years; Muhammadu Kanta, son of Makata, thirty-
eight years; Hummadu, son of Kanta, thirty years; Umaru,
son of Hummadu, ten years; Maliki, son of Umaru, one
month and ten days; Muhammadu, son of Umaru, five years
and ten days; Muhammadu of Sifawa, son of Maliki, two
years; Ibrahimu, son of Muhammadu, two months and one
day; Tomo, son of Ibrahimu, grandson of Kanta, who was
the first to reside in Birnin Kebbi, seven years;
Ibrahimu, son of Ka'abu, ten years and one month; Umaru,
son of Muhammadu, thirty years and two months; Muhammadu
Dan Giwa, son of Umaru, seventy years; Kanna, son of
Umaru, sixty years; Hummadu, son of Kanna, five years;
Sama'ila, son of Ibrahimu, ten years; Abdullahi Toga,
son of Sama'ila, twenty years, ten days; Salaima (sic),
son of Toga, fifteen years; Muhammadu Hodi, son of
Salaima, two years; then came the Fulani invasion and
capture of Birnin Kebbi; Isma'ila, son of Salaima,
younger brother of Hodi, five years, one month and
ten days; Yakubu Nabame, son of Sama'ila, five years
and six months; Yusufu Mai Nasara, five years; Muhammadu
Ba'are, son of Nabame, one year; Abdullahi Toga, son of
Sama'ila, eighteen years; Sama'ila, son of Yakubu Nabame,
during whose reign the Europeans arrived (after he had
held office for twenty years). They have been at Argungu
now for nine years; which gives Sama'ila a reign of
twenty-nine years.

I obtained this account from the hand of Malam
Masallachi*, son of the chief snake-charmer, who was
himself son of Malam Musa.

*Cf. II/CIII.

THE ORIGINS OF KANTA (I/VII)

This is the beginning of Kanta's power. It all began
one day when he was a boy herding cattle. For he used
to be the slave of the Filani and he used to herd
their cattle.

Well, that day one of the cows bore a calf when
they were out grazing. When they returned in the
evening, Kanta's master was walking round looking at
them and saw that the cow had a calf. Said he "That
cow with the new calf--whoever eats that calf all by
himself, the whole world will learn of him, and everyone will grow to fear him." Well, Kanta was in among
the cattle and heard what his master was saying.

Next morning, Kanta drove the cattle out to graze.
And when they were out in the bush, he caught the calf
and, slaughtering it, ate up its meat, every bit of it,
leaving nothing.

His capital towns were three: Gungu, Leka and
Surame. He died at Surame, and his tomb is there.

During his time, sand was brought from Azbin to
sprinkle round his horse's tethering-post, such was
his power. But there was never a ruler at Kabi (Kebbi)
before Kanta. And he ruled for thirty-eight years.
And of the rulers of Kabi since him, none have done
the like of what he did.

KANTA, WHO WAS THE FIRST RULER
OF KEBBI (II/XLIII)

Kanta was the first King of Kebbi. The other rulers
that I have mentioned all held the title of Magaji;
none of them was King. From Cairo Kanta made his way
to Firzan (?Fezzan) and lived there for seven years.
There they became apprehensive that he would take over
the town; for the young men began to follow him. Per-
ceiving this, the leaders expelled him. Then he went
to a malam, who advised him to come west.

So he came west and reached Azben. There, the
King of Azben (Tuareg ruler) gave him his daughter,
Kyawo*, as wife. She bore a son, Muhammadu. But Kanta
remembered what the malam had said to him, and he told
the King of Azben that he was going to continue his
journey westwards.

He reached Gande and came to a slave-encampment of
the Fulani. He joined them and took up his dwelling
there, and saw how the Fulani regularly came and exacted
payments in lieu of working, from their slaves. And
when the slaves' children matured, they would seize them
and take them off to their village. Then Kanta asked
them "And what do you receive in exchange from these
men?" "We don't receive anything" they answered, "We're
their slaves." Then he said "Very well. From this
year on, there'll be no more taking anyone from here;
and they'll not be given anything again."

Well, the time came and they came for the payment
in lieu of work. "You're not getting it" said Kanta.
And all the others came and gathered round the Fulani
(tax-collector) in a crowd. Then said Kanta to the
people of the slave-settlement "Let everyone go and
get himself a branch from a geza; then sharpen them to
a point." And they did so.

Then the Fulani gathered their forces and came to
where he was. "Grip your sticks, all of you" said Kanta,
and taking one himself, went ahead, calling "Everyone
follow me." And so they launched themselves at the
Fulani. And the Fulani fled back to their encampment.

Then the men of the slave-settlement caught a mare,
and, bringing it, put Kanta on it. So Kanta became
their king, and they began calling him by the title of
"Sarki" (king). Next he moved his residence to Tudun
Leka. That is why his descendants are called "Lekawa".
While he was at Leka, his strength increased greatly.
From there they went on to clear a site for the city
of Surame; and after Surame, he built Gungu.

The reason for the building of Gungu was that
Kanta's wife, Kyawo, daughter of the King of Azben, ran

---

*"Beauty".

away from her husband, when her parents were at Gungu.
And she went and stayed at Gungu, and there complained
that the air did not suit her. So that was how Gungu
came to be built.

A TALE OF MUHAMMADU KANTA, KING
OF KEBBI (II/L)

Makata and Kotai were the parents of Kanta; it was
while he was in Firzan (?Fezzan) that Makata begat
Kanta. When he was forty, he came to Azben; he was
there ten years and then came to Gande, and was there
for twenty years. Then he started hostilities with
the Fulani and took their slaves away from them.

KANTA'S CITY THAT THE NUPES BUILT (II/XLVII)

It began when the Nupes were late arriving. Kanta
ordered them to bring shea-butter, for him to use in
the building. They refused, so he rode forth. He
reached Yauri on the river and ordered the Nupes to
bring canoes and take his army across. But they answered that they hadn't any canoes in which to take
his people across. So there he spent the night. But
next morning he gave the order "Fetch the horse from
Zazzau (?)", and they saddled it up. Then he ordered
"Zagi, lead the horse forward." The zagi did so, and
so crossed the Niger, with the water no higher than
the horse's knees. And so the army poured across.
    Then the Nupes expressed their contrition and
besought him to return, promising to bring the shea-
butter and to build a city. Then* he went back, and
presently they brought shea-butter, and using that,
built the city.

_____
*Reading Ran for Yan.

THE REIGN OF KANTA AND WHAT HAPPENED
DURING IT (II/XXXVIII)

What is now the city of Surame was first built by the
men of Kebbi. Next came the men of Sanwaya* and built
in their turn. After then the men of Gurma*. Next
the Dakarkari built. Fifth came the men of Kwanni*,
and they built. After them the men of Zamfara. And,
seventhly, the Nupes built their city. They used shea-
butter** to build with.

Now all these seven cities were all one city. As
each tribe built their city, another would come along
and put up theirs--until there were seven cities altogether. And the seventh was built with shea-butter†.

They sent to Azben and fetched sand in palm-leaf
bags, and they brought water from Tanshama--which is a
lake in Azben--in goatskin waterbottles, all the way
to Surame. There they stopped and gave the water to
the horse to drink. And they poured the sand round its
tethering-post, and it lay down and rolled. Then said
Kanta to his horse "Now Azben reaches right to here,
and from now on you're an Azben horse!" And even today
the places can still be seen--the tethering-post, the
sand, and where the water was poured out.

Kanta also made them build a well in Surame. Now
this well had a chain in it--which no one has ever been
able to pull out from that day to this. Then again,
there is a rooster in Kanta's compound, whose cackling
is to be heard even today--but no one has ever seen it.
And in the space in front of Kanta's compound there is
still drumming and trumpeting. Moreover, even today
no Fulani will sleep the night in Surame; if he tries
to, he will have missiles thrown at him.

On another occasion, Kanta's wife complained of
the heat. So they built a hill of rocks for her, and

---

*The last syllable of the place-name is tentative, as
   the H. has -awa (= "men of").
**Instead of water presumably!
†There seems to be a lacuna here.

she went to the top of that and enjoyed the cooler air.
Kanta's corn-bins are over there, to the east of Gungu.
Well, there was once a Fulani grazing his cattle there
who said to himself "I wonder what's in Kanta's corn-
bins." "Who knows?" said his friends. "Well" he said,
"I'm going to climb up to have a look and see what's
in them." They tried to stop him, but he persisted.
He climbed up and--well, he and his straw hat, they're
both there, by the lip of the corn-bin, to this day.
For he never came down again.

Also, between Gungu and Silame there is a mortar
and a pestle and the mark made by the slave-girl of
Kanta's wife, where she knelt, pounded* cola-nuts and
gave them to her mistress, when she was on her way from
Surame to Gungu. She took them (chewed them), and spat
out the pieces. And those pieces of chewed cola-nut
are there, to this day--gravel that looks just like
cola-nut.

KANTA'S ORDER TOUCHING THE FULANI (II/XXXIX)

In olden times, the King of Katsina and the King of
Gobir were overlords** of Muhammadu Kanta. And Muhammadu
Kanta addressed them both thus "Look you, if we don't
beware, the medicine men have warned us that some fair-
skinned people will take our power from us. See then,
King of Katsina, that you do not permit the Fulani of
Katsina to build any huts--only temporary shelters.
And you too, King of Gobir, don't you permit the Fulani
of Gobir to build huts--only temporary shelters. And
in addition let us make a practice of taking their
animals, and let us start buying horses." And he repeated "For the medicine men have warned me that some
fair-skinned people will appear, who will take from us
what we now control."

Thus did those three kings plan together, and
that--so I have heard--is how Kanta came to give this

---

*I.e. treating a luxury as if it were a staple.
**The H. is perhaps weaker.

order, "The Fulani are not to build any huts, still less
found a town." And, you know, when the Fulani did appear, they did conquer the whole country. That's all.

THE ORIGIN OF THE TWO LAKES
AT GUNGU (II/XLIX)

When they were building Gungu, Kanta asked "Where will
we get water for building?" His workers answered "There's
a well here, we'll make do with what we can scoop out
from there." "Then there are no true men of Kebbi left"
said Kanta.

But an old Kebbi man jumped to his feet. His name
was Jabaka and he said "No, Kanta. There are no true
rulers left, but there are still some Kebbi men." Now,
he had a son called Dalal Bangi. Then said Kanta "Well,
since you say that there are still some men of Kebbi
left, what does this Kebbi man want?" And fetching a
blanket, Kanta said "Give it to the man of Kebbi to
cover his body and keep the mosquitoes away." He was
given the blanket, and he said to his son "Dalal Bangi,
where's your younger brother, Lobaji?" "Here he is,
with me." "Good! Then let's go to that water at Silame.
But first get me some perch*, Kebbi perch." So they
went and got him perch--a lot of it--and brought it
along. "Old man" they said, "Take what you need." He
selected one fish and told them to sweep up some cattle
dung and grill it for him. They did so, and when it
was done, he took it and fell to, eating it, and ate
until he had eaten his fill. "That's just right" he
said, "Fine--where are Dalal Bangi and Lobaji? Both
of you, follow me."

So they followed him, until he reached the river-
valley, and the bank of the river itself. There he said
"Dalal Bangi, you two go ahead and take a direct route
to Gungu." But the old man himself laid his harpoon to
the bank of the river, and so, dragging it behind him,
followed his sons. And so he made a way, right up to

---
*Tilapia Nilotica.

the city of Gungu. This isn't just a fable, for every
year the water would bring fish as far as Gungu.

And that is how there came to be two lakes here
at Gungu, one called Dalal Bangi, the other Lobaji.

THE DEATH OF MUHAMMADU KANTA, KING
OF KEBBI (II/XLVI)

Kanta conquered the whole of this world (!), except
for the pagans of Rini na Ashita*. He said he was
going to attack their place. Then the malams told him
not to go, but he insisted on going, and went off to
Rini na Ashita. Now the town was on top of a rocky
hill.

So Kanta went there. But when he looked at the
hill, he could see nothing but rocks**. "Let's get up
it" he said. So up they went and conquered the pagans,
conquered them completely. But it chanced that a handful of survivors escaped their notice. These shot an
arrow, which took Kanta in the neck and killed him.
He died at Jirwa on the 9th of Ramadan, 962 AH.

They put him on a camel and so he came to Sokoto.
At that time Sokoto was nothing but trees and wild
beasts, and no one imagined that there would one day
be a town there. But there the camel that was carrying
Kanta knelt down, and Kanta's feet touched the ground.
Then said his slave-girl "Do you see this place where
my master's feet have touched the ground? Well, there
will be a capital city here one day."

They reached Gungu with him, and made twelve
tombs†. Twelve mud-roofed buildings were set up here
in Gungu, and they put him into one of them. But no
one knows even today which of the buildings contains
Kanta's body. While there is even dispute as to whether
he is still here, or has been taken away.

---

*I have given ashita a capital letter here, and two
   lines below. This seems inevitable.
**Taking kare = "interposed themselves to his view".
†Cf. II/XLII.

MUHAMMAN NA KYAWO AND AMAR, SONS OF KANTA
AND KINGS OF KEBBI (II/XLIV)

Muhamman na Kyawo, Kanta's son, became king, and at
that time it was not possible to travel through the
Rubu bush; for lion and elephant and leopard had cut
the road. Then the new king said to his drummers "Go
to the Rubu bush, beat your drums and make this proc-
lamation--that I say that elephant and lion and leopard
and hyena and all the beasts of the bush which have
been attacking people--all these are to desist. Let
me not hear that they have again attacked anyone so
long as I live."

And it was Muhamman na Kyawo, son of Kanta, also
who ordered them to go and proclaim to the River Kebbi,
at a time when the jinns of the river and crocodiles
and other beasts of the river had been devouring men,
that they were never again to attack men, so long as
he lived.

When Amar, son of Kanta, became king, the men of
Sanwai had taken many of the towns of Kebbi, leaving
the men of Kebbi with only Sifawa, Dogon-Daji and
Gwandu (for Gwandu was a tributary of Karari). Well,
when Amar became king, he drove the men of Sanwai from
the edge of the river valley, and they went back over
the Sauwwa, and settled there. That is how Sauwwa came
to be founded. But he drove them from Sauwwa, and they
moved on and cleared a site for the city of Riya.

And Amar went and settled at Kaikayaje. There he
died, and Hummadu Karami became king.

MUHAMMAN NA KYAWO, KING OF KEBBI (II/LII)

The King of Sanwai attacked Surame, when Muhamman na
Kyawo was king, and was defeated by him. The gawasa
trees that surround the river-valley of Katami are
the draughtsmen of the Sanwai men. During the pursuit,
a warrior named Tungullu fell at the place that now
bears his name.

Further on, they reached Dankal, and that too is named after another warrior who fell there. But when Muhamman na Kyawo reached Batakira, quite close to Dankal there, he reined in his horse and said "Batakira has been torn (?)." And just there, where he stayed, there is today a lake. So Muhamman na Kyawo returned to Surame, and dwelt there.

Sanwai sent in its submission, but Muhamman said "Tell your king to come himself." So the King of Sanwai came to him at Surame. "Well, what is it?" asked the King of Kebbi, and the other expressed his contrition. "I accept it" said the King of Kebbi, "But, if it is true contrition, lift your head and look up." He lifted his head, and instantly there was a rope round his neck. And to this day he has not returned to his home. Then Muhamman na Kyawo ordered that, as from one week from that day, there were to be no more peaks* to the thatches of the huts of Sanwai. And no more there are, to this day.

THE ORIGIN OF GINDI (I/LII)

There was once a man called Gindi, son of Dugaji, who had very big eyes. He was given a maiden in marriage, but she refused to have anything to do with him. Then he left his town, Gundun-Gawa, in anger, and coming here erected his shelter, and lived in it. All he had for company was a broad deleb-palm and the animals of the bush. But one day there came a malam from Gulumbe, called Malam Madubi, and he said to Gindi "One day this place will become a town." Said Gindi to him "Won't you settle down and live here with me?" "Very well" said the other.

That is its origin. Now the first king of Gindi was Homa, son of Madugaji. After him his younger brother Nayi. After him Dakare, son of Homa. Then Na'a'i, then Na'araga, then Alku, son of Na'a'i, then Naburmi, son of Dakare, then Dashira, son of Nayi, then

---

*Presuming tsoro = tsororuwa.

Alku-karami (Little Alku), then Nayi, son of Homa--
that was his youngest son.

It is seven hundred years since the founding of
Gindi. The city was built in the time of Dakare, son
of Homa. In the time of Alku, the river Gindi came
into existence--before that it had been a stream. Later
Hodi, son of the Emir of Kebbi came and occupied the
place. He it was who later became Emir of Kebbi, and
fought with Buhari, son of Abdusalami. He drove out
Hodi, son of Tarana Dugaji. Jatau, son of Tsofo, succeeded Hodi. After him came Jatau Damne, then Jibirila,
then Ganji, then Labbo, son of Jibirila, then Killodi,
then Idi, son of Jatau Damne, then Killodi, son of
Labbo. Finis.

THE MEN OF KEBBI AND NABAME, KING
OF KEBBI (II/XLVIII)

When the Fulani defeated Sama'ila, son of Sulaimana,
the whole country came under their rule. Then the men
of Kebbi had all manner of work to do--cutting grass
and cornstalks for roofing, then making their way to
Gwandu and building their homes for them. And when
they got there, and had finished building a hut and
thatching it--then the Fulani woman would come in and
say "Ugh! This hut stinks of fish. I don't like it.
Take it down and make another--and use upland grass,
not river valley grass." And this sort of thing went
on for nineteen years.

And they had to pay a tribute of rice, one thousand
measures. If they took it and it was found one measure
short, then they had to go back and fetch it. This was
when Malam Halilu was Emir of Gwandu. And if he set
out for Sokoto, he was put in a litter* and carried on
mens' heads. The men of Argungu had to carry him as
far as Bubuche; then the Bubuche men would take over
and carry him to Katami, and so on till he reached
Sokoto.

---

*Slightly extending the meaning of <u>karaga</u> in deference
  to <u>cikin</u>.

Here's how Nabame came to go to Sokoto. A Fulani
was grazing his cattle close to Nabame's farm, when
Nabame said to his lad "Go and drive away those cattle."
The boy went to do so, but the Fulani called "Hi! Go
back, you puppy! Why, I was there when his* father was
killed." The lad returned to Nabame in tears, and told
him what the Fulani had said. To which Nabame answered
that the Fulani was lying** and that his father had
never even been there. The Fulani came a little closer
and called out "Hey there! I was there when they killed
your father!" Nabame had a spear in his hand, and he
threw it at the Fulani and, chancing to hit him, killed
him.

The matter was reported to the Emir of Gwandu,
Malam Halilu, and he said "I'm not handling this case.
You can go to Sokoto and have judgment done there."
So that was how Nabame came to go to Sokoto. That was
when Aliu Babba, son of Bello, was Sultan.

THE TAKING OF SILAME (II/LI)

Nabame launched an attack against Ahmadu Rufa'i, when
the whole area of Silame was flooded. Then Ahmadu
Rufa'i put his horse at the water, dashed into it and
so got through. Nor did he give the beast a breather
till they reached the Dan Kala gate[+]. There he met a
Babambade, who said to him "Tall One, son of Shehu, on
the red horse--so we saw Nabame, and we leapt into the
water, did we?"

---

*Nabame's presumably. The significance of the remark
  is not clear to me. However, the use of the words
  ubanai and ubaka itself constitutes an insult.
**Deleting the quote marks in the H. and making it
  oratio obliqua, in order to keep the reference to
  Nabame's, rather than the Fulani's, father.
[+]Of Sokoto?

THE FULANI OF GWANDU AND THE
MEN OF KEBBI (II/XXXIV)

Formerly the men of Kebbi, the people of Argungu, used
to be sent for to go to Gwandu, and there build a hut
for the Emir of Gwandu's wife. But when it was finished,
and she went into it, she would say "Ugh! This hut
smells of fish. Have it pulled down and another put
up." And they had to do so. Every year they used to
do this.

But the men of Gwandu, when they came to Argungu,
would stay in the compound of a man there, in Argungu.
And they would get him to fetch a ram and slaughter it
for them. But while the master of the house was busy
flaying the ram just outside the door of the hut, one
of the Gwandu Fulani would grab the man's wife, and
going into the hut, have intercourse with her. So that
at that time, if there was any Kebbi man who had a
handsome wife, when the Gwandu Fulani came, they would
take her from him; and it wasn't till after they had
again departed, back to Gwandu, that the Kebbi man would
get his wife back.

But at last the Kebbi men got a king, who said
"Men of Kebbi, what these Fulani have done to us in
the past--from now on I shan't permit!"

Presently a message came from Gwandu, telling them
to go and build a hut. But the King of Kebbi said
"No! We're not coming! Seeing what trouble and pain
you have caused us in the past, we no longer agree to
come." Again they sent back from Gwandu, and again
they refused; and yet once more.

Then the people of Gwandu gathered their army and
marched against the men of Argungu. And the latter
went out and defeated the Gwandu forces. There ensued
a state of hostility between Gwandu and Argungu. The
Emir of Gwandu sent to the Sultan (for help). And so
the men of Argungu carried on the war, destroying towns
and capturing people, and the state of hostility continued. Nor did it come to an end, until the Europeans

arrived. As for Isma'ila, when he became King of
Kebbi, he took many of the Fulani's towns. That's the
end of the account that has reached me.

HOW HALIRU, EMIR OF GWANDU, ATTACKED THE DISTRICT OF AREWA ("THE NORTH") (II/LXVII)

Haliru, Emir of Gwandu, took an army and set out for
Birnin Kebbi. He passed Digi and Tilli and, making for
the district of Arewa, at last appeared before Makwaruwa;
and attacked that town. Reinforcements poured in, and
all joined battle with the Emir of Gwandu.

So the battle continued. Then the Emir of Gwandu
upbraided his people, saying "What! Didn't I bring you
here to fight for me? And now you're refusing to fight."
And jumping up, he was about to join the fight himself,
when one of the men of Arewa, a hunter, shot him in the
neck with an arrow; and the Emir of Gwandu retired again.

Thereupon the men of Arewa set about the rest of
the enemy's force and overcame them; for, having brought
low their leader, they began taking horses and men in
large numbers. And then they drove the army before
them nearly to Tilli. From there the men of Arewa returned home.

They found Haliru, Emir of Gwandu, dead. They took
his white burnous off him, chopped off his head and
stripped him of his clothes. Now this was when Dadin-
Kai held the title of King of Arewa at Baibaye; and
Toga was King of Kebbi at Argungu.

Then they brought the head and the burnous here,
to Zazzagawa. Then Toga, King of Kebbi, rode over to
Zazzagawa and was shown the head of Haliru, Emir of
Gwandu, who had led his army against the district of
Arewa, only to be killed by the men of Arewa. Then
said the King of Kebbi "Fine! My thanks to you, men
of Arewa, for killing him. But, had you but taken him
alive and brought him to me, I should have said something to him, the likes of which he never heard in all
his life--and till his death he would never have brought
an army against us again! However, as it is, so be it,
and my thanks to you!" Well, that's all that account
as it reached me.

ANOTHER ACCOUNT OF THE SAME (II/I)

Haliru, Emir of Gwandu, attacked Karakara with his
army. He suffered defeat, and was himself wounded.
He fell from his horse to the ground.

    Some time passed after he had fallen, and presently
up comes a pagan with his axe. Says he fiercely "Look--
there's a malam fallen from his horse," and coming up,
the pagan hit him with his axe. As he did so, the Emir
said "No, not a malam--I'm the Emir of Gwandu."

    At which another pagan there said equally fiercely
"Then hit him again, if it is true that he's the Emir
and not just a malam." But the Emir of Gwandu said
"No! No! Don't hit me again, for I've had enough."
Up comes a friend of the first pagan and says "Let's
kill him, if he really is the Emir of Gwandu, as it
seems." Says the Emir again "Will you spare my life,
if I promise not to attack you again?" But they refused,
and killed him. And, cutting off his head, they took it
with them and made their way to Argungu.

    When the Emir of Argungu, Muhammadu Ba'are (lit.
"man of Arewa"), heard that they had killed the Emir of
Gwandu and cut off his head and brought it, he said
"Leave him there at Zazzagawa. God has delivered us
of an enemy."

ISMA'ILA, KING OF KEBBI, AND SULTAN ABDU, THE "UNBAKED POT" (II/XVI)

This happened in the reign of Sultan Abdu, "Unbaked
Pot". When he became Sultan he set out from Sokoto
and went to Gandi. There he was reinforced by Tukur,
Galadima of Kano; Abubakar, Emir of Katsina; Mai-Gardo,
Emir of Daura; the Yarima of Kazaure; Umaru, Emir of
Bauchi; the Emir of Zazzau; the Emirs of Katagum, Misau
and Hadeja; the kings of Zamfara, Kaura, Gumi and Bakura;
the king of Gobir from Isa; and the Emir of Gwandu.
Then Sultan Abdu set out from Gandi and returned to
Sokoto, where he spent two nights. On the third day

he set off to invade Argungu, with this whole force.
The Sultan's army, horse and foot--if any one* were to
say what their number was, he would be lying. So Sultan Abdu went forth against Argungu.

Now at this time Isma'ila was king of Kebbi. He
was reigning at Argungu. And news reached him that
Sultan Abdu, "Unbaked Pot," had collected a great army
and was on his way to Argungu to destroy it. Then
said Isma'ila, King of Kebbi "Abdu, 'Unbaked Pot,' has
been a long time a-coming. What was that other Sultan
at Sokoto long, long ago who was coming to destroy
Argungu, and he too was a long time a-coming? In fact,
I'm still waiting for him." He went on "But I've got
allies too. Let me summon them, for they and I are
one." And Isma'ila, King of Kebbi, continued "Let the
men of Zabarma come; and let the King of Arewa come
too. For he was a friend of my father, and they liked
and trusted each other, and discussed matters freely.
At such a time as this I'll not reject their friendship.
Go and summon them." So his allies set out to join him
and came and entered the city of Argungu at night.

As for Sultan Abdu, when he got there he camped
at Farin Dutsi by the gawasa trees. And early next
morning, he took his army up to the gates of the town.
The women, concubines and camels were left behind in
the camp. Then the Sultan called to Tukur, Galadima
of Kano. "May God give you the victory" answered Tukur,
coming up. "You're to attack there, at the corner, by
the Majidadi's compound, from there as far as the Mala
gate." Then Sultan Abdu, "Unbaked Pot," went up close
to the Tudu gate--where the market is now. That was
his objective. Abubakar, Emir of Katsina, attacked the
Durumma gate. Maiturare, the Marafa, attacked around
Dan Koji, supported by the Emir of Gwandu. So Argungu
was surrounded--except for one gate where there were no
horsemen attacking.

Then word was brought to Isma'ila, King of Kebbi,
who was in his compound "May God give the king the
victory. The Fulani are over there, and have started

---

*Inserting ya between kowa and che.

to fire the town." (It was Galadima Tukur's attack
that they spoke of.) "Oh" said Isma'ila, "Now we'll
rout them. My eye or Abdu "Unbaked Pot's" eye. Either
he dies, or I. Bring me my horse--the dun." So they
brought him his horse and he put foot to stirrup and
mounted, saying "Praise be to God! I, Isma'ila, give
thanks to God and to his Messenger. All is well!"
And the dun answered him, neighing three times. And
the King of Kebbi said again "See how they have attacked
us without rhyme or reason, but now God will enable us
to prevail over them."

He went forth, asking as he went "At which point
is Abdu?" But the people of the town didn't know. For
the one they thought was the Sultan was Galadima Tukur.
On the side of his attack they had breached the town
wall and entered. But the men of Kebbi took their harpoons, and from where they stood within the town, stabbed the horsemen, stabbed them and drew out their weapons
again. Out comes Isma'ila, King of Kebbi, with a spear
in his hand. Now the spear had a charm tied to it, and
wherever he went, killing men as he did so, he would ask
"At which point is Abdu? My eye or his eye. Either
he takes Argungu, or else today I'll drive him all the
way to Sokoto." And he killed and killed, and they
couldn't stand against him and broke. Some--both horse
and foot--fell into the river and were killed by any
who saw them. No, the Fulani couldn't stand against
him. For they said "Good God! This is no normal man!
If we don't run away, he'll kill us all."

But wherever the King of Kebbi came on horsemen,
he would kill them; till they began to plead with him
for their lives. Maiturare, the Marafa, was over near
Dan Koji and heard that the army was defeated. Says he
"Come on then, all my men! Let's see if we can slip
along the bank of the river and so make it back home."
So they went that way, but the men of Kebbi cut them
off, and catching up with them, began killing them,
stabbing and stabbing, until horses lay in a heap.
They went on to the camp, and there found that Sultan
Abdu, when he reached the camp, had gone straight
through it at the gallop, without looking at it.

So the men of Kebbi went into the camp, and set to
capturing the women and the camels. On that day Majidadi
took five camels, and Umaru Dandani took one.

The number of Fulani killed in this fighting is
beyond numbering. But of the men of Kebbi, only six
died. As for the Sultan, he did not stop to drink
water till he reached Silame.

Meanwhile Isma'ila, King of Kebbi, went on stabbing
people with his spear until it became quite bent; and
the weapon has been preserved to this day in the keeping
of the Emir of Argungu. He keeps it in one of his
buildings, and allows nothing to touch it, taking care
that termites do not eat it.

As for Argungu, they couldn't drink the water of
the river for three months, and had to dig wells--all
because of the dead of the Sokoto men. And for three
months too, if a man was sitting anywhere in the city,
he had to hold his nose for the stench of the men of
Sokoto that had been killed. And if anyone arrived outside at the travellers' camp and viewed the city from
there, he wouldn't go any nearer than that--the stench
would be quite enough for him. The Rupell's griffons*,
hyenas and vultures, they too were glad for what the
King of Kebbi had done--for they got a sufficiency of
food.

And here's what people say about it all: "Isma'ila,
King of Kebbi is a faithful Muslim and a warrior. What
he did that day was from God. So let no one try con-
clusions with Isma'ila, King of Kebbi. As for Sultan
Abdu, he is Abdu the unbaked pot, which won't hold water
even as far as out of the hut. And Isma'ila, King of
Kebbi, showed that he was the great storm which dis-
solved the unbaked pot, so that the earth returned to
its fellow earth."

There is plenty more on this subject, but we'll
stop there. This with peace.

---

*? more plentiful in those days.

ISMA'ILA, KING OF KEBBI'S
DUN HORSE (II/XXII)

There was once a horse at Argungu, the like of which
has never been. It was brought from Arewa to Isma'ila,
King of Kebbi, who bought it and kept it in his compound. It was the one he would ride himself, and it
was a dun.

If the King set off for war, he would ride it. And
when he camped against another town, to attack it, if it
was going to fall, the dun would neigh three times. And
the King of Kebbi would ride out from his camp against
the town, and without delay burn it to the ground, and
so return home. Now when the King of Kebbi perceived
the quality of this horse he tied three charms to it:
one on its neck; one on its forehead; one on its tail.

And so it was--if he set off to war, he would make
his camp in the bush; and if he was to take a town that
day, then the dun would neigh three times; and Isma'ila,
King of Kebbi, would rise and mount, and attack the town.
And he would quickly conquer it, and so return home.

But on another day, he would set off to war, ride
out and set up his encampment in the bush, and the dun
would not neigh. Then there was no victory. Even if
they went on, they would not take the town, but would
return no richer than they had come. And so the people
of the town too perceived the quality of that horse and
and the men of Kebbi said "Well! That horse of Isma'ila,
the King--he's a jinn, not a horse. You know, that
horse--whenever the King leads us to war, if the dun
neighs three times, we take a town. But if he doesn't
neigh, we don't take the town."

Well, one day Isma'ila, King of Kebbi, set out to
attack Sainyinna, the town ruled by Jeyo's husband.
This is the war that the men of Kebbi refer to as the
"Dono* War". They went and attacked the town without

---

*The context does not indicate which of the several
 meanings of this word is here involved.

taking it. Then a relief force arrived from the regions
of Kajiji and Yabo, a large force. And this force went
round behind and cut the route that the King of Kebbi
had followed. Presently the Kebbi army gave up the
attempt to take the town and withdrew--to find their
way blocked by these reinforcements. This was reported
to Isma'ila, King of Kebbi. Now, it was some little way
off that they were blocking his road and the King exclaimed "Where are my warriors? Where's Dangaladima
Dobi? Where's Sule Auta?" (At that time Majidadi Aliyu
held the title of Galadiman Magaji.) The King went on
"You're the best fighters. Hasten on to reinforce those
in front, for the Fulani relief force has held them up."
"May your life be prolonged, King of Kebbi" they answered,
"Consider it done," and they set off at a gallop. But
he called them back, telling them to stay behind him and
follow more slowly. Then* Isma'ila, King of Kebbi, stroked
his dun and said "Give me shield and spear." These were
given him, and he spurred the dun and went off at full
gallop.

   And when the relief party saw the King of Kebbi
coming, they didn't wait, for they knew it was he. They
broke and fled. But he caught them, and stabbed and
stabbed. He stopped there, and his dun began pawing
the ground, wild with rage. Then presently the others,
Dangaladima Dobi, Sule Auta, Galadiman Magaji Aliyu
and the rest came up with the King. And so the battle
ended and they returned home.

   But as for Isma'ila, King of Kebbi's dun, there has
never been a horse his like in the whole world. Men
said he was a jinn. His fame reached far and wide, and
even the Fulani would come to Argungu, just to see that
horse, the dun. And the King of Kebbi loved the horse
beyond measure and kept a special lad to tend a fire by
it to keep the flies away from it.

---

*I have omitted gudummowan na, da which is an irrelevant
 anacoluthon, and I suspect a case of diplography,
 for the same words occur four lines (of printed text)
 on. I have understood sai in their place.

And when his dun horse died, Isma'ila, King of
Kebbi, was sore grieved in his heart, and the men of
Kebbi, the people of Argungu too grieved at his death.
Now the cause of the horse's death was that he was
given a bolus made from <u>maiwa</u> flour. For they were
ignorant that horses cannot endure <u>maiwa</u>.

Then the King of Kebbi said "Well, now that the
dun is dead, neither hyena, nor vulture, nor Ruppell's
griffon will eat him. Come and dig a pit here in the
compound and bury him, and then let them put up a
building over it." And they carried out his orders.

Well, Argungu will never see a horse like that
again--yet we can't know that, for there is no limit
to God as creator, and maybe in the future, they'll
see another horse like it. But Isma'ila, King of Kebbi,
grieved for years over the death of his dun. That's
all. This with peace.

ISMA'ILA, KING OF KEBBI, AND THE
ZABARMA MAN (II/XVII)

Here's another. Isma'ila, King of Kebbi, summoned
reinforcements from Matankari, Chibiri, Doso and Hoga,
and they all came to him. Says the King of Kebbi "I
have summoned you, as I am going to invade Gwandu.
People of Zabarma, do you understand?" And the men
of Zabarma answered "May the King of Kebbi's life be
prolonged--we understand*." And the King asked the
people of Arewa if they understood, and they answered
"We understand, King of Kebbi. May God prolong your
life--let us be going!"

So the King of Kebbi set off with his army and
made his way to Gwandu. And the men of Zabarma looked,
and saw a large city. At this one of the Zabarma men
said "Hey, King of Kebbi, you're too greedy. This city!

---

*I have not attempted to render the minor slips in
 the H. that the writer has inserted to add verisimilitude to the speech of the Zabarma man.

And just the few of us! And you've brought us here!
Well, you'd better swallow your desires and take us
back home--for then you'll live to fight another day."
So the King of Kebbi went home, and stayed there. That's
all. That's the end of that account.

ABUBAKAR KARARI, ELDEST SON OF ISMA'ILA, KING OF KEBBI (II/XXVI)

There was once a son of the ruler of Argungu whose like
has never been. This was when Isma'ila was King of
Kebbi, and he had a son called Abubakar Karari. The
King's other sons and younger brothers made free with
the possessions of the people--but not Abubakar Karari.
Now Isma'ila, King of Kebbi asked his people whom
he should appoint to take charge of the state, who would
discipline his sons and younger brothers and prevent
them from their extortions; for he said that he feared
they would drive people away from his town. Well,
Abubakar Karari heard this and went to the King and
said "God give the king the victory. Be pleased to
gather all your nobles and tell them that you have
given charge of the state into my hands." "What!" ob-
jected Isma'ila, "But even I, who am older and more
experienced, have found this burden too heavy." But
Abubakar Karari answered "May the life of the King of
Kebbi be prolonged. Nevertheless, I ask you to give
this charge to me, even if only for one year. You'll
see if the King's sons or younger brothers or grand-
sons or their servants lay their hands on the possessions
of the people any more." "Are you sure?" asked the King.
"Yes" said his son.
Then the King of Kebbi had the Galadima called,
and the Magajin Gari, and the 'Yan-Nami, and the Diko,
and the Kunduda, and the Lailaba, and the Kaura, and
the Kokani, and the judge, and the treasurer--all the
nobles he collected, even to the Dangaladima of the
town, and his own younger brothers and sons--all. Then
the King of Kebbi addressed them thus "Well, my people,
I've sent for you to tell you this. I am very troubled

by the extortion that is regularly inflicted on the
people--so I am giving the Gago charge of the state.
If anyone practices extortion, Gago will arrest him
and, with the assistance of the judge, punish him."
And the sons of the King expressed obedience to his
will. So did his younger brothers. So did all his
nobles too. And Gago, Abubakar Karari, rose and went
home.

That evening he had a proclamation made, announcing
that if a son of the King, or a servant of the King, or
a grandson of the King, or slaves of the King, or any
servants of the King's sons took something belonging
to one of the people, the owner should go quickly and
take him before the judge. And he directed the judge
to go to the mosque and there take his seat, saying
that he would bring to him anyone who committed an offence, so that he might judge him before God and His
Messenger. "Very well, Abubakar Karari. I understand"
said the judge. Abubakar had his proclamation repeated
for three days, and had posts cut and brought in, and
made into spits for impaling and set up at the city gates.
And three of them he took and set up, one at the Kaura
dye-pit, close to his house; one by the old market, near the
home of the chief butcher; and the third in the market
near the entrance to the compound of Dangaladima Dobi,
Isma'ila's younger brother. Then Abubakar Karari said
"Now, men of Kebbi, if any man wrongfully takes another's
possessions, I'll have him impaled on those stakes." He
went on "Leave the people in peace. For there can be no
kingship without people to rule over! Now, I have seen
how the King's sons and servants extort and steal. But
I will not allow people to have their possessions taken
from them wrongfully, I won't allow theft here in Argungu.
For if such things continue I can see that the sons and
younger brothers of the King will force the dwellers of
our town to emigrate." And all the poor people said
"Abubakar Karari, we approve this proclamation that you
have made. May God prolong the life of the King of
Kebbi for giving you charge of this state. Life has
become pleasant for us now."

Well, from the day that Abubakar Karari made his
proclamation, for a whole year, not a man interfered
with the possessions of another. And the people said
"My! But we have benefited from the King's appointing
Abubakar Karari! For look! Wherever you please now,
you may leave your things, and go off and come back and
collect them again. Even the termites won't touch them--
let alone the hand of man remove them. This is something that indeed gives us pleasure!"

The effect of the proclamation extended to Zazzagawa,
to Gulma, to Sauwwa, and from there to Arewa, to the
pagans; thence to Chibiri, the town on Samna; from there
to Doso, away in Zabarma district; from there to Foga,
where the salt comes from; to Kyangakwai, to Ilo. For
all these people, subjects of Isma'ila, King of Kebbi,
were embraced by the ordinance that Abubakar Karari had
made. Whatever you might leave somewhere, when you returned you would find what you had left and take it up
again. For if anyone took wrongfully what was not his
and was caught, he was taken to Abubakar Karari. He
would arrest him and take him to the judge, saying
"Judge, punich this man, for he has taken wrongfully.
I'm just one of the King of Kebbi's guards." And the
judge would execute justice, and the man would be taken
and put in prison.

But this affected the relationship between Abubakar
Karari and his father. For one day they rode forth to
visit Zazzagawa. Isma'ila, King of Kebbi, approached
the town and the people, men and women, young and old,
came out to watch. The king reached them and was passing
and the women were about to shrill with joyful welcome,
but the people stopped them, saying "Don't shrill yet,
for this is only the old king" and then "Now, where's
Abubakar Karari, who made the proclamation and freed us
from theft and extortion? Ah, there he is! This is
what we came to see!" And along comes Abubakar Karari,
and the women start to shrill, showing their joy. For
this was the man whose proclamation had ended extortion,
and theft too. Then the King was told "May the King's
life be prolonged--just see, Abubakar Karari will take
the kingship from you. For look at the people--he's

the one they want to see." "Hm. Is that so?" said the
King of Kebbi. Thus people sowed dissension between
them, until the King of Kebbi said "All right, Gago--
what you have done is enough now." Abubakar Karari
answered "May the King's life be prolonged. I've just
tried to help you, but since it seems that I have done
wrong, take back your state; I wash my hands of it."
He went on "King of Kebbi, it is now seven years since
I asked you to give it into my charge so that I might
assist you. And now you see that I have been of assistance to you for seven years, in which there has been no
extortion and no thieving. You see people who are going
out to their farms put their cloths down at the city
gate and go off and spend the day at their work. Then
in the evening they come back and find the cloths right
there where they left them by the gate; pick them up
and go on into the town. But now--take back what is
yours, for I'm going home, to live my own life, privately
and to myself."

One day a servant of Abubakar Karari went and bought
a ball of _fura_ for thirty cowries, but had no money. This
was reported to Abubakar Karari, who fetched thirty cowries and gave them to the _fura_ seller. As for his servant, he drove him from the town; for Abubakar Karari
never oppressed anyone--that is why he was so popular
with the people.

After the Europeans arrived, people could do work
and ask payment for it, and they were not deprived of
their rights. Then they said "Ah! Here are those who
rule as Abubakar Karari ruled. For we haven't enjoyed
secure government since the period that Abubakar Karari
held office--until now that we enjoy the peace of the
Europeans."

This is an account of something that happened in
Argungu and is true--not a tale. That's all. This
with peace.

SAMA'ILA, FATHER OF NABAME,
OF ARGUNGU (II/XXXVII)

When Sama'ila, father of Nabame, died, for nineteen
years there was no king of Kebbi, only local district
kings; for the Fulani conquered them. Then Nabame
became king. It was at Augi that he assumed the office,
at the season when the corn was up to the chest of a
horse. But at the time the grain was formed in the
heads, Sultan Aliyu defeated and routed them, and re-
took Argungu.

MARAFA MAI-TURARE'S MAN AND ISMA'ILA,
KING OF KEBBI, AND THE MEN
OF AREWA (III/XV)

Isma'ila, King of Kebbi took an army to Gandi and attacked the people of Gandi. Then one of Marafa's men,
called Alaburo, brought along all Marafa's horsemen and
came to the assistance of the town. But when Alaburo
got there, he found that Isma'ila, King of Kebbi, had
fought with the men of Gandi, and taken them captive.
His force had then moved away and dismounted and were
watering their horses. At this point Alaburo arrived
with a large force of reinforcements.

Isma'ila, King of Kebbi was sitting on his shield,
when word was brought him to mount at once, as Marafa
Mai-turare had arrived. But Isma'ila, King of Kebbi,
merely said "Go and water the horses."

Then Galadima Aliyu (who now holds the office of
Majidadi) galloped up to the king and took his stand
beside him. Dangaladima Dobi did the same; after him
Sule Auta did the same; and after him Magayaki, who
ruled the town of Farin Dutsi; next Abubakar Karari--
all these warriors came to where the King of Kebbi was
and took their stand by him.

Alaburo, Marafa Mai-turare's man, aimed his gun
to fire into the King of Kebbi's camp. But it misfired,
three times in all. Then he held the gun under his

horse's stomach and fired. Then it went off. He had
a leather collar with a charm round his neck, and the
bullet hit no one, but lodged in a dum-palm.

Then the King of Kebbi mounted, and they went right
into the reinforcements that Alaburo had brought. Karari
spurred his horse and went and hurled his spear at Alaburo.
The spear hit him. There was another of the Zazzagawa
warriors too who pursued Alaburo and threw a spear at
him, and it hit his horse on the quarter.

Isma'ila, King of Kebbi, took many horses and then
went home.

As for Alaburo, when he got to Gwadabawa, to Marafa
Mai-turare, he showed Marafa his own wound and also where
his horse had been hit. And Marafa took a horse, a
slave-girl, a slave-lad, a kit-bag, three hundred thousand cowries and bundles of corn; also two cows, and he
gave them to Alaburo, wishing him a speedy recovery.
And Alaburo was delighted.

So he set off again and taking the Yabo route, made
his way round to Tambawel. From there he went to Gwandu
and was given a force. He took a large force and went
to Kuduru. When he got to Kuduru, he attacked it, and
even penetrated into the town. The men of Kuduru at
first thought it was the king of Doso and his men who
had come. And it wasn't until they saw that men were
being taken prisoner, that they knew it was the Fulani.
Then they started up and joined battle with the men of
Gwandu.

Now at that time the king of Yabo (he's District
Head of Giddere and a son of the King), was lying down,
ill. But a man--he's alive too--called Galadima--went
and said to him, to the District Head of Yabo "Hey!
Get up, there's an army got into the town." Then he
did get up and mounted his horse.

Now Alaburo too was on his horse, holding his gun.
He fired it once. And then a boy who was up a kalgo
tree shot Alaburo in the wrist. Then Alaburo began
saying "All withdraw from the town, for I've been wounded
in the arm." So the men of Gwandu withdrew from the
town, back to the mouth of the well. There they stopped. They had even at one point captured the District

Head of Giddere and slashed him with swords--but they
didn't penetrate.

Presently a relieving force arrived. Someone else
shot Alaburo, and he fell. Then his force was pursued,
and men and horses captured. The people of Kuduru took
many horses and so returned home.

But when the King of Karakara heard that Alaburo
had been killed, he called an Arewa man, one of his
people, and said "I hear that they have killed Alaburo,
Marafa's man; I want you to go and bring me his head
now."

So two of them set off, riding horses, taking a
bag (made from palm fronds). One of them dismounted
and cut off Alaburo's head and put it in the bag, and
did the same with his feet and his hands. Then they
picked it up and took it to the King of Arewa, Mai-
Karakara. And the rest of the force went back without
its leader, Alaburo. That's all. That's all that I
have of that account.

THE KING OF ZABARMA AND THE SON
OF SULTAN ABDU (III/XVI)

Sultan Abdu, "Unbaked Pot," produced a son, called
Mahe, who ruled the town of Dandi.

One day Mahe took a force and travelled by Dogon
Daji and Tambawel until he reached Birnin Kebbi. From
there to Jan Tullu, which he attacked. And next,
Zarmakwai. Now at that time Zarmakwai had been given
guns and ammunition by the French. And he mounted at
once with the guns they had given him and went to
Baibaye. There he said "Usumana, come, let us go to
Jan Tullu. For I have news that that son of Abdu,
"Unbaked Pot," has attacked Jan Tullu. Let us go and
lay them low." So they mounted. And the King of
Arewa, Mai-Karakara, also mounted and the King of
Arewa from Dumega, he too rode with them. And finally
the King of Fala Birni also joined them. They all
went and found Mahe here at Jan Tullu.

But Mahe, as soon as he saw that he was hard pressed, used a disappearing charm and vanished. As to the rest of his people, they were captured and killed, and his younger brother Barayar Zaki, was also captured. Then Zarmakwai, King of Doso, took Barayar Zaki away to Doso, and he took him to the Frenchmen. The Frenchmen said "Zarmakwai, let him be killed." But Zarmakwai said "No. We, if we've had a battle and we capture the son of a King, we don't kill him, but we send him home and he is taken back to his parents." And the Frenchmen said "Very well, Zarmakwai. Very well, we'll leave him to you. Do whatever it pleases you with him." "Very well" said Zarmakwai.

Zarmakwai kept him there in Doso and he brought a gown and trousers and a turban, and he gave them to Barayar Zaki. Zarmakwai said "Now, men of Zabarma, I know you, that you're hot-headed and foolish. But don't let me hear that you have touched this king's son. For the man who touches him will have me to reckon with." Then Zarmakwai said "Barayar Zaki, any day that you want to go home just tell me and I'll have you taken there." But Barayar Zaki said that he had no wish to go home at present. And Zarmakwai said "Very well."

There came a day when the Frenchmen sent from Yamai and said "Go and tell Zarmakwai that that son of a king that was captured is to be brought here to be killed." And then Zarmakwai answered "Oh, he's already gone home." And the messenger went back.

Zarmakwai brought a horse and two gowns and trousers and a turban and four cows and he gave them to Barayar Zaki. And he had Barayar Zaki escorted all the way to Sokoto. Now Barayar Zaki is still living at the present day in Sokoto. That's the end of that account that I got.

HOW THERE CAME TO BE MEN OF ZAZZAU*
IN ARGUNGU (II/LIII)

There was once a man called Zaure, who was son of the
King of Zazzau. Kanta took Zazzau and killed the King
of Zazzau. Then Zaure went as a follower of Kanta,
and coming to Alwasa, first settled there, and remained
there until the death of Kanta.

The men of Azben (Tuaregs) drove him from Alwasa,
and he moved to Gandiyal. Then from Gandiyal, he moved
to the city of Kyasuwa. In those days Argungu didn't
exist, neither did Gulma, nor Sauwwa, nor Augi, nor
Bubuche.

Presently a malam persuaded him to move again,
saying "Let me help you found a town, from which nothing
will ever drive you; nor will it ever be invaded." And
the malam led on. Zaure followed him, and so they came
to the site of Zazzagawa. The malam marked out its
circumference. Then Zaure gave him a thousand (bags of)
cowries, and entered and made his dwelling there. And
there he continued to live with his people, until he
died.

Darhu, his son, succeeded him. When he died,
Hassan, his younger brother, succeeded him. He died
and Abdu was appointed to the office; when he died,
Bawa succeeded, and, on his death, Abdullahi; and, on
his death, Gero Kwankwando; and on his death, Hasan.
Hasan died and Kichira succeeded him. He was succeeded
by Maitaru, who died and was succeeded by Kadaura.
Kadaura resigned**, to be succeeded by Kato, who is
the king of Zazzagawa today.

LIST OF HEADS OF SAUWWA DISTRICT,
IN ARGUNGU (II/LIV)

They are called Dagelawa. From the time they were in
Baghdad until they came to the land of Gobir, there

---

*Or, more likely, "the origin of Zazzagawa (=Men of
   Zazzau)".
**? under pressure from the British?

were fifty-seven heads. And since they came to the
land of Kebbi, there have been twelve heads: first,
Sa'idu; second, Goga; third, Ibrahimu; fourth, Sa'idu;
fifth, Abubakar; sixth, Abdu Salami; seventh, Abdullahi;
eighth, Almustafa; ninth, Aliu; tenth, Abubakar, eleventh,
Muhammadu; twelfth, Salihu, who is the present district
head. These, all told, ruled for 106 years.

DANDANGUNA, WHO INTRODUCED RICE
TO KEBBI (II/XCIV)

There was once a man here in Argungu who was a hunter.
If he was setting out hunting, on the day before setting
off, he would seek a loan of a thousand bags of cowries,
against a promise to pay when he returned from hunting.
This man had fifty dogs and many servants who would follow him to carry the game he shot. Now whenever he
went hunting, each of his dogs would kill some fifty
beasts. And when he got back he would go and repay all
the money he had borrowed.
   There was also a man called Dandanguna, a Kebbi
man, who had two younger brothers. These it was who
first grew rice at Argungu. All the way from Sokoto,
along this valley, they cleared land and grew rice.
From Argungu here they extended their planting on to
Birnin Kebbi, and further still--till it reached between Tilli and Digi. One of the younger brothers came
along behind, pulling up all growth and leaving it to
rot and fertilize the land*. The other trees that you
see here now, and the deleb-palms, are the ones that he
missed, not seeing them. Had he seen them, you would
not now see any trees at all in this valley, for on the
route that he followed, there is nothing growing. Look,
it is quite clear and open where he went, between Felande
and Gulma, as far as Sauwwa--an open plain, with not a
tree growing there. Moreover, over there, close to

_____
*To make sense, I have inserted a full stop after
  dono and altered the semi-colon in the next line
  to a comma.

Birnin Kebbi, where he went, he cut down all the grass
and trees, and there too there is open country. And
beyond again, between Digi and Tilli, there too nothing
grows, for he cut down all the trees there were there,
and it is quite devoid of vegetation. Yes, he* it was
who started rice-growing. And still, the Kebbi men of
today, they still grow it. And the rice grown in
Argungu and Birnin Kebbi derives from that of Dandanguna,
who began it.

His course took him from Sokoto to Wamako, to
Gwamatse, to Jekanadu, to Tozo. From there he made his
way to Dan Kala; then Silame, then Gande, then Katami.
Next to Augi, Bubuche, Dan Barke, and thence Maguna,
then following the river to Kwararo and Argungu. Next
he came to Tsillallal, then Sarkawa; then he passed just
here, close to Felande. Then Gulma, Sauwwa and Ambursa;
and so, along the river to Birnin Kebbi, Kola, Digi and
Tilli. So it is that today, throughout this whole land,
there is nowhere where rice is so plentiful as in these
towns that I listed to you. They are the most abundant
rice-growing areas.

But, in addition, ever since they first got it from
Dandanguna, you can see how the rice seed has multiplied.
For it has spread into Gungawa; and to Yauri; and even
to the land of Bida. As for the Bida people, they came
to get hold of the rice seed, as they were regular
visitors to Gwandu, since they were under the Magaji of
Birnin Kebbi. That's how they obtained rice seed. And
the people of Birnin Kebbi were ready to give the Bida
people the rice seed, as the latter were subject to
them. So they too got it, but still, even today the
men of Argungu are greater rice growers than the Hausa.
This is all that I have found out, from Samna, son of
Mai Yaki. That's all.

THE ORIGIN OF THE KINGS OF KARAKARA, OF
THE DISTRICT OF AREWA ("THE NORTH") (II/LV)

The first King of Karakara was Sawani, who ruled for

---

*Subject reverting to the elder brother, presumably.

twenty years and then died. Chiffa ruled for twenty
years too, and died. Goje succeeded him and ruled for
two years. Now the city of Karakara was being built,
because of the warfare against the Fulani; but the
Fulani made an attack (and left it in) ruins*.

Chiffa himself didn't go to Karakara, until he
had first made Kuka his base. Kuka was a Fulani town,
but there were pagans living in it, who had formerly
been ruled by the King of Kebbi, but had themselves
preferred Fulani rule. He spent a year at Kuka and
then moved to Karakara, where he died. Their (?his)
tomb is at Kwakka.

Next Kibiya became king. He ruled for twenty-one
years, nor was any attack made on him, until he died.
Tankari succeeded, and he too was left in peace to rule
for fifteen years, until he died. Bisalla succeeded
him, and ruled for twenty years before he died. Chibiri
was attacked during his time; he reinforced it, but it
was taken nonetheless. Next Jintori became king. During
his time, Haliru, Emir of Gwandu, attacked Karakara, but
Jintori defeated his forces, killed the emir and took
many horses. He ruled for fifteen years and then died.
Muhamman** succeeded. While he was king, Shehu, son of
the Magaji of Birnin Kebbi, attacked one of his towns,
called Kuduru, but Muhamman killed him and took many
horses. He ruled for twenty-nine years and then died.
Next Manomi became king, and during his reign, Aliburo,
the servant of Mahe, attacked Kuduru; but he was killed
and fifty horses taken. Manomi was king for sixtten years
and then died. Next Hakimi became king, but then the
Europeans arrived, and there was no more fighting. The
French confirmed him as king, but our Europeans gave the
title to Yabo. Mai-Gizo sought the title of Yabo's
Dangaladima for himself, but now that title has been
given to Bozari. And it was from Bozari that I obtained
this account.

---

*I have interpolated the words in brackets, as the
   brevity of the H. is obscure to me. But I may be
   wrong.
**The first Muslim name.

THE KINGS OF AREWA ("THE NORTH") (III/VI)

When Hodi was king of Arewa (in the land of Argungu)
there was an alliance with the King of Kebbi (and this
was continued by) every subsequent king. Two generations
followed and, finding the alliance (already established)
maintained it. And when Hodi was king of Arewa--he was
father of Gama-dadi--Gama-dadi had a son, who is the
present ruler of Arewa at Tullun Dabaga, who is called
Mai-doka.

In the days of his grandfather, Sultan Alu Darkakau
brought an army and attacked him. Whereupon Hodi, King
of Arewa, went out to meet the Sultan and routed him,
utterly and completely, taking his riding camel, and
seizing people and horses beyond number.

Then Hodi, King of Arewa, said "Now! (Men of)
Arewa, come here all of you. I shall send messengers
to Sokoto with this camel and her trappings, and with
the horses." So he handed them over to be taken to
Sultan Alu Darkakau, and he told his messengers, when
they got there to tell Sultan Alu Darkakau that he
sought peace and friendship from him.

Obediently, the messengers set off and made for
Sokoto. When they got there they told Sultan Alu
Darkakau the message that Hodi, King of Arewa, had sent
by them. Whereupon the courtiers who were sitting in
the presence of the Sultan said "Sultan, may your life
be prolonged, how can this be? We go to someone's town,
and attack him; he defeats us, and takes our possessions,
and then sends us our possessions back and says that he
seeks peace from us? Well--we don't accept this proposal."

But there was one of Sultan Alu Darkakau's sons
there and he said "May young men speak?" He was told
that they might, and went on "You made war on them and
they took your possessions by force--or did they come
and steal from you? Or did they, on the other hand,
come out and meet you (fairly) on the road and take
your things? Or did they steal them? You know that
you attacked them and they defeated you. And now, when

they send to you, saying that they seek peace, will you
refuse to accept it? Hodi, King of Arewa, has sought
peace from you, because he saw that you couldn't prevail
over him and that he was going to destroy you." He concluded "Now, since he sent, saying that he wishes peace--
give him what he asks for."

Then the Sultan said "Now, since Hodi, King of
Arewa, has sent to us, let us accept his offer of peace.
For if we don't--on the day we return there--on that
day he will destroy us."

And Sultan Alu Darkakau said to the messengers of
Hodi, King of Arewa, "Go and tell Hodi, King of Arewa,
that I grant him peace."

The messengers set off, and when they reached home,
coming to Hodi, King of Arewa, they told him.

Later the wife of Hodi, King of Arewa, produced a
child, and the boy was given the name of Gama-dadi. Now
it was this one, Gama-dadi, who is the father of Mai-doka,
the King of Arewa, this one who is at Tullun Dabaga.

Now, when Gama-dadi became king, at that time, the
king of Kwonni brought an army, with horsemen, in great
numbers, and attacked Chibiri. Now Chibiri is the seat
of a king, called Samna Kwando.

When he saw the army he said to his people "Make
haste and go to Gama-dadi, King of Arewa, who's at the
city of Fala, and tell him that an army has come upon
my town; and that I want his help and reinforcement."

Hodi, King of Arewa, had the drum for mounting
beaten, and in a very short time the horsemen had collected. They mounted and galloped till they reached
Chibiri. They came upon the king of Kwonni's force and
scattered it. They took seven hundred and sixty slaves,
and three hundred horses--which is, all added together,
horses and slaves, a thousand and sixty.

The King of Arewa, whose seat was the city of Fala,
Gama-dadi, gave out twenty horses with orders that they
be taken to the King of Kebbi. At that time Toga was
the king of Kebbi ruling in Argungu. Says Hodi "Here
are some firstfruits*, to take to Toga, King of Kebbi;

---

*Lit. "the first ripe heads of millet roasted".

an army was brought against us, but we drove it back
and scattered it completely."

When Hodi was King of Arewa, the Fulani attacked
regularly but not a single man of Arewa was taken by
them.

Now the son that Hodi, King of Arewa, produced,
the single one, was one whose like everyone would like
to have. For indeed in the forces of Sokoto, there was
no one who didn't know Mai-doka; for he, Mai-doka, would
take an army and go into Hausa country, wage war and
return.

On one occasion he took a force--twenty horsemen
went with him to war on that day--and they drove home
some three hundred cattle. Presently a new force caught
up with them, and Mai-doka said (to his men) "Go on
slowly as if we were in Fala city." Then he waited till
the pursuit came right up to him, then turned and attacked them and continued killing men until they scattered,
each one taking his own way.

Then Mai-doka rejoined his men and presently came
to Fala city. He went and showed (what they had brought)
to his father, saying "Gama-dadi, king of Arewa, see
what I have won. Moreover a relieving force caught up
with us--but they ended badly, for we inflicted a heavy
defeat on them."

Again he--Mai-doka--took a force and went into
Hausa country, and attacked them, capturing men and
cattle. Reinforcements came and caught him, but he
attacked them, inflicted great loss on them and it was
with difficulty that they escaped.

And from that time forward, if Mai-doka was leading
the army, no enemy relieving force would approach--for
they knew Mai-doka.

Once he went with Isma'ila, King of Kebbi, to war
and they attacked a town, where he got an arrow in his
left eye. And when the King of Kebbi took a force
against Hizna, Mai-doka was wounded in his right thigh.

Again, when Sultan Abdu, "Danyen Kasko" ("Unbaked
Pot"), attacked Argungu, Isma'ila, King of Kebbi, sent
to the kings of Arewa, saying "I want you to come and
help me, for our alliance is not merely a thing that

began yesterday; the friendship between us, us and you, dates from the time of our grandparents and parents. And we, in our turn, have not annulled it." So they proceeded to mount and go to him. And on that occasion Mai-doka was given a cut on the right of his head.

Now when Isma'ila, King of Kebbi, saw how the Europeans had divided the land and the city of Fala had been left on the French side, he said "Now, since they have divided the land, if one of Gama-daɗi's elder brothers crosses over to this side, I'd make him King of Arewa." Then Mai-doka heard of it and said "King of Kebbi, as for me, although they have divided the land, I'll never stay under the rule of Zarmakwai*--for I'm your man, King of Kebbi, Isma'ila." Isma'ila, King of Kebbi, answered "But, Mai-doka, I'm looking for one of your father's elder brothers to come over this side that I may appoint him King of Arewa," but he went on "However, since you've come, I'll give you the position of King of Arewa."

Then Isma'ila, King of Kebbi, took Mai-doka and went with him to the Europeans in Argungu, and so Mai-doka was appointed King of Arewa, at Tullun Dabaga--and here he is, still king in Tullun Dabaga. That's all. This with peace.

BUBEN SHIKO AND THE EMIR OF GWANDU AND
THE EMIR OF BIDA (III/XIV)

In the days when Hanafi was Emir of Gwandu, there was a king at Giro, and his name was Gudurega, Buben Shiko.

The men of Gimbana took an army and attacked Giro; and Buben Shiko went out and drove them off; took their horses, captured their men, and then returned home.

Hanafi, Emir of Gwandu, went to attack Giro, but didn't take the town. When Buben Shiko came forth, he drove them off, took horses and men, and then returned home.

When the Emir of Gwandu got home he sent a letter to Bida, to the Emir of Bida, Umaru Majigi. And the

---

*?

Emir of Bida brought reinforcements from the men of
Bida, horse and foot. He set out and arrived in the
land of Gwandu. He reached a town called Zakuwa and
stopped there.

The Emir of Gwandu set off and made his way to
where the Emir of Bida was. And together they moved
to Giro, halted there and attacked Buben Shiko--he was
the father of the present Gudurega. The men of Gwandu
and the men of Bida attacked together. So there were
two great kings together attacking one small town.

And it wasn't until seven months had passed, that
the men of Giro came and said "Buben Shiko, we have no
corn, and now, look, it is seven months that you have
been fighting with two of the world's great kings, who
have been besieging us for seven months; there are
even men from Sokoto in their army." They went on
"Now, see--our corn is finished. We have no millet,
no guinea-corn, no _maiwa_, no beans--we haven't even any
water. Well, what shall we do, Buben Shiko?"

But as they were speaking thus to him, the army
took the town. Buben Shiko was taken and killed. Then
the whole town was destroyed. But some people never
even heard of the fall of this town, for there were not
many inhabitants, and it was only a small town. Had
Buben Shiko been reinforced, he wouldn't have been
defeated. It was because he was not reinforced that
they were besieged for seven months and eventually,
through lack of food and water, overcome. That's all
I know about Buben Shiko. This with peace.

THE ORIGIN OF LEMA AND THREE OF
ITS KINGS (II/XXVII)

The town of Lema in the land of Argungu was founded
when a man called Na-Kwaido arrived there. He was its
founder, in the days when Bello was Sultan.

Presently the town was attacked by the Fulani.
They fought and the people of Lema defeated the Fulani.
It was Bature who was King of Lema during the time Toga
was King of Kebbi, and when Bature died, Gyambe, his

younger brother, was appointed. When Gyambe died, his
son, called Wasakwai, was appointed, and he is still
king.

Well, Mai-Turare, Marafa of Gwadabawa, made an
attack on Lema, and caught the town with only a few
men there. There was the King of Lema, also Kyuya--
who is now Yarima of Lema--and Tudu, and Dangaladima
Arzika. Some twenty fighting men in all--that was what
Marafa Mai-Turare found in Lema; all the rest had gone
into the bush. The force arrived and Lema was attacked.
The attack came from the north, the east and the south.
Only on the west was there no fighting.

The battle had continued, for some time, when
Wasakwai, King of Lema, took his spear* in his hand.
Wherever he hurled it, it found its mark. He moved
from place to place in the town. Then a huge fellow
from Marafa Mai-Turare's force rushed at Tudu, and Tudu
shouted "Lema, come here!" The King hastened over.
The arrows were flying thick and fast, but he interposed
his shield; he reached where Tudu was, and the big
fellow from Marafa's men came on into the town and
grappled with the King of Lema. They wrestled for a
while, and Marafa's man drew his knife and wounded Lema
in the arm. Lema threw him to the ground, but he lifted
Lema off his feet. At this point the King of Tudu ran
up with his arrows. Says he "Lema, where can I (safely)
shoot him?" But Lema answered "Don't try to distinguish
him from me; just shoot at us both!" Unwillingly, Tudu
put his arrow to his bow, and shot--and hit Marafa's
man in the left eye. "Draw your knife" said the King
of Lema, "And cut his throat, as you would a ram." Tudu
did so, and they both set off to join the fight again,
leaving the other there dead.

Presently one of Marafa Mai-Turare's men called
out to those of his own side, saying "You know that
Marafa led you here to fight, don't you? Well, how is
it that you're not fighting?" But the King of Lema
shouted back "That's not true--but they don't see this
as a place to fight. They don't want to fight here.

*A local, Argungu type.

So you'll be going back where you came from empty-
handed." The King continued "But we, we're hoping
with God's help to get horses and slaves from you.
We'll be taking them very soon. But you, you'll get
no profit out of us! For God is against that. See,
already we've killed numbers of your people, and we
are going to capture others very soon--whether you like
it or not!" So they drove the attackers away from their
town and pursued them, taking the horses of Marafa's
men. Afterwards the King of Lema said "Here take these
horses to Isma'ila, King of Kebbi. An army came against
our town, and we killed its men and took their horses.
And here, King of Kebbi, is the proof to distribute
to your men." And so, right up to the time that the
Europeans came, the Fulani never attacked and captured
any of the people of Lema--not during Wasakwai's period
of office. He is still king at Lema, has been ever
since he was a young man, and now as you see, he is old
and there has been no warfare. That's all. This with
peace.

ISMA'ILA, KING OF KEBBI, AND BAKO KUNDUDA*, KING OF AUGI (III/XXXIII)

Isma'ila, King of Kebbi, took an army and went to Gande.
Marafa, Maiturare also mounted and went to war. And
word was brought him that the men of Kebbi had attacked
Gande, whereupon Marafa went to Gande, to their assistance. And a fight developed with the King of Kebbi's
men.

Then Bako Kunduda, King of Augi, put his horse
forward and went in among the men of Marafa, at once
killed one of their horsemen and returned to the King
of Kebbi. Then back he went again, but was shot in the
chest with an arrow. Controlling his horse, he returned
to Isma'ila, King of Kebbi, and gave him the salute with
his weapon. Says Isma'ila, King of Kebbi "Bako Kunduda,
stop a minute for them to pull out the weapon that is

*Kunduda is a title.

in you." "No" replied the other, "King of Kebbi, I won't let them pull it out, when the battle isn't over yet." Again "Let the battle be finished first, and then I'll let them pull the arrow out of me."

Then Bako Kunduda took a hold of (?) his horse, spurred it, and went back and aiming at another, thrust at him with his spear so powerfully that he pierced the pommel of his saddle, went right through the man, and hanging him over his horse, grabbed the other horse and led it back to the King of Kebbi.

When the Fulani saw this, they didn't wait, and the Kebbi men went after them, capturing them. Then the King of Kebbi laughed and pulling down his turban, covered his mouth*, saying "The Fulani met with Uwar** Kebbi and he brought them low." And the King of Kebbi returned home and settled down again.

On another day the King of Kebbi set off with an army to attack Birnin Kebbi. They fought the men of that city. Now the King didn't know it, but some of those he was fighting against were of his own kin, and they said "Shame on you, Isma'ila, King of Kebbi, does a man seize his own brothers?" That ward was called Taka-lafiya. But presently reinforcements arrived and attacked the forces of Isma'ila, King of Kebbi.

Whereupon Bako Kunduda said "King of Kebbi, I beg that you will stand to one side and let us fight this battle for you." "Very well, Uwar Kebbi" said the King of Kebbi, "I agree." Then Kunduda dismounted, tightened his girth, securing his saddle on the horse and mounted again. Kunduda set off and went in among the men of Gwandu, slashing them, until he had captured five horses and put the men of Gwandu to flight. Then the King of Kebbi returned home.

Time passed and one day Kunduda set off to go to his farm, over there by Maguna--there's a tamarind tree there, which is called Mafasar Doki (?place of horse-robbery). Kunduda's people were working, and he was

---

*? to hide the undignified mirth.
**Uwa, "mother" has many idiomatic meanings expressive of importance and essentiality.

walking through his farm, carrying three throwing spears
and a sword. Along come some hostile horsemen, and one
of them gallops over to seize Kunduɗa's horse. Whereupon Kunduɗa takes one of the spears and hurls it at
him--it hit him in the lower part of his back and came
out through his thigh. Then Kunduɗa took his horse--the
horse of the man he had felled--and getting on to it,
went for the others, and, all on his own, proceeded to
give them a drubbing. He took three horses, plus the
one he was riding, four. Then he set off home along the
road, and showed them to the King of Kebbi. The latter
questioned him, and he told him what had happened. Says
the King of Kebbi "Congratulations, Kunduɗa! Our thanks
to you for what you have done."

A little later, the King of Kebbi set off to attack
the land of Zabarma, a town called Kwalo. They got there
and fought with the people of the town, who fought back
against the King's men, inflicting wounds on them. Kunduɗa had his horse killed. Then said the King of Kebbi
"Bring up one of the led horses and give it to Uwar
Kebbi to ride--for his has been killed. Moreover, I,
King of Kebbi, know that today I shall have to take part
in the fighting myself; for I know that if I don't, we
shan't return home today." "God forbid!" says Kunduɗa
in grief, "Let them rather kill us before they reach
you! If things come to that pass, there'll be no one
left alive of those gathered here."

And when Kunduɗa went forth and into the people
there, at once he scattered them and dispersed them,
and took four horses. Isma'ila, King of Kebbi, smiled
with pleasure, and said "Uwar Kebbi, we thank God, we
thank His Messenger, and we thank you, Uwar Kebbi--for
if you hadn't acted thus, we should have lost many men.
As it is, in fact, see, we have had men killed; but, but
for your deeds, our losses would have been incalculable."
Then Isma'ila, King of Kebbi, and his men turned and
returned home.

For there was never a war in which Kunduɗa Baƙo
showed cowardice. Then came the European conquest.
That is the end of the account I have of Baƙo Kunduɗa,
Uwar Kebbi. That's all. This with peace.

THE ORIGIN OF THE (TITLE OF) UWAR KEBBI, KUNDÙDA (III/XXXIV)
(See last story for the meaning of <u>Uwar</u> <u>Kebbi</u>)

Here is the origin of the Kundudas. Saleman (<u>sic</u>--
?Suleiman) was King of Kebbi, living at Birnin Kebbi,
and at that time Toga held the title of Kunduda.

Saleman, King of Kebbi, set off from Birnin Kebbi
for Gurma to make war against them, but the men of the
town drove him away and he didn't take the town. So he
returned to Birnin Kebbi and stayed there.

But Kunduda Toga heard what had befallen the King
of Kebbi, and set off, cutting straight through the
bush, went to Gurma and attacked them. He took the
town, burnt it to the ground, and turning, set off home.
He reached a lake and halted there. Then he took some
of the slaves and gave them to someone, saying "Here
are some slaves--take them to the King of Kebbi, and
tell him that these slaves are the people of Gurma that
I have captured and brought home." And the slaves were
taken to Saleman, King of Kebbi, and he was told "Kunduda
says, here are some slaves, and they are from the town
of Gurma." Then Saleman, King of Kebbi, said "Go quickly
and tell Kunduda Toga to come, as I am sending for him."
They went and told Kunduda Toga that Saleman, King of
Kebbi, said that he was to come to Birnin Kebbi as he
had sent for him. "Very well" said he.

Then he mounted and made his way to Birnin Kebbi
and came before Saleman, King of Kebbi. The King of
Kebbi gave Kunduda a very warm welcome indeed and said
"Very well, Kunduda, from today you are 'Uwar Kebbi'.
And from today, from now on, whoever holds the title
of Kunduda shall also be Uwar Kebbi." And now you have
heard why it is that the Kundudas are also called Uwar
Kebbi.

And whenever they went out to war, if the fight
started to go badly, then the Kundudas' drum theme would
be played "There is Gulma (<u>sic</u> ? = Gurma) with a horse
that has no speed; nor can the rider of the horse escape." And wherever a Kunduda might be, if he heard the

drum-theme of the Kunduḍas, he would know that there was
a fierce fight on, and come along at a gallop. Even if
there were a thousand bows against them, and only five
of the Kunduḍa family, they would put the bowmen to
flight and with no delay. And then the men of Kebbi
would be able to advance.

Kunduḍa Toga had fifty children, all male, and
everyone of them mounted on a horse and wearing the
quilted armour. His eldest son was called Bature. On
one occasion the Fulani attacked them in three ranks and
held up Saleman, King of Kebbi's advance. So the Kunduḍas'
drum-theme was beaten, and Kunduḍa Toga called out "Where's
Bature?" Up gallops his eldest son, with his brothers
behind him. Then Kunduḍa Toga said "Bature, over there
where those men have formed three ranks--that's where
we want to break through." And Bature answered "It's
already accomplished."

And he spurred his horse, and his brothers after
him, and at once broke up the enemy, who scattered. And
they took many captives of the Fulani, went through to
pursue them, and then returned home. Kunduḍa went on
to Augi and settled there.

And the Kunduḍas still have this position of high
respect, so that the King of Kebbi--whoever may be the
current holder of the title--will never take counsel on
his own, but will always have a Kunduḍa with him. And
now you know why Kunduḍa bears the title also of "Uwar
Kebbi". I have this account from Kunduḍa himself.
That's all. This with peace.

KUNDUḌA BAK͟O, UWAR KEBBI, KING
OF AUGI (III/XXXV)

Isma'ila, King of Kebbi, went to attack Dankala. But
the town was reinforced, and the Kebbi men gathered in
one spot whereupon the drum-theme of the Kunduḍas was
beaten. When Kunduḍa Bak͟o heard this, he galloped up,
and as he came, took a spear and a shield. He put
spurs to horse and didn't rein in until he was in the
midst of the relieving force; he made for one horseman
and hurled his spear at him; he fell to the ground and

Kunduda Bako seized his horse and took it to Isma'ila, King of Kebbi.

Back he went again and the relieving force was scattered. And the men of Kebbi pushed forward their advance, captured some people and then returned and went to Maikulki. Then entered that town, but the king of the town collected some people at the entrance to his compound and began firing at the men of Kebbi. The stout resistance was reported to Bako Kunduda, and he came galloping up on his horse. When he got there, he spurred his horse and went and captured the king of Maikulki, complete with his mare. He captured him lock, stock and barrel, and all the people of that town too were taken, and then they returned home.

On another occasion they went off to attack a town called Binji. And Ba'are came to relieve it. Now when Bako Kunduda saw Ba'are, son of the King of Binji, and the whole gathering of the horsemen of Binji, then he charged at them and broke them up, straight away killing one of the horsemen and capturing his horse. The rest of them, when they saw this, didn't stay but made off at a gallop. The men of Kebbi fought on, took prisoners and then returned home.

Then Magajin Gari* went to Isma'ila, King of Kebbi, and asked that he might be given a force to go and take prisoners. And the King of Kebbi granted his request.

They set off and took a route to the east of Gwandu, travelling all through the night till dawn came. Then Magajin Gari said "Kunduda Bako, let us return home." But Kunduda Bako answered "No, Magajin Gari--now that we have come out, we're not going home without a fight," and he went on "I'll take over command of the force; it is now under my orders."

On they went, past Gwandu and began fighting. The men of Gwandu got news of it and came out to a little town there in the bush and halted. All the men of Kebbi had gone on. The men of Gwandu didn't see them, but they saw Kunduda. He turned back and routing the men of Gwandu, went after a horseman. The latter tumbled off his horse, and Bako Kunduda took the horse.

_____
*Title.

When they got home Magajin Gari saw Bako Kunduda
with the horse. Says Magajin Gari, Muhammadu "Bako
Kunduda, where did you get the horse?" and the latter
answered "Magaji, when you were coming along, I was
behind you. The enemy's reinforcements overtook me at
Bela. I turned on them, but they didn't stay--they
ran away. I went after one horseman. He, when he saw
I was going to catch him up, tumbled off and let the
horse go. And when I came up, I grabbed the horse and
turned and came on back." So they came back to Argungu
and settled down again.

Presently they heard that the men of Gwandu had
ridden out to war again. Then Lailaba* went up to
Isma'ila, King of Kebbi, and said "King of Kebbi, I
have news that the Fulani are coming to attack. So I
have come to you to ask that you permit me to go and
set an ambush for them." Says the King of Kebbi "Go
along Lailaba, your request is granted."

Then Lailaba sent off his messenger telling him to
go and ask Bako Kunduda to mount and come and join in
the ambush. They set off together and going, waited at
Bunguji. Presently the men of Gwandu arrived. Bako
Kunduda promptly started out, but the men of Gwandu, when
they saw the ambush, turned and fled, at once, without
staying. Bako Kunduda pursued them and taking a horse,
returned. When he got back, he gave it to Lailaba. And
that was the origin of the friendship between Lailaba
Umaru and Bako Kunduda--his giving him the horse he had
taken in the fight.

Again they went off to war. The horsemen divided
up and Bako Kunduda made for the land of Yabo to set
an ambush. The rest of the force returned, but not
Bako Kunduda--until two days had passed. He had, in
fact, stayed to capture a horse. Bako Kunduda's compound began to mourn for him, thinking that he had been
killed. Then they saw him--with the horse that he had
taken from the men of Yabo! And the people of Argungu
were more amazed than ever at Kunduda Bako.

---

*Title.

Again Lailaba went up to Isma'ila, King of Kebbi, and said "King of Kebbi, I pray you, give me a force to take to war," and the King of Kebbi answered "Lailaba, go along--your request is granted." Lailaba sent to tell Bako Kunduda, and they made their preparations and set off to attack Ambursa. But they found that a relieving force had quickly come to the aid of Ambursa. They fought with the men of Ambursa, and Kunduda's horse was wounded by arrows seven times--but he still took two horses, and so they turned and set off home. Kunduda Bako's horse didn't die until they reached Wuyan Nufawa. There it died.

Abdu, "Unbaked Pot," attacked Argungu and Bako Kunduda said to Isma'ila, King of Kebbi "When anyone comes right to our home, we don't fight him in the town, but go and meet him outside." And Bako Kunduda was the first to be away outside the town. Before the fight broke up, Bako Kunduda captured a horse and said "Here's a horse--take it to Isma'ila, King of Kebbi. The victory is ours." And Isma'ila, King of Kebbi, at once mounted his dun and came out, following after Kunduda. The rout lengthened into a pursuit, and Bako Kunduda took five horses on that day.

Then Isma'ila, King of Kebbi, took a force against Katami. The men of Katami gathered and put up a stout resistance, but Bako Kunduda came along and charged them and broke up their group. But they shot Bako Kunduda's horse. The horse didn't die till he reached Tungar Kwanni. Then it died.

Bako Kunduda was a real warrior. Nor was it till the Europeans came that the men of Kebbi ceased fighting against the Fulani. That's all the account that I have of Bako Kunduda. This with peace.

THE ARRIVAL OF A EUROPEAN
AT ARGUNGU (III/XX)

When the Europeans were at Jebba, one of the artillery officers received an order from the Governor, and he-- the European in charge of the guns--collected artillery soldiers up to the number of 33 men.

He took them to Wushishi, and from there went to
Zunguru. At that time Zunguru was just bush. Next day,
a letter was sent after him, and he, in his turn, from
there, wrote a letter and sent it to another European
of the artillery. The latter European collected together
some artillery soldiers and when he had picked them out,
he said to them "You are to go together with the European who has taken the 33 soldiers and the gun. When
he's taken them to Wushishi, he's going on and you're
to accompany him to Argungu." He went on "Whether you
spend four months, or whether you spend six months, I
don't know which it will be, but that European will be
in charge of you."

So we set off from Jebba, and we made our way to
Kontagora. When we got there, we met some horse soldiers
and some foot soldiers. We were travelling with four
European officers and one doctor. Setting off from
Kontagora, we went until we met with a European sergeant
from the artillery. We set off from Yelwa and reached
Bahindi. There, when we arrived, we found another
European with his soldiers. We set off again and came
here.

When we reached Bashe, the European who was in
charge of us said "Now!" and came and picked out some
soldiers who were some of the most efficient ones, and
took them and put them in charge of the gun. He said
"Now you see, we're in the land of Gwandu, and perhaps
they will attack us, so I don't want you to relax for a
minute."

From the time that we set out right until we reached
Kalgo, we didn't find a single town were we were accepted
by the people. But Haliru, when he heard that the Europeans were coming, said "You people who are in Kalgo
have food prepared, and _tuwo_ and _fura_ and let all sorts
of food be prepared; I am going out to meet the Europeans
since they're going to stop at my town today."

As we marched along, presently we met with the king
of Kalgo. Says he "I've come out to meet you, European.
I am very pleased to see you." Then he went on in front
and took us to just outside the town and there we camped.

Then the European collected the soldiers and the
laborers and said "Now! This is what I've got to tell
you, both soldiers and laborers. You see this town.
This is a town that is at peace with us. Nobody is to
touch anything that belongs to them. If anyone touches
anything, King of Kalgo, you're to arrest him and bring
him to me, and I'll punish him." And the King of Kalgo
fell to the ground and said "Thank you, European. Now
that you have given me this instruction, I, for my part,
if anyone does anything, I'll arrest him and bring him
to you." Then the European gave Haliru, King of Kalgo,
his hand, and the latter mounted and went back home.

When he got there, he sent back about thirty chickens, about 100 eggs, and two large calabashes of milk,
and a ram and about 50 loads of wood. The European
said "My thanks to you, King of Kalgo, Haliru." He went
on "I am going to Argungu, but in the evening come back
and I'll give you a paper for you to keep." The King
of Kalgo answered "Very well, I understand, European."
The evening came and he returned. The European got the
piece of paper and gave it to him.

Next morning when it was light we set off and went
to Birnin Kebbi, and there we spent the night. Next
morning we set off again, and came to Gulma and there
we camped. Then the European sent on a messenger and
said "Go and tell the King of Kebbi, Isma'ila, that I'm
on my way. He's to prepare a lodging for me."

The King of Kebbi, Isma'ila, said "Very well. I
understand and agree to what the European has asked."
Then he said "Now, let the people who live in Tankoji*
move out and let them leave the place. We'll let the
Europeans have that place to stay."

The King of Kebbi had tuwo and fura prepared and
plenty of food got ready. And, when the Europeans
arrived, the King of Kebbi, Isma'ila, sent out to meet
them.

As soon as the European had dismounted, the King
of Kebbi, Isma'ila, got on his own horse, and went out
to where the European was. They met and they greeted
each other enthusiastically.

---

*I have given it a capital letter.

Then the European said "King of Kebbi, get on your horse and go back home now. I'll come later to visit your home." And Isma'ila, King of Kebbi, answered "Excellent, European." And then the King of Kebbi got on his horse and went back home.

Next, the European mounted his horse and came as far as Farin Dutsi, and had a look at the place. He went back from there and said to the King of Kebbi "I've seen a place and I should like to set up a government station there outside the town, because where we are now, you have to turn some people out in order to make room for us there." The King of Kebbi answered "No, European, you stay where you are. It doesn't matter." But the European refused.

When evening came, the King of Kebbi had a proclamation made in Argungu, and said "Men of Kebbi! I know you, and I know that you are hotheaded. Well, don't let me hear or see any man who has laid hands on one of the soldiers. If I do, I'll have something to say to you."

Then the European said "King of Kebbi, I want you to give me donkeys and donkey drivers and I want to take them with me and load them, but I'll pay wages for them." And the King of Kebbi had donkeys fetched, and gave them to him.

The European left some soldiers here in Argungu, and went off to Baibaye. He left soldiers there and went on to Matankari. There, too, he left soldiers and went to Chibiri, where he also left soldiers. Then he took some other soldiers and camels and went on to Matankari, and went to Kwonni, and Tawa, and Adar, and Tsibiri, which is the city of Gobir. And he went as far as Maradi.

From there he came back, having got news that the town called Giwaye had revolted. Then he sent a letter telling two of the European officers to go and subdue that town. They set off and went and attacked the town, Giwaye. And the King of Giwaye ran away and went on to another town. Now the name of that town was Karakara, and when he got there he stayed there.

The European returned and reached Argungu and
found a -fort prepared. So the move was made into the
fort, and there they stayed.

But one day the European got news that the King
who had run away had gone to Karakara and was living
there. So the European took some soldiers, a company,
and some artillery and went to arrest him. Whereupon
he ran away and went into French territory.

Next the European came back again, and when he
got here he learnt that some of the soldiers had committed an offense. Whereupon he arrested four men and
put them in jail, and others he greatly reduced in pay.
When he got back this time, he stayed for seven days.

Then he set off from the town again and went to
Lema and spent the night there. From Lema he went to
Baibaye, and spent the night there. From Baibaye he
set off and made his way to Goro and spent the night
there. He set off at night and entered the bush of
Yelu. It was evening when we reached Yelu. Setting
off from there we went to Bana, and from there to Tunuga,
and from there to Kyangakwai. From there we made our
way to Illo and spent the night. He then spent seven
days with another European.

Next we moved off and went to Kurukuru and spent
the night. From there we went to Yantala and spent
the night. From there we went to Gwamba. At Gwamba
the European said "Where are the canoe men? I want two
canoes." And he got into the canoes next morning. Now
it seems that he was going to meet some other Europeans,
five of them: a colonel, a major, two captains, and one
other officer. And we came back with them.

We got back to Illo and when we got there we found
that another European had arrived with the soldier's
wives. Them we met at Kyangakwai.

Setting off from Kyangakwai, we went to Fingilla;
then to Bunza; to Sabon Gari; and Kalgo. Haliru, King
of Kalgo, came out to meet us.

Now Haliru said to the European that he wanted to
attain the office that belonged to his family; but his
father had never been king. At the time that he died,
he had held the title of Dangaladima. "Is that so?"

said the European. "Yes" answered Haliru, king of the
Kalgo, adding "Now I'll obey you; I'm your man, and I
want you to appoint me to the title that belongs to our
house." The European said "I see. Did I give you a
letter previously?" The other answered "Yes." Then
the European said "Very well. As for that former letter
that I gave you, if any European comes and spends a
night in your town, take it and give it to him in order
that he may pay you for any food that you bring him."
He went on "But let me give you a paper which you are
to hide and not give to anyone. If there is a war with
Sokoto, another European will be coming here and he's
the man you're to give this paper to. You mustn't give
it to anyone else except him, and you must hide it away
carefully." And we spent the night there.

Next morning we set off and came to Birnin Kebbi,
and spent the night. Next morning we set off again and
reached a point between Gulma and Sauwa, by a large
baobab tree in a valley. There we spent the night.
Next morning we set off again and reached Argungu, where
we spent eight nights.

Then one day the European said "Let someone go and
tell Isma'ila, King of Kebbi, that I want him to give
me some men to show me the way, for I'm going to travel
to the land of Gwandu. But I shan't fight them unless
they attack me first."

We set off from there that night, but we didn't
reach Gwandu until sometime past midday, in fact it was
the early evening when we reached Gwandu. We skirted
the town to the west, and went round to the south of the
town, and there we camped in the low-lying valley by
the water. We spent the night there. Next morning very
early we set off towards the south, then we turned
sharply and made west. We went to a town called Kardi,
and there we spent the night.

Next morning we set off again and came to Birnin
Kebbi. We crossed and, going on into the bush, spent
the night there. Next morning we set off and made our
way to Gulma, and spent the night there by the Dyepit
Gate. We set off from Gulma and so came to Argungu.

Next some Fulani brought a complaint to the European that they had had some cattle stolen. Now these
Fulani were people from Digi and also from Tilli. We
spent four nights there, and then the European set off,
taking infantry soldiers and gunners and departed.

When the people of Digi heard that the Europeans
had come against them with an army, they sent out their
old men, and these came and met the European out in the
bush and said "European, let there be no fight, for we
are sorry and we don't want to fight." The European
didn't spend the night at Digi, but passed on and went
to Tilli. There he spent the night by the gate on the
east of the town. He set off from there and went south
and didn't stop for the night again until Bunza.

He picked out some of the Company's soldiers and
one European and ordered them to go to Raha, for he had
heard news that there was a woman there who was causing
trouble. She it was had made the men of Raha attack a
(? the) European. "Go and fetch her" (he said). But
it seems that in the meanwhile she had heard news that
the Europeans had spent the night at Bunza, and had run
away without waiting.

Next we went to Sabon Gari, and spent the night
there. From there to Kalgo; from there we moved on and,
passing by Birnin Kebbi, we went into the bush and spent
the night. Next morning we set off and came to Gulma,
and from Gulma back to Argungu. When we got here, we
spent ten days.

The European set off with the soldiers again, and
we went to Silame, and then returned. When he got back,
he spent four days and then set off again and so went
to Gande. He returned again, spent another seven days,
and then set off again in the direction of Katami, and
there we spent two nights. But before we came back from
there the King of Kebbi sent some horsemen to inform the
European, saying "One of the artillerymen has gone mad."
So we came back and returned home.

Then the European said "Now! Both the soldiers and
the laborers, all of you, be off into the bush and hunt
for this artilleryman." We spent five nights looking
for him in the bush. Eventually, after seven days, a

man from Argungu spotted him in the bush, very thin,
nearly dead. Then the European said "Now this man is
mad, and I don't want his gun and his knives, or anything metal to be left in his hut." He went on to say
"A close watch must be kept on him so that he doesn't
go back again into the bush." Eventually he wrote a
note about him and he was taken away.

Now the reason that he went mad was that he used
to visit Farin Dutsi, the place where they had their
fetish, when he wanted to relieve himself. And that is
why that man went mad, for that place has a lot of
fetishes. But afterwards, another one got into the
habit of taking his gun in the evening and going and
shooting in that place. And so, because of this shooting
the place there, Farin Dutsi, became a little less evil.
Now, there used to be two crocodiles there at the time
when we made a fort in that place, and these two crocodiles used to wear, one of them a snow white burnous,
white as paper; and the other one used to wear a pepper-
and-salt gown.

Then there was another place where the men of Kebbi
would bring meat and fish and money and would throw it
into the place, saying that this was in supplication.
Now, inside, there was a snake, as it seems, and he
wouldn't come out except on a Friday and on a Sunday*.
Those were the only two days in the week when he would
come out.

Next, when the European was at Argungu, and when
there was a fort at Farin Dutsi, every evening he would
get on his horse and go to the town and ask whether any
soldier had gone into Argungu and taken anything by
force. If, when he had asked, he was told that it was
so, then he would say to the man (who claimed to have
been robbed) "Now, however many people are gathered,
can you be sure that you recognize the man who took
this by force?" If the other answered "Yes, I'll know
him," then he would say "Very well, tomorrow morning
you'll come along." But if it was in the day, then he
would say "Come along with me and don't be frightened."

---

*Cf. the Daura legend.

If, as he was coming, the man would be trembling, the European would say "Hey! Don't be afraid. Say what you have to say straight out. Whatever you say, I'm listening. For you see, I won't have any interpreters for myself, I don't want it to be told me in English. Say what you have to say straight out in Hausa, and don't be frightened because you see that I'm a European."

Then the European would take the man around among all the soldiers and laborers until he spotted the culprit. Then the European would send away all the rest of the people, and as for the culprit if he were a soldier or if he were a laborer, he would take him and do justice. And that's what he used to do all the time that he was here in Argungu.

While we were living here, one Wednesday a note came that Kano had been attacked. When the Europeans halted at Shagari, on the edge of the low-lying valley, horse soldiers were sent, two of them, and they brought the European the note. It was sunset when they came.

Then the European said to the soldiers and the laborers "Let them all come tomorrow and get the money for their food, and let them go into the town, and let every man get rations for himself. Tomorrow after midday we're going to set off and we're going off to meet the Europeans in another town called Shagari."

Now this was in the month of the Big Festival, the day before the Festival. Well, we set off from here, after midday, and on that day we didn't get any sleep. It wasn't until we were to the east of Sainyinna that we settled down for the night.

Early in the morning we set off and met with some Europeans, about 15 of them. We went on and came to a halt at the camp. Then our European gave them a piece of paper and they went to the "judge". Next they were given distinctive badges. And it was because they were on the side of the Europeans that they were given these signs, made of red cloth. They tied them on their arms, so that, when they were in the area of the fighting, the soldiers should not think they were of the Sokoto people and shoot them. That was why they were given these pieces of red cloth, which they fastened on to their arms.

We spent two nights there, at Shagari, and then
set off and went to Bodinga. There we spent the night.
Then, setting off from there, went to Kasarawa, and
halted there. There two companies of the Lokoja artillery were taken out, and departed. Then the horse
soldiers had a battle with the men of Sokoto, but no
cannon were fired. When evening came, they returned,
and we spent the night at Kasarawa.

Next day when it was light, our European was told
that he was the advance-guard, together with his troops
and two guns (cannon). As for the Lokoja artillery,
they were told to stay behind as the rearguard.

On Sunday, when we went out, we found the people
of Sokoto, gathered in large numbers near a deleb-palm.
Now at that time we had 156 soldiers, 25 officers, and
in command there was a general and a colonel. Those
were the commanders and we had two millimeters (? French
machine guns ?) and four machine guns; and 1,100 laborers.

We made our way to a _gawo_ tree, to the south of
which there was a _kurna_ tree. Then the general and the
colonel took up a position in one place, and picked up
their glasses and looked. They ordered the artillery
officer "Take action with one gun and shoot towards that
large group of horsemen over there." We went into action,
and he ordered "1900, fuse nine nine*."

One round of shrapnel (?) was fired, and it fell
beyond the people. Then the European ordered "1850,
fuse eight!" Said he "Corporal, fire three rounds at
that target (?)." Then the colonel ordered "Cease
firing!", and we stopped.

Next a man wearing a white gown came running towards
us and the soldiers shot three bullets at him. Then
Nakaiyama--he was the chief headman of the laborers--said
"Hey there! You laborers, hit that man there."

And then one of the Sokoto men picked up a stick
and drove back some of the laborers, Yoruba men, towards
us, hurling sticks and stones at them. The Yoruba began shouting "Hau, Gambari ashere!**" He drove them

---

*I.e. 1900 yards range. The Hausa phonetic equivalent
  of this order makes interesting reading!
**Gambari (Yor.) = "Hausa".

towards us at the run, and they came running right past
us. At this point one of the soldiers shot the Sokoto
man.

We went up the hill. Marafa* had some soldiers (sic)
with him who continued firing guns at us and hit one of
the artillery laborers in the hand. This laborer's name
was Mai-tsamiya. Then the European gave the order "Everyone lie down, both soldiers and laborers. Everyone lie
down." So the Sokoto people believed that we were dead.

Then the Majidadi* of the Vizier came galloping up.
Whereupon the European ordered us "Halt! Action front!
Case-shot (?)!" In no time we had our guns ready to
fire. Now we had a European sergeant who came running
up with the case-shot, and gave it to us. We loaded it
and fired and immediately the Majidadi of the Vizier
fell, both he and his horse.

Next the European ordered "800, fuse three!" We
aimed at where the Sultan was and continued to fire.
But they quickly set off running away.

Next we went to where there was a spring, just there
by the Taramniya Gate and halted there. When we reached
the deleb-palm where the Sultan had been, we found his
flag, which he had run off and left.

Presently a man riding a camel came out of the west
galloping. The soldiers were pursuing him and shooting
at him. They got him in the foot, but he didn't fall
off. After the fight was over and everyone had gone
home, then that camel rider came along to the doctor who
treated him, and his foot got better.

Some of the Company's soldiers and artillery were
taken and they went into the town and then came back.
Next we went to the east and came to the edge of the
place called Mai-Bindiga, where the Sultan would go for
the Festival prayers. There we halted.

We spent a night and next morning word was taken
to the General, and he was told that the Sultan was at
Wurno. So on Monday we set off and went to Wurno, but
the Sultan wasn't there. We spent the night; next
morning we came back again. On that day the soldiers

---

*Sokoto titles.

and the laborers had a tough time, for three of them,
one soldier and two laborers died of thirst. Water was
brought out to us, and Nakaiyama took some laborers and
went from tree to tree giving the soldiers water. Then
we returned here and came to the fort.

Two days passed and then the Governor* arrived, and
he set off for Katsina taking with him the General. And
one of the European soldiers went on to arrest Aliyu,
Emir of Kano. That's all. That's all that I saw.

---

*I.e. Lugard.

XI
Kebbi Customs

THE MEN OF KABI AND THE MEN
OF KATSINA (I/XXXIII)

There was once a Katsina man who came to the Emir of
Gwandu, Umaru-Bakatara, and became his servant.

Time passed and one day he went to Argungu, where
he stole a horse. But before he could leave the town
with it he was caught. He was brought before Sama,
Emir of Kabi. Said the Emir "Take him away and kill
him!" But before they could take him, he said that he
was a Katsina man. Now the men of Kabi and the men of
Katsina are in joking relationship, and one will never
let the other down. So the Emir of Kabi said "Very
well, since he is a Katsina man, we mustn't shed his
blood."

Now there is a lake there, which is so deep that
ever since Argungu was founded no man has ever reached
the bottom. Then the Emir said "Take this Katsina man
and throw him into that lake." They took him--but when

he was thrown into the lake, the water became so shallow
that it barely reached his buttocks, and the Emir of
Kabi was amazed. And from that day the men of Kabi have
never again illtreated the men of Katsina.

Similarly when Toga was Emir of Kabi, a raiding-
party returned with slaves that they had caught. They
were sorting out the Emir's share of these, when a foot-
soldier came up with a Katsina man. Said the Emir "Hey--
what about that Katsina man?" "He was taken in the
fighting" answered the people. "Take the shackle off
his neck!" said the Emir. So this was done and he was
released.

Now the reason that the men of Kabi and Katsina
will not ill-treat one another is that originally they
were related. And so one will never harm the other.

Similarly if either sees that the other's gown has
been slightly burnt, he'll snatch it away--this is part
of the joking relationship. Moreover it is said that
if you eat fish in front of a Kabi man, if you don't
invite him to join you, a fish-bone will stick in your
throat. Then you will have to beg his pardon, and he
will give you medicine to drink which will help the
fish bone on its way.

Thus too, there's a stretch of water at Argungu
called Gamdi, which is fished every year. And if they
are going there to fish, the whole town collects, and
the Magajiya of the town goes into a state of bori-
possession. When she gives the word to enter the water,
everyone goes in and fills his gourd with fish before
coming out. But if she doesn't give the word, and anyone goes in, if he goes under the water, he won't come
out--he'll die. It is said there are a lot of jinns in
the water there.

THE MEN OF KEBBI (II/XCIII)

The fishermen of Kebbi, if they are going to begin
fishing, will perform magic for the occasion and then
gather all the fishermen together. Their head is the

town homa* of the King. After him the Judge's homa,
then the Kunduɗa's homa, the Majidaɗi's homa, the Karari's,
the Lailaba's, the Galadima's, the Magajin Gari's, the
Kokani's, the Yannami's, the Muza's. All these gather,
and then take the road to the river. When they get there,
they stop and ask "Where is the Magajiya's homa?" Then,
when someone says that he hasn't come, they send off a
young fellow to fetch him. ·While he is being fetched,
the town homa--who is "King of the Water"--performs the
fetish rites. Then he says to them "Let everyone enter
the water with his people." And everyone goes into the
water and sets to fishing, catching fish.

But if, back at home, there was ill-feeling between
two of them, and one of the two catches a fish; if the
other is present, then the fish will turn into a frog,
or else the stone of a deleb-palm.

In olden times, the men of Kebbi would, if one of
their women gave birth to a child, take the child down
to the river and throw it in. They would leave it there
for seven days--then, on its naming day, they would come
and fetch it; and it would be named and a ram slaughtered.
But when Isma'ila became King of Kebbi, he forbade the
practice, telling the men of Kebbi to desist from leaving
their infants in the water. But for his prohibition,
they would still be doing this today.

And when the child has grown and reached years of
discretion, and has begun to get around, then he will
begin to go down to the river himself; there he will
bathe, and learn to swim and to fish. And he will acquire also the knowledge handed down in his family. They
will show him how to prepare "medicine" from little bits
of chopped-up wood (?); and another for catching all
sorts of fish; and yet another for use if a man gets
a fish-bone stuck in his throat. These are some of the
pursuits of the men of Argungu--and they still are to
this day. That's all.

---
*Lit. "net".

ARGUNGU WATER CUSTOMS (III/XXI)

The men of Argungu have a river where they go fishing.
There is one pool that they call "Swallower of Strangers";
another that they call "Magajiya's Pool"; and another
they call Gamdi.

The day they go off to fish Gamdi, they first perform fetish rites: take black goats there and slaughter
them; also a red billy-goat; and a red rooster, a black
hen, a white hen and a speckled hen.

Then they go along to fish Gamdi taking <u>gumba</u>
(pounded bulrush-millet and water), diluting it and
pouring it into the pool. Next those who are to do
the fishing gather. One man will put his net (?) in,
and it will be as if he had gone and put the fish there:
he'll catch a lot and fill his gourd with them. Anyone
who knows the nature of the place, if he is lucky at his
first entry, and gets a lot of fish, he won't go back
into the water again. But one who doesn't know it, will
keep going on in, trying again; but his net (?) will
just float straight to the surface. And the men of
Kebbi, without saying anything, will just push aside
the net of the man who hasn't reappeared--for they know
that he is dead.

But if Gamdi is fished, without anyone dying, and
the fish are taken into Argungu, then there will be a
conflagration in the town, and the whole of Argungu will
burn down.

This Argungu custom is carried out every year--right
up to the present.

And the people of Argungu say that this Gamdi has
many jinns living in the pool. And the same is true of
Magajiya's Pool. If someone goes there and enters the
water, he'll be drowned at once. There are a lot of
jinns in Argungu.

Each year the <u>bori</u>-men of Argungu slaughter black
goats, and red goats, and then white chickens, and then,
having slaughtered them, pour the blood into the water
for their fetish rites. For thus, they say, they "make
the water right".

MARRIAGE AMONG THE MEN OF KEBBI (II/XCVI)

If a man of Argungu intends marrying the daughter of
one of the common people, while she is still quite
young, he will go regularly and work on the farm of
his future in-laws. First he will help hoe there.
Later he will go again for the reaping and cutting off
the heads of corn. Then again later to the rice pad-
docks, to turn over the soil and to sow the seed; and
back again to thin; and again, when it is time to cut
the rice. Moreover, he will go and make zana mats for
his in-laws, and take them to their compound. Then off
again to cut wood and bring it back; and going round
their compound, renew all the fence posts; and fetching
the zana mats, fix them to the posts, and so right round
the compound, until he has completely surrounded it with
zanas. Next, when the Lesser Festival* comes round, he
must find five thousand cowries, and take them to the
compound of his in-laws. And the same again when the
Greater Festival** comes.

Also, when it is the harvest of the bulrush-millet,
he must fetch ten bundles of millet and take that to
their compound. And at the rice harvest, he must take
them one large hide bag full of rice. And every year
he must do these things, until she is old enough for
marriage.

When she is old enough to be married, the marriage
price must be paid. This is thirty thousand cowries,
at least for the daughter of common people. She is put
in henna for three days. Then the bridegroom is also
put in henna for four days. So the bride, in all, is
in henna for seven days.

Then when they come to seize her and take her, she
runs off and goes to the drummer's compound. And he,
the drummer, slaughters a kid and gives it to the bride
and her accompanying girls to eat. After this, the
bridegroom's friends go to the drummer's compound and

---

*'Id al Fitr.
**'Id al Adhā.

fetch the bride and take her to the groom's compound.
But the groom will not approach her for two days.

Then, on the third night, he goes to the bride's
compound* with his friend, and when they get there, they
must give her money before she will speak to them. This
is what they call "Buying the bride's mouth". If they
don't give her the money, she won't speak to them. They
must give it to her first. Presently the groom's friend
departs and makes his way home. But the bridegroom will
sleep there. Next morning, before it is light, he too
will get up and go off to his friend's compound.

If he finds her a virgin, he will present a sheep
and a white cloth, to be taken to the compound of her
parents. And in the morning too, an old woman will make
an early start to visit the bride. If she has kept her
virginity, the old woman will go to her parents' compound, and when she gets there, announce that the bride
"Has preserved her loin-cloth." At this announcement
her parents will be very pleased.

But if she has lost her virginity, then the husband
may drive his bride out--unless he feels for the shame
of her parents. In this case he will begin abusing her
roughly and continue to do so day and night, mocking
her, all so that she may say that she dislikes him. If
she repudiates him, then he will be refunded his marriage
payment. But if he, the bridegroom, repudiates her,
then she will return to her parents' compound, but not
a single cowrie of the marriage payment need she return.
Well, that's all I have to tell of marriage at Argungu,
at least so far as concerns the children of the common
people.

MARRIAGE BETWEEN THE CHILDREN OF ROYAL FAMILIES AT ARGUNGU (II/XCVII)

As for the daughters of noble houses at Argungu, to
marry them a marriage price of two hundred and ten
thousand cowries was payable--or alternatively, two
cows. On payment of two cows, the bride would be taken

---

*Presumably her new one.

to her husband's compound. If the bride repudiated her
husband, they would pay him back a hundred and five
thousand cowries of the marriage price; but the balance,
of a hundred and five thousand, they would keep and not
return. As for the husband, he wasn't in a position to
say anything; he was afraid, for the girl was of royal
family, and, were he to say anything, they might come
and extort more money from him. While some of the brides,
who repudiated their husbands, would return and live at
home, without a single cowrie of the marriage payment
being refunded. That's all about the marriage of the
children of royal families in Argungu.

And now for the marrying of the kings of Argungu.
If they saw a beautiful girl of the common people formerly, before the Europeans came, they would seize her
and take her to their compounds. There they would sleep
with her, and not till afterwards would they send money--
twelve hundred and fifty cowries--to her parents' home,
saying "Here's money to complete the marriage with your
daughter." That's what they used to do in the old days,
so that they acquired a large number of wives.

Of the kings of Argungu, one would have five wives;
one ten; one fifteen; one twenty; one twenty-five; one
thirty; one thirty-five; one forty; that's how they
were, some even had fifty-five!

But, now that the Europeans have come, most of
those wives have left the king's compound--for you see
their parents now maintain them and give them cloths
to wear. For now they have returned to their parents'
compounds, and I'll tell you the reason, which is that
the Europeans will not allow a common man to suffer,
unless he has committed an offence. This is why nowa-
days the kings of Argungu have only a few wives. That's
all. That's the end of what I have discovered on this
subject.

THE FETISH OF THE MEN OF ARGUNGU (II/XCVIII)

In the olden days at Argungu this is what they used to
do in time of war: having been out to fight and captured

some Fulani and brought them home, they would take
them to Gamdi, where there is a lake--just here to the
north of Argungu; and there they would put them to
death and practice their fetish rites.

There was another fetish place, just there, close
to the city, beside the river. They call it 'Ci-Baƙi
(Devour-Strangers). There too they would put to death
those they took there. There is yet another place too,
over there to the east of the city, where they get earth
for plastering the walls of city buildings, there too
they had human sacrifices. There is a place there,
where there is water, they call it "Mala". That is
where they put them to death. And yet another place
they had of human sacrifice, the place they call "Dagwal".

Another practice was for the king to take some five
people into his compound, and there kill them and skin
the bodies. Then the flesh would be cut up into small
pieces and taken and made into what they called "kilishi"
(type of biltong); spices and oil would be added, and
it would be put in the sun to dry, until it was completely
dried. As for the bones, they would be chopped up and
put into a cooking-pot. Soup would be made, poured on
to tuwo, and the whole taken out to the entrance of the
compound and there given to the people to eat. But the
kilishi was only brought out, when they were going off
to war. Then they would fetch it out, and, dividing
it up, give it to the people. Every man would put some
into his wallet. That's what they used to do. So you
see, that's the reason that the men of Kebbi are such
warriors. That's all of that account of Argungu.

A FETISH OF THE MEN OF KEBBI (III/XXXVI)

There is a place, a rocky hill here, to the south of
Argungu, near the city, close by the low-lying land of
the river, which is called Dan Koji. This is where the
men of Kebbi have their fetish. When they have been to
war and captured some Fulani, they will stop and pick
out a beautiful maiden and then take her to Dan Koji and
there slaughter her.

And if they have been and captured a beautiful
woman--who is not yet old--then they'll take her to
Dan Koji and slaughter her there. At first they used
to do this secretly, but later the matter became open,
and everyone knew about it.

But if they hadn't just been away to war, then
they would catch a black bull and take that to Dan
Koji and slaughter it.

Nor did they cease this practice until the Europeans came to Hausaland. Then they did.

Moreover, the King of Kebbi, in the days of old,
when they had been out to war and brought captives, would
look out a beautiful woman, a Fulani, and would slaughter
her there, in his compound; the flesh would be cooked
and the men who went to war would be given it to eat.

I got this account here in Argungu. This is what
they would do in the olden days. That's all.

A CUSTOM OF THE RULERS OF
AREWA ("NORTH") (II/XXIX)

If a ruler of Arewa dies, a bull is taken, slaughtered
and skinned. Then there is drumming with large numbers
of drums, announcing that the king has died. Meanwhile
the women of his compound are crying loudly in his compound. Then the king's body is wrapped in the hide of
the bull and placed on a bed*, and some big, strong
fellows brought and made to lift the bed on to their
heads.

Then the leading men of the town gather, offer
words of consolation and instruct that the king's sons
and younger brothers, also his elder relatives of his
father's generation be gathered in one place.

There lies the corpse on the bed, carried on the
heads of the four big fellows. Then the leading courtiers address the corpse thus "Show us who is to become
king, so that we may live in peace with our wives and
children; and may reap our corn, and prosper. Show us

---

*The H. gado has, of course, no legs.

the man, who, if he becomes king, will insure that we
enjoy these things, and the whole district prospers.
Point him out to us, that we may make him king." And
all the people walk round the body, which is in an open
space in the midst of them, alone but for the four
bearers.

Then the body begins to go round the people there,
till it reaches the one it has chosen. When it reaches
him, it bumps into him. Then the leading men express
their joy at having a new king, under whom their district will enjoy peace and prosperity. Meanwhile bulrush-
millet has been pounded with water*, and the corpse is
carried away and buried.

But they send the king elect to Argungu to the King
of Kebbi, saying "Our king has died, but we have followed
our usual custom for selecting a king, and this is the
one chosen." Or else they will say "Here's the man that
the corpse bumped into." And the King of Kebbi will
wind a turban on his head, and fetch trousers, sword
and horse, and give them all to him. Then the party
will set off back and so return to their town.

But the new king won't go into his compound. He
will have a grass shelter put up, and going into it,
live in that for six days. Then, on the seventh day,
a feast is held, and money and gowns and cola-nuts and
horses and cattle are brought and given to the new king.
Now all these things come from his relations who show
their pleasure at his appointment to the kingship by
giving them and so making large contribution to his
possessions.

As for the deceased king's wives, no man of the
family that hopes to become king himself will take them
in marriage. But some other, an outsider, will come
and marry them. Some of the wives will remain in
mourning** for one year; and if one of them had been
married to the king for a long time before he became
king, when he died, she might prolong her period of
mourning for two years, before she married again.

Well, there's one custom of the kings of Arewa.

---

*Why? For the people to drink, presumably.
**Lit. "washing".

A CUSTOM OF THE COMMON PEOPLE OF
AREWA ("NORTH") (II/XXX)

They have a custom in Arewa, that if a lad sees a
maiden that he likes, he will proceed to court* her.
If she likes him--even if her parents have pledged her
to someone else--she will not say anything, but hold
her peace--although she is in love with the other one.
Sometimes this young fellow will make her pregnant.
When this becomes known, he will be arrested and taken
to the king**, who will fine him a hundred thousand
cowries; and the girl's parents will be fined one hundred thousand cowries too. That is, totalled, both
parties will be fined two hundred thousand cowries, for
the boy making the girl pregnant.
    But if the young man is careful[+], he won't make
her pregnant, and (his parents) will go to the girl's
parents, taking money--perhaps thirty thousand, or
forty thousand, or fifty, sixty or even a hundred thousand, but the common people won't give a higher marriage
price than that.
    When the girl is taken to the compound of her bride-
groom, on the day that she is to be taken to her new hut,
the families of both gather, and the bridegroom summons
two friends to come and hold the girl's legs for him.
Then he starts to insert his penis and she to cry. Presently, when they don't emerge, someone else--his elder
brother, or his father's older or younger brother--comes
in and strikes his buttocks, saying "Get on with it!
Damned, good-for-nothing boy! You lazy fellow, you're
keeping people waiting, hanging round, waiting for you
to come out." Then the bridegroom renews his efforts
and penetrates the girl. As he withdraws, blood follows,
and there is blood to be seen on the girl's belly too.
Then a piece of white cloth is brought and taken and
shown to her relatives, on both her mother's and her

---

*Tsarance, see Glossary.
**Cf. I/XI.
[+]Or "wise" or "patient".

father's sides. And they fetch money, and a roll of
white cloth and kids, which they give away. And people
throng behind them and drum for them, and they dance
joyfully, with the piece of white cloth in their hands.
They shrill to show their joy that their daughter has
kept her virginity and that they have nothing to be
ashamed of.

But a bride, whose groom finds that he penetrates
easily, as with a woman that has been married before--
he will collect a calabash (from those that have been
presented for the marriage), a gourd-ladle, a wooden
bowl, a mat-cover and a cooking-pot in one place. Then
he will go into the bush and cut a tall post and bring
it in and dig a hole and set it up at the door of her
hut, or at the entrance of the compound. Then he will
pierce holes in all those things, bring them, thread
them on to a piece of rope and hang them from the post.
So everyone who sees it, knows that the girl hasn't kept
her virginity. As for her parents, they are much grieved
at their daughter's unchastity, and when the groom an-
nounces it, they will go to him and try to persuade himself to resign himself and not to pierce the utensils.
If then the girl wishes the marriage to end, her parents
will pay back the equivalent of the marriage price. But
if it is the husband who wishes it, then the girl leaves
his compound, but the parents don't have to pay anything
back.

Well, that's the custom of the people of the North,
which they still follow, to this day. That's all.

WHEN THE CHIEF BORI-MAN DIES (II/XXXII)

Here, in the district of Arewa, if the chief bori-man
dies, all the bori people are collected, men and women,
young and old. Then they get goats--a young red billy
or a young red nanny, and a young black billy or a young
black nanny; and big roosters, a red one and a speckled
one; and threshed corn, grain, and intaya--what people
call "acca". They pound this up with water. Then they

get buttermilk and honey. Then they slaughter the kids
and the chickens, <u>tuwo</u> is prepared from the pounded
grain and water, and--while they speak words of con-
solation--they pour it out on the ground.

Or else they take the fowls and go either to a
large baobab tree, or to a tamarind, or to a mahogany,
or to a <u>tsiriri</u> (<u>Combretum Kerstingii</u>), or to a <u>k̂irya</u>
(<u>Prosopis oblonga</u>), or also to a rock, and there they
say the words of consolation. Then they return and
bury the dead man. Their idea in gathering, they say,
is to contribute alms to the dead man, so they eat <u>tuwo</u>,
and take their fill of meat and everything else; and
they consume the pounded bulrush-millet and water, and
the honey--all, they say, as alms to the dead man!

And there you have the account of what they do
when the chief <u>bori</u>-man dies. That's all.

XII
Other Hausa Customs and Beliefs

THE CHARACTER OF ALL HAUSAS* (I/XXXVI)

This concerns Hausa customs. When they begin eating,
they say "In the name of God" and when they have finished, they say "Praise be to God".

Similarly, too, when greeting one another, they
touch hands, and if the first inquires "How does the
cold weather suit you?" or perhaps "How's the tired-
ness?", the one greeted will answer "Praise be to God."

Then if a Hausa comes on his friend eating, the
friend will invite him, saying "Time for food (lit.
we're at calabash)" and the other will say "Praise be
to God".

Again if a Hausa comes upon his friend seated,
after he has made formal salutation, he says "Greetings
at your sitting". Others say "Greetings at your resting."

Kano women who are going into another compound will
say "Afuwo". But Sokoto folk, both men and women, when

---

*See ABR 2, p. 58.

they are going to enter a compound will make formal salutation.

If a Hausa dies, people will say "Let us go and condole with So-and-So." (This condolence is what they call ta'aziya.) Then they go to his compound and say to his relative--be it son or father or brother or grandfather--"I am told that So-and-So has died, is it true?" "Yes" he will answer, and the visitor will say "God have mercy upon him and give him pardon and lighten for him the darkness of the grave!" The other will reply "Amen". And when they are about to leave, they will say "May God calm your spirit" and then depart.

And this is the Hausa way when a woman bears a child. Two days after the birth, women will come and visit her and give her "Greetings on your good fortune" and the new mother will answer "Greetings to you too." For giving birth is no easy thing. Then if the birth is on a Friday, on the next Friday, the child will be named. For this, there is a gathering of malams, neighbors, and relatives both of the father and the mother. They arrive early in the morning, the child is named, and the malams make intercession for it "May God give it life, may God hide it in the hole of bitter-ness*, may God bless the mother's milk!"

Then cola-nuts are divided out and everyone is given some. And a ram must always be slaughtered be-fore a naming ceremony. When it has been flayed, the midwife is given the head and the skin and the feet. And the barbers who shave the infant's head are given the saddle of the ram.

As for the new mother, she will wash with hot water daily for forty days. And when she washes, she doesn't use her hand to dip out the water to wash her-self, but leaves are picked for her, either from the rumhu** or from the cediya, and these she dips into

---

*Edgar's note says "so that witches can't get at him. If a mother sees a witch, she says that her child's flesh is bitter"--so discouraging an appetite for it.
**Species of cassia.

the hot water and sprinkles it on her body. At this
time she is said to be "doing the forty", and when the
period is finished she is said to have "cast off the
washing".

If a boy sees a maiden he likes, he will begin to
invite her, secretly, to come and talk with him, and
bring her presents of money or cola-nuts and give them
to her. If she then says he is the one for her, he
tells her parents.

Then if they set out to arrange the marriage, they
approach her father's younger brother--it is his responsibility, for her father has no say in it. Then they
take money and pay their respects to her mother's younger
sister and to her mother herself. Then they go round
her family, paying their respects to all of them, so
that all may know that she is to get a husband. And
after that her father's younger brother gathers together
the relatives and they collect. The boy's parents bring
a calabash of cola-nuts and ten thousand cowries to the
girl's parents, who then say "Very well. We give her to
you." The boy's parents say "We accept her" and a day
is fixed for the wedding.

If the appointed day comes, some ten girls are
collected together secretly, and she is summoned into
a hut. When she is inside, the girls are beckoned in
to come and surround her. Then an old woman, ululating
for joy on her behalf, plasters her with henna--and she
herself starts to cry, but only in play. Then the other
girls also begin to cry. And they keep at it for three
days, while she is kept wrapped in henna. Then the
marriage is officially performed. This occurs in the
morning, and there is a party in the evening.

Meanwhile the boy also, in his home, is wrapped
in henna. And his best man will keep giving the
bridesmaids money for food until the party has ended.
It is on the day of the party that the bride is taken
to her husband's hut.

Next morning--if she is the child of wealthy
parents--the wedding presents are brought. But in some
places this is not done till three months later. Next
morning too, both bride and groom are unveiled. Then

the groom's friends all borrow horses and ride to the
door of the groom's home. Now, among the presents a
fine gown is brought for the groom, and fine trousers,
also a turban and every other finery, in which he dresses
himself, and, going out, mounts his horse. The other
youths follow him and they spend the rest of the day
riding round the town. Then, at sunset, they return
home and dismount.

Late that night, when everyone is asleep, accompanied by his best man he enters the hut. But when the
best man speaks to her, she refuses to answer, until he
gives her the cola-nuts "to open her mouth"--then the
bride will allow herself to smile.

The best man goes out, and when the husband touches
her, she strikes him. This happens several times and
they struggle. And only with difficulty does he have
intercourse with her. Then, if he finds her a virgin,
without experience of men, he will buy a silver dollar
and give it to her. But the groom, as soon as it is
dawn and before people are awake, goes out and making
his way to his best man's house, hides.

But if he finds that she has had experience of
men, then the other girls will laugh at her. Her husband will make a hole in a water storage pot, a mat and
a drinking calabash; and, grasping the string door-
curtain, cut a piece off--for she has acted shamefully.
Then, when everyone knows what she has done, he does
nothing more to her, and they go on living together.
But people will say "Well! So that girl never made it!
Devil take her!" But we are speaking of the girls of
old, not those of today.

SOMETHING ABOUT ALL HAUSA* (I/XLI)

The Hausas say that you shouldn't trust five things:
don't trust a horse, don't trust a woman, don't trust
night, don't trust a river, don't trust the bush! All
these five things are not to be relied on.

*See ABR 2, p. 54.

Then the Hausa say that, if a man dislikes you,
you should like him, thus making him feel ashamed. If
a man is mean towards you, make him a present and make
him feel ashamed. If a man offends you, be patient with
him, thus again making him feel shame.

Again, they say, if you want to know who is not
your friend--if you lost someone through death, your
son, your father or your mother, then the man who fails
to come and give you his condolences, he's the man who
dislikes you. Or if you're ill in bed, well, if a man
doesn't come once to visit you, during your whole stay
in bed, he's the man. Or again, if you escape some
danger, it's the man who doesn't come and congratulate
you on your escape.

Similarly too, if you're going off on a trading
journey, it's the one who gives you some food for the
journey that you should bring a present for when you
return. But if someone waits till you get back and
then brings you something for your return, but when you
were setting out, never gave you anything for the journey--
he's just after a present from you.

Again, if there is a search for a thief and he is
not found, if anyone sees a gambler--arrest him. And
if you're looking for a liar and don't find him, if
there is a talkative man to be seen--arrest him. While
if you're looking for a double-dealer, and you see a
man who hangs his head--arrest him!

And even if a man is treated with great respect
among the Hausa, if you see that he gambles, or visits
brothels, or any other place that he ought not to--have
nothing to do with him.

Also the Hausa say don't make your choice of a
wife on the day of the Festival, or on any other fes-
tive occasion; for at such times, they are all dressed
up, and you cannot distinguish the goodlooking from
the ugly ones. And among the Hausa if a man goes in
for spirit-possession, respectable people won't mix
with him.

The people of Kano say that if your superior is
setting off, either for a ride or for a visit to the

country, they will say to him "Safe return*!" Then
when he gets back, they will say "Welcome, sir." If
a guest visits you, at the end of his stay, when he is
going home and you're saying good-bye to him, you say
"Alight safely!" and he answers "God grant it!"

If an itinerant trader gives you a present of something he has picked up on his travels, you must say
"God give profit!" Or if a hunter gives you game that
he has shot, you must say "God open the bush to you!"
Then if a farmer gives you the first ripe heads of
millet, or some other treat from his farm, you must say
"God give strength for the farming!" Or if a man is on
his way to market to sell something, cola-nuts or anything, and he takes some of it and gives it to you, you
must say "God grant a market!"

And this is what the Hausa mean by "contemptuous"
behavior: a man who has no idea of what is proper
behavior, or who regularly fails to give his superiors
due respect, in fact who respects no one except himself.
Of him they will say "He is contemptuous of other people."

And what the Hausa calls "insolence"--a man always
provoking others to quarrel, even those who are more
powerful than he. Of him people will say "He's a regular insolent fellow."

If the Hausa see a pregnant woman, they will say
"That one has eaten beans."

And lastly they say "All craftsmen are liars, but
the biggest one is the blacksmith."

THE BEST SORT OF HAUSA WOMEN (III/X)

Here's something about Hausas. If they are about looking
for someone to marry, an experienced man who knows women,
will look for a woman with small heels, long toes, long
fingers, small loins, light-colored (? bright) eyes and
a little mouth. Nor should her head be too big. She
should have a head of hair; dark-colored gums; teeth

---

*Using an unusual H. word for "return".

not too close together; no elbows. She should have
hair in her armpits, and a woman's voice, not a man's
voice. She should walk slowly, not too fast. Moreover she should have a bridge to her nose and a long
neck, but not a thick one; large breasts; but not a
large umbilical hernia; nor should she have broad loins,
nor large buttocks. She should have neat little feet
where the anklets go. Her body should be smooth and
soft. Her color should be light red--not white and not
black, but between the two--what is called "wankan
darza"; she should be neither short, nor tall; of few
words; one who does not go out and about much; very
languid, not active. Yes, if a man marries such a one,
he marries a woman indeed, and if (in addition) she
loves him, then is he indeed fortunate.

But a woman with big heels will have a big vagina
also; a woman with a broad mouth will have a broad
vagina. As for a woman of broad loins, a man cannot
effectively copulate (?) with her. As for a woman with
large buttocks, she cannot stand having a man; whereas
a woman of very small buttocks can never be satisfied.
A woman with a hollow between the eyes and no bridge to
her nose, is a quarrelsome woman; a woman with little
eyes is a senseless creature. As for a woman with a
tiny head, she will not bring one good luck. Even when
she has put the water on for the miya, if she looks into the cooking-pot and sees her small head, she'll say
"I haven't put enough water in for soup, let me add some,"
and so she'll fill the pot up with tasteless miya. A
woman with a big stomach is no pleasure to sleep with,
for she takes up the whole bed. As for a woman with
an umbilical hernia, a little food won't be enough for
her! A woman without hair, she too is not a bringer of
much luck--neither is a woman with scars on her body.
A woman with a small forehead will do nothing except
quarrel. A woman with big feet who walks fast, putting
the earth behind her (?), she too will not bring luck.
A woman with a rough body gives no pleasure to embrace.
A woman with no hair in the armpits, or who lacks pubic
hair, so that she is like the outside of a water-pot--
if a man is going to sleep with her, he will have to pat

(her) with the back of his hand (?)*. A woman with an overdeveloped clitoris will be always after men, she'll never tire of them. In one day she'll go to fifteen men. But a fat woman will have a small vagina, and a man will have difficulty entering her. Well, now you've heard about Hausa women.

THE JINNS TO WHOM THE GOGE-PLAYERS PLAY WHEN THE CHIEF BORI-MAN COMES (III/XXIV)

This is what Hausa people who perform bori do. They go and collect men with goges, and start playing castanet-gourds and drumming on calabashes. Then one of them says "Let a black goat be brought for Doguwa and slaughtered for her." And again "Doguwa-of-the-compound wants a white fowl or a red goat brought to her." And again "'Yar-Zanzana says that she wants a kyalla goat brought to her." A red and white goat, that is what they call a "kyalla". Or else they will say "Let a speckled hen be brought." Such are for 'Yar-Zanzana.

Then there is another (jinn) called Maiyya. They go and buy meat and give it to her to eat.

Another too there is called Ladi, and they will bring her fowls, of any type, and when they give them to her, she comes awake.

Yet another there is, called "Fulani woman who keeps cattle". To her nothing is given, save only cowrie shells, strung on a thread, which she hangs round her neck.

Then there is one who lives in the water, who is called Hajo-in-the-water. And another similar one Maibujaje-in-the-water. Then there ie one on the land called "Gwari woman", and another called Jiko.

These last two eat onions, beans and cassava--that's their food. Those are the female jinns that I have told you.

Of the males, there is Kure (? = male hyena)--he is given a cock. There's another called Dan Musa, and

---

*Presumably = "stimulate manually".

he's a snake, and a black billy-goat is slaughtered
for him, so that he may drink the blood and eat the
meat. Then there's another called Babbako (? = "gathering storm"); another called Lion; another Malam
Alhaji; another Alhaji Kalgo; another Malam Gayya; another Ubandawaki*; another "the Dark-eyed one"; another
Dunaga; another Janzari (? = whirlwind), and he is the
dirtiest of the lot, for he eats excrement. Then there
is Bako (= stranger, guest); and Mai-dawa; and Na-matuwa;
and another called Drinker-of-Water; and another called
Bird. There's Dangaladima*; and Sarkin Rafi*; then
there's Barber; and Danyarima*; and another, Dan Daudu
(= homosexual male); another that lives in the water
called Dandu; and another similar one, Harakwai. Then
too there is Sambo-in-the-water. And there is Dikko,
and Leper, and one called Red-Chewstick-Tree; and there's
Sambawa; and there's Rakato. That's all that I know of,
of the jinns that appear when they play the goge. That's
all.

THE STREET-PERFORMER CALLED GWALAJE (I/XLV)

I saw some performers in one of the town streets. One
of them had a gown made from a grass mat and they were
calling him "Gwalaje, great dodo**." There were women
and small boys, using bottle-gourds as castanets. They
had gathered round and were watching him, giving him
money as he danced. He had a cap of chicken-feathers
on his head and a long staff which he was holding, and
he was singing these words "Gwalaje, great dodo! Who
won't be dispersed!"

DISEASES AND THEIR CURES (I/XXIV)

It is said that the Hausa believe that if a man suffers
from hiccoughs, he will be cured, if the names of seven

---

*Titles.
**For dodo, see Vols. I and II passim.

liars are written down and he drinks the solution when
they have been washed off.

Or, again, if anyone suffers from boils on the
knee (lit. "a divorced man's urine"), if he kneels in
front of a dog, he will be cured.

Then there's mumps. If a man gets that, he should
lift a mortar on his back and walk around in his compound with it--then he'll be cured.

THE CHARACTER OF THE MEN OF KWANGWAMA (I/XI)

I'll tell you about the people of Kwangwama. In origin
they were from Zazzau, but their customs are those of
pagans.

When a man dies, if he reached old age, they rejoice, and dance and beat their drums, for there is
nothing amiss in his departure. He has begotten children, his children have been born. But if one dies
young, then they bewail it, for his promise has not
been fulfilled and they are very sad.

Also at Kwangwama if a youth makes a virgin pregnant, the king fines* the boy's parents six hundred
thousand cowries and takes another six hundred thousand
from the girl's parents--making twelve hundred thousand
cowries that he collects in all from the parents.

Among the leading men of Kwangwama, and many of the
ordinary people too, it is a custom not to wear a cap
when paying a formal call on the king in his compound.
Exceptions to this are the imam of the town and the
chief butcher, also malams and any visitor who is not
aware of the custom.

When a child is born, a boy is circumcised while
still an infant, and a girl is given a husband when she
is seven years old, and it is publicly known who this
is. Moreover the girl has freedom of choice who it is
to be, even if it is a stranger or a foreigner. She
will be given him as his wife. This is because it is
feared that if she is given to someone that she doesn't

*Cf. Vol. II/XXX.

like, she will cause them worry. And when the time
comes for the marriage to be performed, on the same
day that she is covered in henna, she is taken to her
husband's home. There, at his home, she spends her
week in her wedding wrappings. Then, on the eighth
day, she is unwrapped, and that night everyone plays
and dances until morning. Then they all go home.

I have observed them do that at Kwangwama, for I
saw there a stranger, a butcher who came to Kwangwama
from the land of Katsina. And settling there he carried
on his trade of butcher, and sought the daughter of the
King of Kwangwama. And when she said she would have no
other, she was given to him and he married her.

When the new moon indicates that the Festival has
come, here too they differ from Kano practice. At the
end of the Fast month, next morning, some hours after
sunrise, the king has still not gone out to the place
of prayer. Rather, all the leading men come and greet
him. Then he gets on his horse and goes off to the
mosque that is used for the Festival prayers, and there
he waits for the _imam_. When the _imam_ comes, two guards,
who have been given the duty, come forward and kneel,
one before the king, one before the _imam_. Then they
change places, criss-crossing in front of the king and
the _imam_, like people setting up the threads for a
loom, until they have knelt some seven times.

Now, in front of the king is a great basin full of
money and covered with a red cloth, and just by it a
maiden and a small girl, lying on their faces, covered
over with large cloths. Then the _imam_ rises and goes
to his place. When it is time for prayer, the king
and all his people rise and come to the place for prayer.
When the prayer is finished, the _imam_ preaches a sermon
and prays, and when that too is finished he spreads out
his blanket, and someone goes and uncovers the girls.
Then the money in the basin is brought and placed in
front of the _imam_. Then the king gives his alms, and
the others after him, giving cola-nuts of different
varieties, cowries, or--since these are the days of
European rule--threepences, sixpences and pennies. Everyone gives alms in proportion to what he has, and then the
congregation rises and goes home.

Then, when the king reaches the entrance to his
house, he stops and speaks, thus "I thank God, I thank
Muhamman the Messenger of God and I thank the Emir of
Zazzau." He says this, because formerly they were
ruled by the Emir of Zazzau. Then everyone goes home
and dismounts.

But, of course, the people of Kwangwama are Haɓe--
for these are the sort of practices of Haɓe people. The
people of Kano, or Zaria city or Katsina--or any other
town--they don't act thus. Then when the king has rested,
a large ram is slaughtered and cooked whole, and tuwo
is prepared, and all taken to the Ura people (who are
nearby poor people). Every king of Kwangwama does this
for them. These are the practices of the Kwangwama that
I have observed.

They also have a game called "takai". Drumming for
this is done on a drum with two drumsticks, while the
dancers circle round with short pieces of wood in their
hands. First one will dance, then the other; then,
turning, they strike the pieces of wood against each
other. This is what they call "takai". The experts at
it dance in one place, and the others in a different
place.

HOW THE PEOPLE OF KAMUKU TURN
INTO HYENAS* (I/XIII)

It is said that the people of Kamuku turn themselves
into hyenas; their kings into lions; and their old
people into bush-cows. Both men and women do this.

When someone comes to them during the day, if he
is a stranger, when night comes, they wait till he goes
out, then follow him and seize him and bite him severely,
but they don't kill him. In the same way, a stranger
may not chew at a bone near the people of Kamuku, for
they will tell him "Hey, stranger, we don't like that.
Don't do that any more!"

---

*Cf. R. No. 20.

One day the King of Kusharki's dog was lost, and
people said "A hyena's got him." But three days later
he returned, and then people said "You see? The hyena
that took him was really a human being."

Then there was a woman called Tadidi at Kusharki,
who was taken once in war and carried away to a town in
the land of Katsina. There she served as a slave for
two years. But one day she felt a desire to return
home. It was then the rainy season and dark had come
after a rainy day. So she asked for someone to come
with her while she went out to relieve nature. Someone
was sent with her and they went out of the town. She
squatted down accordingly and her escort stood near
waiting for her. When she had finished, she opened her
eyes very wide and stretched open her fingers--and turned
into a hyena. Then, howling like a hyena she tried to
seize her escort. But he fled, and arriving home with
difficulty, said "Guess what, that slave-girl turns herself into a hyena. I've been lucky for she nearly got
me." The people all rushed out of the town, but when
they got to where she had been, they found she had run
off. But they heard a howl in the bush. These are the
ways of the people of Kamuku.

THE DEATH OF A KING OF THE GWARIS, THE DAKARKARIS AND THE KAMUKU MEN (II/XCV)

Here's a custom of the Gwari people that I have observed.
If their king dies, they send to tell his relatives,
wherever they may be, that they must come for the king
has died. Then the chief men gather, and two days are
spent in digging a grave. To this they make a mouth,
like a well. Down inside, they hollow the earth out,
so that it is like the inside of a mud-roofed hut. Meanwhile a beautiful woman, a concubine is chosen, and a
slave-lad, and one of the king's riding horses. Then
they kill these, and adorn their bodies with finery; the
horse too is equipped with full accoutrements. Then a
couch, mats and bed-coverings are brought, and taken into the grave. After this, they lift the king and carry

him into the grave; so too the concubine, dressed in
her finery; and the slave too; and lastly the horse too
is lifted into the grave. The king's body is placed, in
a sitting position, on the couch, and his back leant
against the wall.

Next firewood is collected and taken in; so too
grass for the horse--and corn too. Then the elders of
the town come forward and make a speech to the king,
thus "And now, oh king, see, here is a horse, and if it
is your wish to ride, this lad will saddle it for your
ride. If you wish to drink water or to eat, here is a
woman, this concubine, to give you water or food. She
too will come to you, if your desire is for a woman.
Remain here, then, in comfort, with these to look after
you. If you feel cold, here is firewood, let them light
a fire for you. Do you hear? Well, we are going back
out now, to go and resume our daily round." Then they
cover the mouth of the hole, bringing a large piece of
earthenware, which they place upside down on the opening.
Or else a water storage pot, which they place on the
mouth of the grave. Then all of them, the living, return to their homes to resume their lives; but the
festivities continue until the new king has been appointed.

And so, wherever you go in the land of the Gwari,
if you see a large piece of earthenware overturned,
lying, or a water storage pot--that is the grave of a
king of that town. So too in the land of the Dakarkaris,
they do the same, having the same custom as the Gwari.
So too the men of Kamuku over there, in the region of
Maruba--they too have the same custom as the Gwari.
That's all.

XIII
Kiraris (Praise-Songs)

Sometimes rendered into English as "praise-song", the
scurrility of some of these hardly justifies the name.
Those of kings, shouted by professional panegyrists,
are, of course fulsome in the extreme. Those of cities
and tribes, quoted by citizens of other cities and men
of other tribes, are more likely to fasten on what are
felt to be characteristic weaknesses. The H. is context-
bound, epigrammatic, often archaic and obscure, and the
translations offered tentative. For other examples, see
Fletcher, R. S., Hausa Sayings and Folklore, (Oxford,
1912); and Prietze, Rudolf, Haussa-Sprichworter und
Haussa-Lieder. 1904 and "Haussa Preislieder auf Parias",
Mitteilungen des Institut fur Orientsprachen 21 (1918),
1-53. For a modern kirari, that of the United Africa
Company, heard in Kano in 1967 may be mentioned:

> Yu'esi, gwafa matokarar duniya! Idan
> kuna yi, ba mai yi.

> "U. A. C., Forked stick that supports
> the world! If you are involved, no one
> (else) can be."

A sociological study of Hausa praise-singing by M. G.
Smith is to be found in Volume 27 of Africa, pp. 26-45.

THE KIRARI OF ZARTU*, KING OF RABA (I/LXIII)

From the people of Wamako--"Let the minds of the Muslims
be at rest, let the world go on peacefully farming!"
From the people of Kubodu--"If (Sultan) Abdu wants the
war finished quickly, let him write a letter summoning
our Zartu, killer of the infidel." From the men of
Bunkari--"Our protection is our brave leaders, others
rely on high walls, while their leaders take tithes
but shrink from war." From Magagari--"We Hausas enjoy
peace and prosperity nor do we fear hostilities." From
the Hausas of Gande--"If Abdu hadn't stopped our hero,
he would have devastated Argungu." From the men of 'Dan
Kala--"Welcome with shrill cries, tireless hero** whom
all long to see--tonight we shall sleep deep, even to
snoring." "Aliyu, the Muslims depend on you. Heir of
Abubakar, east and west, they tell tales of your great-
ness as a ruler, and the pagans submit⁺, for yours is
the majesty, power like Bello's, even in his sleep he
prepares war on the pagans--Ali Zartu!"

KIRARIS OF THE MAJIDADI OF SOKOTO AND ZARTU⁺⁺OF RABA (I/LXIV)

Here's a praise-song a drummer made up for Majidadi.
"Stay of the freemen of the people, Usumanu# son of
Bawa, Shehu## Majidadi, treacherous river, only the
wise man, son of Alhaji, can cross you. You people
follow him without rash haste. No man was able to
kill you, Shehu of Garba's people, no man to make you
do his will or prevent your purpose. The protection

---

*Perhaps from zarto ("saw" = "fierce man").
**Reading magagari for Magagari.
⁺Presuming maladam = ladabi.
⁺⁺Perhaps from zarto ("saw" = "fierce man").
#Shehu and Usumanu are here synonymous and used
  indifferently.
##Shehu and Usumanu are here synonymous and used
  indifferently.

of Shehu is greater than the security given to a farm
of forty bundles of corn. My lot is more pleasant than
the caravan-leader from Illo, for he feeds me, he gives
me to drink and he clothes me--there is none like Shehu
among us Hausas. Stay of the freemen of the people,
Usumanu, son of Bawa, Shehu Majidadí, of unbending
courage, son of Bawa whom all praise, Shehu Majidadí,
son of Maje Hajji*, Usumanu, rainy season that does no
damage! Shehu has ten characteristics, which I will
itemize. Count them for me, my brothers! Shehu knows
exactly what must be done without any showing him. He
does not chatter; Usumanu doesn't backbite; slanders
no one, for Shehu has the nature of the Kwatawa**. He
never sets an example of being contemptuous. Shehu
observes all men and their deeds. With his own eyes he
beholds them. And so it is that he is loyally respectful to those who are above him, knows not insolence,
only truth, and loyally serves the Vizier's house. No
worthless servant he. If he is giving a present, he
does it without speaking of it. For you find suddenly
as you sit there, he gives it you with 'Here you are'.
Importunity has no effect on him. If Shehu says 'Yes',
he will not change his word to 'No'. This I know well--
if he likes you, set your mind at rest, for you will
prosper and need seek help from no other. There is no
falsehood with Shehu, nor does he like lying men to
hang around him cadging. Stay of the freemen of the
people, Usumanu, son of Bawa, Shehu Majidadí."
    There are many songs about Zartu, King of Raba.
"Even in his sleep he prepares war on the pagans, Ali
Zartu, crocodile's hide that defies kneading, slave
of Bara'u⁺, even in his sleep he prepares war on the
pagans, Ali Zartu. Let Abdu summon his armies together
to war on the house of Sama; we set out from Sokoto,
and camped by the water of Kware; alas I feel pity for
Argungu, for the house of Sama is to fall low, say the
men of Kware. Come quickly, Zartu, and finish the war,
say the men of Jiko."

---

*He who died while on the pilgrimage.
**Or "a nature to be copied" if we emend to kwatantawa.
⁺Presuming Ba-Magujen = bawan.

THE KIRARIS OF ALL THE HAUSA TOWNS (I/LXV)

Every group of people has a verse about them that is
well known.

About a Kano man they say "Kano man, bow of beni-
seed, Dabo's thin bowstring, learning that doesn't prevent thieving, gourd whose fruit spreads far abroad.
At early morn a dyer, at mid-morn a malam, after midday
a middleman trader and at night a thief; who comes in
with 'Peace be upon you' and goes out leaving people
calling on God in horror--your hands are in the purses
of those who give you a ride." That's what the Zazzau
people say of the Kano people.

The people of Kano have a joking relationship with
the people of Zamfara and say of them "Ali's Zamfara--you
are propped-up cornstalks, in the darkness you become
deceitful." That's what the Kano people say of the
Zamfara people.

As for the men of Zazzau, if the Kano people see
one, they will say to him "King whose father was a com-
moner--while you are growing your father is reducing his
farmlands. You of Turunku, you grew up in confusion
saying 'I saw your mother and thought he was mine*.'
You don't carry home any bundles of corn, but if someone prepares tuwo from one, you'll eat it--man of
Zazzau, groundnut-oil that doesn't get thick."

And the men of Zazzau say of the Katsina men "Katsina
abode of keeping up appearances, eating groundnuts and
washing hands**!"

And of the men of Gobir they say "People of Bawa
treating fences like a saddle, you enjoy fine corn, and
you burn them, Gobir home of fighting."

Of the Kanuri they say "Fanna's Bornu, great numbers, you seek and you destroy, Bornu, house of royalty"--
that's what they say cf them.

Then of the Nupes they say "Anufa'u (?) cattle
excrement, wet inside, dry outside, it's unlucky when
you kneel down, excreters in the water."

---

*Using the masc. nawa, ?, laughing inter alia at the
   Z. dialect?
**Pretending to have had a meal that was worth washing
   one's hands after.

While of the men of Keffi they say "Keffi, most
obstinately persistent of Hausas, you're up to a Dala
and a Gwauron Dutse, remains for you to reach the place
whence you go forth to kill and return to."

Of Bauchi they say "Squat town of battles, God too
is with their town*."

The kirari (praise-song) of Adamawa is as follows
"Fried meat in great demand, Adamawa, great market**
of slaves, it is known that the men of Maradi go to
Bauchi⁺, Adar, hard for Hausas to reach."

Of the men of Sokoto they say "Dagyal (Degel),
horse-tomb, the one of Bello which turns flour-water
to honey⁺⁺; were it not for the buying and selling of
corn, you would be pleasanter than Kano."

The people of Kontagora they call "Gwamatsawa"
because Nagwamatse was their ruler, also "Yamutsawa"
because they caused confusion (yamutsa) throughout the
land; also "Dimawa" because they threshed (dima) the
land. These are their kiraris in Kontagora.

As for the travelling traders as they go along,
people say of them "Scattered of God, death this year,
lamenting next year. Trader, whose word is twisted#,
you are the fire, your wife is the smoke, of Bawa,
younger brother to the dog, selling your wares in un-
promising places, the cutting of trade routes your good
fortune, who consults with those from others' compounds,
who is at enmity with those from your own compound."

As for the kirari of the Filani, this is it--"Skinny
little blade, wearer-out of shoe leather, always saying
'I can see them, come along, I'll take you,' starting
quarrels and then running off. From afar, like a lump

---

*This trans. is v. dubious, and dada not known to me.
**Lit. Gwanja, ie. the great market for cola-nuts.
⁺The word "Bauci" seems to be connected with bauta
  (slavery), but its appearance in a kirari of Adamawa
  seems to need explanation.
⁺⁺Reading kasari for Kasari.
#A pun in the H.

before the fire, like a shoulder, you are fat, rotten
meat-before you're done you put out the fire." So much
for the Filani.

Again, Muslims dislike those who are paupers,
orphans and bachelors.

Lastly here is the kirari of women--"Without you,
there is no home; with too many of you, the home is
spoilt; women, the snare of Satan."

A KIRARI OF HAUSA WOMEN (II/XI)

Women--hanks of grass that smother one with burrs; little
black knife that cuts up one's capital; without you,
there is no home; if there are too many of you, a home
is ruined. King of "If I come to your compound, what
will you give me?" But I take my wealth to your compound, and as soon as you see that you have devoured*
my wealth, then you try to drive me away.

THE DOG'S KIRARI (I/LXVIII)

The Hausas say of the dog--"Dog, canine one, your break-
fast is a club to your back, your flour-and-water a
stick, dog who makes null two things, who nullifies
prayer and who nullifies excrement**, hyena's cola-nuts,
that needs no packing, with ribs like the plaiting of
a mat, and a tail like a stick of tobacco, ears like a
spoon for snuff, anus like a sucked lime, and nose ever
wet."

AUTA (I/LXX)
(Edgar says this is about a blind slave, at
Bida, called Auta, a lazy cadger.)

---

*Deleting the comma after ga.
**Apparently, but the meaning of this idiom escapes me.
  If we read ƙashi for kashi, the phrase might mean
  "who splinters bones". But it may merely be a zeugma,
  using the verb karya in two senses, not translatable.

Auta who never does anyone else a service, but visits
houses where he will be given something. Any money he
gets goes to women.

A LITTLE SONG (I/LXXI)
(Composed, Edgar says, by the Fulani, against
the Kebbi men.)

I hear a rustling in the grass--who's there? "Oh, I'm
the king of Argungu town and I am gnawing the corn. Put
me in a song if you like--for millet, my boy, is tasty,
tasty, tasty."

XIV
Anecdotes and Letters

(The latter mostly sent to Burdon as Resident of
Sokoto Province.)

THE HONEST FILANI WOMAN AND ABUBAKAR,
KING OF BEBEJI* (I/56)

In the days when Abubakar was king of Bebeji, one day
he strolled forth from the entrance-hut of his compound
to take the air with his followers. He noticed, away
outside the town, a Filani woman selling milk. She had
a child strapped to her back. She swung him round in
front and was suckling him, when the child regurgitated
into the milk. When she saw what had happened, the
Filani woman picked the milk up, went to a midden and
poured it away. Then she washed her calabash.
　　Then she set out for home. She didn't know it, but
the king was watching her and saw that she was going home

---

*(Kano Emirate).

243

without having got any food. He had her called. She
came and knelt before the king, and he said "Where's
your calabash of milk?" "Here it is" says she. Then
the king made his _jekadiya_ take the calabash. She took
it into the compound and it was filled with guinea-corn.
Then he gave her twenty thousand cowries and said "May
God give you his blessing! Accept my thanks for refusing
to give the Believers an unclean thing to drink." And
she thanked him.

THE DONKEY-MARE AND THE HYENA (III/68)

There was once a female donkey, in foal, who was driven
out to graze, her front legs hobbled. And there, in the
bush, she dropped her foal.

The sun set and night came. Presently along came
a hyena to where the donkey was, hoping to seize the
newly-born foal. But the mother wouldn't allow it.

When the hyena came up, the donkey kicked her with
her hind legs, and bit her, until the hyena, tiring of
this, leapt at the foal to seize it. Whereupon the donkey seized the hyena by the neck and bit right in. The
donkey's owners searched and searched until they were
tired. Nor was it till next day when it was light that
they came and found the donkey, firmly attached to the
hyena's neck. The hyena was dead, and so was the donkey--
only the foal was still alive. And they actually had to
go and cut through the hyena's neck, for the donkey's
jaws refused to open. That's all.

THE KING OF ZAUMA, HIS COURTIERS AND
THE FROGS (I/XXIII)

One day the King of Zauma was sitting in conversation
surrounded by his courtiers. That day there was a
storm, and the rain came down in buckets. It began
in the morning and didn't let up till evening.

There was much water everywhere. The borrow-pits
around were all full, and the frogs were croaking "Kwa

kwa." Then the King of Zauma asked his courtiers "That
croaking the frogs are making--what do they want?" And
they answered "May God prolong your days! It's _tuwo_
they want." Then said the king "Go into the compound
and get twenty bowls of _tuwo_, and take them to them to
eat, so that they can shut up." Then the courtiers got
themselves the bowls of _tuwo_, and each took a bowl back
home with him; and picking up a large stone, they threw
it into a borrow-pit. Then they returned to pay their
court to the king, and sat down. But the frogs went on
croaking.

Then the King of Zauma asked again "What do those
frogs want now? They're _still_ croaking." And his
courtiers answered "May God prolong your days! They
want something to cover their bodies. They feel the
cold." Then said he "Go into the compound and get
twenty-five gowns and take them to them." The gowns
were brought, the courtiers took them away and divided
them up. Every man got one for himself and took it
home and left it there. Then they returned to pay their
court to the king and sat down. But the frogs went on
croaking.

Then the King of Zauma asked again "What do those
frogs want _now_? They're _still_ croaking." And his
courtiers answered "May God prolong your days! That
croaking that they're doing now--that's thanks that
they are giving you for the present you've given them."
"Oh! Excellent!" said he, "Give them my best wishes
in return."

THE CARAVAN-LEADER, MIJINYAWA-MAI-AKOKARI*
AND ALL THE OTHER CARAVAN LEADERS (I/XXXII)

This was a highway robbery that happened at Gwamba. It
began when the caravan leader, Mijinyawa-mai-akokari
left Kano one Tuesday, the fourteenth of the month of
Safar, with some twenty-five other caravan leaders, in
the twenty-fourth year of the reign of Abdu, Emir of
Kano.

---

*Majinyawa the Fortune-Teller.

Now Mijinyawa had a home in Kano, and another at
Kalgo, and he would travel via Sokoto and Gwandu till
he came to Kalgo. There he would spend four days and
then set out again, travelling via Yelu (? Yelwa), with
large numbers of animals, about two thousand five hundred, three hundred baggage mules, some two
hundred riding horses, and some four thousand five
hundred people.

They reached Gwanja safely, and were returning
through the land of Borgu, when they reached a place
called "Rafin Tukuruwa". There they were met by the
pagans led by the Magaji of Kayama, who attacked them
with a shout, shooting and slashing. Then the caravan
leaders closed up and joined battle with the men of
Borgu. And the men of Borgu killed some twenty-two
of the caravan leaders, and some two hundred and twenty
of the other men; and captured some three thousand five
hundred of them. Though I was told by a man called
Musa that they killed some fourteen hundred and captured
some sixteen hundred. But, in any case, the caravan
leader, Mijinyawa-mai-akokari was killed, and of the
others, some were killed and some taken.

Presently news of this reached the King of Gwamba,
Muhammadu, son of Sambo, son of Udulu. Mounting with
his people he went to the place, but before he got there,
he began meeting with the fugitives. These Muhammadu
Sambo Udulu had collected as they turned up in their
ones and twos and threes, sometimes five at a time.
Among them were the caravan leaders, Mai-Yaki, Isa and
Bako-ba'u; also some three hundred and twenty women,
and, later, about three hundred and fifty donkeys. Then
as they were going away, they found the caravan leader,
Na-gulbi, with his family, all safe. Then Muhammadu
Sambo had them taken over the stream there. But, other
than those who joined him, none escaped. Some, scattering, perished in the bush, and others reached Illo.
If you lived there, you might see five mules appear
with their loads, and no one driving them, or perhaps
groups of fifty donkey-drivers, without a fragment of
a cola-nut or a single gown between them--the whole
lot were scattered far and wide.

But the man who planned the seizure of the caravan was Bakin-jaki, he and the Magaji of Kayama, together with a great crowd of Borgu men, and other pagans too. But the downfall of the caravan leader, Mijinyawa-mai-akokari was originally caused by treachery. Bakin-jaki, son of the king of Borgu, had been trying for some twelve years to overpower one of his caravans.

Whenever they heard that Mijinyawa was on his way, they would rally, horse and foot, a great crowd of them, some five thousand men. And when they saw him, they would block his road. Then Mijinyawa would say to them "Hey, you bastards! Get cutting grass!" And everyone of them would bend to it and pull up grass. The caravan would go by, and then, when it had passed on some way, they would follow after it to attack it. But when they got close, if Mijinyawa saw them, he would shout angrily at them "Hey, you bloody beggars, bend down and get cutting grass! Bastards!" And down they would get again, hard at it, cutting grass.

This would go on until the caravan had eluded them. They would tire of this and go home in despair. But Bakin-jaki and the Magaji of Kayama continued to pursue him, until they got him. For there arose rivalry among them, as is the way with caravan leaders, and two of them became treacherous. And Bakin-jaki sent to them, promising to spare their lives and those of their families and animals, if they would agree to help him overpower the caravan. And he sent them an evil charm to give Mijinyawa-mai-akokari. They gave it to him—and that was that! For he didn't know about it, and that was how the caravan was taken. No one escaped, for they killed every single one of them. And all their families were carried off. Indeed, in the whole of that party of travellers none escaped, save those whom Muhammadu, King of Gwamba, had taken over the stream.

It is now twenty-five or six years since they set out on that journey—the caravan leader, Mijinyawa-mai-akokari and his five sons, Bako, Zangi, Zango, Momman and Sulaimanu. And the year the caravan was destroyed was 1278 AH. As for Muhammadu Sambo Udulu, he became king in the year 1275 AH. That's twenty-eight years ago. This with peace.

THE MADWOMAN AND THE PARTY GUESTS (I/68)

There was once a madwoman called "Kagoma" who wandered through the villages of Zazzau, scattering people.

As she was going once she met some women taking a large calabash of tuwo to a party at the home of their in-laws. The madwoman said to them "Here you! Put down that calabash!" And they put it down, in fear and trembling. Then she said "You eat that tuwo! And if you don't eat it, I'll kill you here and now." So they started eating, and they ate and ate, till they were full. Says she "Go on eating, don't stop!", but they said "But we've had enough, we're full." "Oh" says she, "Really? Don't you feel like eating?" "Oh, yes! We feel like eating." Then she jeered at them "We want to take it to a home where there's a party!" and she left them there with the remains of the tuwo in the calabash. Then they went off home, grumbling as they went.

IBRAHIMU, KING OF WUSHISHI AND HOW HE
SAW THE WOMAN WITH THE BUN* AND CALLED IT
"THE ORIGINAL BUN" (I/XXXIX)

One evening, Ibrahimu, King of Wushishi, had come outside the gate of his compound and was sitting there, when a woman, a stranger from Kano, came by with an enormous bun on her head. In the whole of the town there was no one with a bun as big as it was, it was beyond description. Then said he "Well!! Now I've seen the original bun!" It was because he saw how big it was, that he called it "the original bun".

---

*I have used "bun" for the translation, but doka is a hair style actually made on the top and front of the head. "Hyena's Forehead" is the name of a particular style of doka.

And so throughout the district of Wushishi this
became a saying, and if anyone saw some wonderful thing,
he would say "The original bun! The King of Wushishi
has seen the 'Hyena's Forehead'."

THE BOYS OF WURNO (I/LIX)

Yesterday I saw some boys coming from Wurno, with their
mothers. With them were their four rams and I heard
them saying "If we manage to sell our rams today or
tomorrow, let us hasten to get some cloths, both those
with stripes of black, white and blue, and the large
headcloths, so that the Festival doesn't catch us in
Sokoto. But if we don't manage to sell them, let's go
and look for a loan, buy the clothes and leave our rams
there; then hasten home, for there are only three or
four days left to the Festival, and it is better that
we hurry and get home and scratch around for some money
to pay for the Festival meal." Finis.

THE OX (I/LX)

I went to the market and was walking round it in the
evening, when I saw an ox who had escaped and run out
of the city. The butchers had gathered, some thirty
of them, and were chasing him with ropes in their hands
to catch him. Outside the town they caught up with him
and began to move more slowly, hoping to grab him, but
he saw them and put on speed and leapt into the river.
Whereupon they too jumped in, all of them, and surrounding
him seized him. He struggled, trying to butt them, but
they tied him up with the ropes while he was still in
the water. Then they got him out, and he snorted as he
went along. Then they brought him to the market and
slaughtered him. Finis.

SOME LETTERS (I/LXXII)

Malam Akali said to take this letter to the Chief European Officer, and say: I send him a thousand greetings.
I am pleased, very pleased to learn of his visit to us
here. May God bring him safely, may he find us all
safe and well. My inquiries about his home, about the
King of England, and all Europeans, both those who have
come here, and those who haven't. If you inquire of us,
we are all well. May God destine our meeting. I too,
Nagwamatse*, greet you and express my pleasure at your
visit. As your head pupil, I am carrying out all that
you told me to do. This with peace.

(I/LXXIII)

From Sultan Attahiru, son of Aliyu Babba, to his colleague and friend, the European. I am delighted that
you have returned, and so are all my people. And I
welcome you with joy and many greetings. Welcome, welcome. This with peace.

(I/LXXIV)

From the Vizier, Muhammadu Buhari, to his friend, the
European, many greetings and a thrice joyful welcome on
your safe return. Welcome! Welcome! This with peace.

(I/LXXV)

From Sultan Attahiru to his colleague and friend, the

---

*Reading Nagwamatse for na gwamatse. This is the scribe
putting in his bit. Burdon had started a school in
Sokoto which in 1906 had eight pupils of whom one of
the brightest was Nagwamatse, son of Malam Akali.
Nagwamatse died after a distinguished career as a
teacher in 1966.

European, many greetings and a joyful welcome on your
return. We are overjoyed and welcome you heartily.
May God insure our safe meeting. This with peace.

(I/LXXVI)

From the chief adviser, the Vizier Buhari, to his
friend, the European, many greetings, respect, friendship and trust; next--we and all with us here are well.
There are no disturbances to report, and no deaths--
saving only Yankwana, and Wambai has been appointed to
his post; and the King of Galma, and his younger brother,
Lamido, has been appointed; also the King of Gobir,
Umaru. We have summoned the elders from there, but
they haven't yet arrived. So we have sent them another
letter. With peace.

(I/LXXVII)

From Sultan Attahiru, son of Aliyu Babba, to his friend
and colleague, the European--greetings and a respectful
welcome. Next, I and my people are overjoyed at your
arrival, we are delighted. May God give you abundant
health. May God give us all peace and security. This
with peace.

(I/LXXVIII)

From the Vizier, Muhammadu Buhari, to his friend and
colleague, the European, many greetings and a hearty
welcome. Next, we are delighted at your arrival. May
God give health! May God keep us all safe and sound.
This with peace.

(I/LXXIX)

From Malam Umaru to the European--a respectful welcome.
Are you in health? And how were your family and rela-

tives at home? Again, I ask about your health, for
health is a thing to be inquired about. One must ask
first about health, before turning to all the other
items of news about the world. Next, after greetings,
here are some Hausa stories that I've brought you. This
with peace.

(I/LXXX)

From the Emir of Kabi, Isma'ila, to the European,
greetings by the thousand, friendship, trust and great
respect. After greetings, the Emir of Kabi, Isma'ila,
asks God to prolong your days; and next reports that
all the people of his land are well, none are in any
sort of distress. Next, the order that the European
sent him has been understood and accepted by the Emir
of Kabi, Isma'ila. And furthermore, the Emir says that
henceforward he will permit no one in the whole of his
land to be oppressed, now that he has understood the
order of the European. May God lengthen your days,
amen, amen, amen. This with peace.

(I/LXXXI)

From the Emir of Kabi, Isma'ila, to the European at
Argungu, greetings and friendship and trust, and sympathy
at the death of the King of England*. The Emir sends
his greetings and sympathy to the European at Argungu
for the death of the King of England. And he is joined
in this by the Judge of Argungu, also Abubakar, man of
God, also Abdullahi of Ibi, also Majidadî, also Umaru,
also the Galadima of Kabi, also the Iname of Kabi, also
the Dan Galadima of Kabi, also the Muza of Kabi, also
the Kunduɗa, King of Augi, also the Lamne, King of
Bubuche, also the Kwaido. And in addition, the Karari
of Kabi and the Lailaba of Kabi, and all the chief men
of Kabi, all send their sympathy on the death of the

---

*? Edward VII, who died in 1910.

King of England. And they beseech the European to
resign himself to what God has done. Also the King
and chief men of Gulma, and Dan Kadu and Tilli and
their chief men, also the King of the North-West and
his chief men; also Kyanga, Gudurega and the chief men
of Dandi, all send their sympathy. All pray patience
and resignation for the European. The Emir of Kabi and
all his chief men are very sorrowful. And this is why
he has come with them to the European, to make their
condolences to him.

(I/LXXXII)

From the Judge of Argungu, to the European at Argungu,
greetings, friendship and trust, respect and thanks.
Next, touching the matter of the girl, Hawa'u, who has
brought a complaint against Riskuwa. Her charge was
that she is not yet adult nor of an age to sustain heavy
work and that Riskuwa has been giving her work that is
beyond her strength. And so she ran away and went to
the European at Argungu. And he told her to go with
Majidadi and Umaru to the Emir of Kabi, who in turn
sent them to the Judge. The Judge learnt that Riskuwa
had beaten Hawa'u as his slave, and threatened to kill
her and throw her in the river. In view of this ill-
treatment the Judge has declared Hawa'u to be free, and
that Riskuwa no longer has the right to treat her as a
slave. Witnesses to this are the European at Argungu,
the Emir of Kabi, Abubakar, the man of God, Majidadi,
Umaru--Majidadi's servant--all these witness that Hawa'u
has received her freedom, because Riskuwa threatened to
kill her and throw her in the river. This with peace.

DIJE'S CERTIFICATE* (I/LXXXVI)

To those whom it may concern, to all rulers, judges
and kings of Sokoto, be informed that Umaru, Majidadi

---

*Lit. "charm" (originally "Koranic verse").

of Geza, in the land of Argungu has freed his daughter,
Dije, from the possession of her master, Mamman Mai Dan
Jiki, of Shuni, in the land of Sokoto, with two hundred
and ten cowries, all of which he has paid in full. Dije
is therefore free, and there are witnesses to this: viz.
Mujaili, Judge of Sokoto, also Mamuda, also Sa'i, also
Maigari, who lives with the Judge of Sokoto. All these
witness that Dije has been freed, and that she is now
the slave of no man--only of God and His Prophet. This
with peace.

IGE'S CERTIFICATE* (I/LXXXIII)

To those whom it may concern. Ige has bought her freedom for two hundred and ten cowries. She has paid the
full amount into the hand of Muhammadu, husband of
Azumi, living at Kauran-diyan-Kimba, which is the name
of the town. Witnesses are: Emir of Kabi, Isma'ila
and the Judge, Ishaka, and the Galadima of Kabi, Ibrahima,
and Majidadi, Aliyu, and Umaru, Majidadi's servant, and
the Majikira of Kabi, and Abubakar, the servant of God,
and Abdullahi of Ibi--and many others, all witness that
Igudu (sic) is now free, having bought her freedom,
and that she is now the slave of no man--only of God
and His Prophet. This with peace.

---

*Lit. "charm" (originally "Koranic verse").

XV
Word-Play and Tongue-Twisters

Except in the interests of completeness, there is little point in trying to "translate" most of these, any
more than there is in rendering "Peter Piper picked a
peck of pickled peppers" into Hausa. However, they
may be of assistance to someone faced with the original
Hausa.

HAUSA DRUMMING (I/XLVI)
(This seems to be a jingle of the 12 Days of
Christmas type. The only point seems to be
the pun on the number and the first word of
the phrase that follows it--which is lost in
translation.)

One for the untanned skin; two for traversing the town
to and fro; three for three of a word (?); four for
ridging cocoyams; five for traversing the town to and
fro; six for six of a word (?); seven for grilling a
dog; eight for the head of an ox's thigh-bone; nine

255

for collecting spun thread on to a large spool; ten
for the roan antelope in the bush.

(I/XLVII)

One..., two... the stem of a white pumpkin; hey, chicken,
what takes you to the river (to lay) eggs?*

THE SONG OF THE HAUSA BOYS
AT SOKOTO (I/XLVIII)
(The boys periodically go round singing songs
making fun of the unmarried men--this may be
one.)

I we-went to the house of a bachelor. I was gi-given
tuwo made from bran. I wouldn't take it, I was frightened. Frightened of what? Frightened of something
with a red beak, a red beak that peck-pecks, pecks in
Baraje's compound. Who's this Baraje? Wash hands.
Let's go. Let's go on which day? On the day for
fighting against spending money on luxury. Luxury,
dog of the idle vagabond (or "of the centipede"), whose
calabash is the best china. Kyarangyaran gidis**.

Or alternatively--I, I shall go to the house of a
bachelor. I was given tuwo made from bran. But I
wouldn't take it, I was frightened. Frightened of
what? Frightened of something with a red beak, a red
beak that peck-pecks, pecks a lump of tuwo; heir of
the hornet. Even if he goes to the river he has his
little tobacco box, his garafuni⁺, his tori⁺⁺, and his
little henna container.

Or alternatively--"The Song of the Boys of Bauchi"
(which closely follows the former of the two preceding
versions).

*? nonsense words to fit a particular drum rhythm?
  There is also alliteration of k (and one g) in the
  second half of this one.
**Apparently untranslatable nonsense.
⁺The plant Momordica balsamina.
⁺⁺??

HAUSA TONGUE-TWISTERS (II/V)

If they get hold of someone who can't speak Hausa, Hausas will tell him to say "I went out early to the farm of Korau, who has ringworm; I came upon some guinea-fowl on the dark-green of the farm of Korau with the ringworm. I said 'You guinea-fowl there, what brings you on to the dark-green of the farm of Korau with the ringworm, raising such a din?*'" And that's how the Hausa--if they see someone who doesn't understand Hausa properly--will teach it to him. That's the end of that one.

ANOTHER ONE FOR A MAN WHO DOESN'T KNOW HAUSA WELL (II/VI)

If there is someone who doesn't understand Hausa very well, Hausas will tell him to say "Hey, you red boy over there, go and pick up the red stick yonder; and go and drive off the red goat that's eating the red guinea-corn of the red man there, who lives on the red bank yonder; drive away that red goat, the one on the red bank over there that's eating the red guinea-corn of the red man there, the one who lives on the red bank yonder**."

And that's how the Hausa will teach someone who doesn't know the language, until he has mastered it. That's all.

---

*I am in some doubt as to the sense of some of the words here. In any case it is probably strained and certainly of less importance than the sound. The main idea is a play on words beginning with kor-.

**Again, of course, the point is in the sound of the H. rather than its sense.

SOME NAMES (I/LXIX)

"Gwallo"--that's a small bundle of corn. "Kurulla" is
when a person eats food in your presence, without of-
fering you some. "Gando" in Hausa means a building to
hold back water (type of dam).

A HAUSA SENTENCE HARD TO SAY
WITH SPEED (I/LXVII)

Here's a tongue-twister for those who are expert at the
language--"A frog and a big chap went to look for something to peck at. Well, will the frog snatch what is
to be pecked from the big chap, or will the big chap
snatch it from the frog?"

ANOTHER HAUSA TONGUE-TWISTER (II/VII)

The Hausas tell of a man who once went to the compound
of another and made formal greeting, thus "Peace be
upon you, wife of Konakota." Konakota's wife answered
"Konakota's not at home. Only me, Konakota's wife."
Says the other "Wife of Konakota, fetch Konakota's haft
(bota) for me, that I may burn (kona) it." But the
woman answered "Oh no! I, Konakota's wife, haven't
burnt Konakota's haft; and how can you, Konakota's
friend tell me to give you Konakota's haft to burn?
Be off with you and let me be! I'll not give you
Konakota's haft to burn. But let Konakota, when he
comes, get the haft and give it to you to burn--that's
no affair of mine. That's between you and him and he
can give it you if he likes." That's the end of that
one.

A KANO TONGUE-TWISTER (II/VIII)

The Emir of Kano sent to tell me to take him the skins
of seven white Kano crocodiles; but I didn't kill seven

white Kano crocodiles. Last year, when I killed seven
white Kano crocodiles, then of course I took him the
skins of the seven white Kano crocodiles. That's all.

A KEBBI TONGUE-TWISTER (II/IX)
(This is almost word for the word the same as
the last but substituting Kebbi (Argungu) for
Kano.)

ANOTHER HAUSA TONGUE-TWISTER (II/X)

Hey, little bird, you're a too bad bird! For you keep
going and doing your dirty droppings where Dad says his
prayers! That's another tongue-twister that Hausas
will use to teach someone who doesn't know the language
how to speak it.
    And here's another they use. "I ran hard*, and
winnowed the river, and winnowed the river's wife, and
caught the testicles of the ram that Dad had to slaughter
for the Festival." That's another tongue-twister that
Hausas use to teach the language, if they find someone
who doesn't know it.
    And here's another they use: "Exactly at the foot
of the dum-palm, there I squashed Mother's crocodile."
    And here's yet another thing the Hausas say--"I
made an early start and went to the durumi of Duru. I
found the people of Duru chopping down the durumi of
Duru. Says I 'Hey, people of Duru, what has the durumi
of Duru done to you that you should chop down the
durumi of Duru so early in the morning (da duru-duru)?'"

HOW THE HAUSA COUNT UP TO TEN (II/II)
(I imagine that the speaker would touch a
finger at each word that I have underlined.)

There was once an elder sister and a younger sister,

---

*The exact significance of mar escapes me, but I sus-
    pect that once again, the whole jingle is largely
    nonsense in the H. too.

and they <u>went</u>; they <u>got</u> what they wanted, and <u>returned</u>.
<u>I</u> too, had I but <u>known</u>, would have <u>gone</u>, and <u>got</u> it
too, and <u>returned</u>. That's how the Hausa count. It
makes ten, you see.

HOW DOGS FIGHT (II/III)

Two dogs went to steal from someone's compound. They
met, and the one said "May God give you <u>tuwo</u>." "Amen"
said the other. Again "May God give you the scrapings
from the bottom of the pot." "Amen" said the other.
"May God give you a bone." "Amen." "May God give you
a dry ball of <u>fura</u>." "Amen." "May God give you a bundle of corn." "Who'll thresh it?" asked the other.
"You will" said the first. "Oh no--you will." "Oh no--
you will." "No--you will." So they had a fight and
then went their separate ways.

Hausas who are clever at words reckon that when
two dogs are quarrelling, that's what they are saying
to each other.

Again, there were two dogs, one of whom had got a
bone that he was gnawing. Up comes the other one and
finds him. Says he to the first dog as he lay there
gnawing "Who gave you that whopper?" Says the one with
the bone "I bought it." "How much did you pay?" says
the newcomer. "A score (of cowries)." "You're lying"
said the second dog, and they joined battle. They
inflicted several bites on each other and then went
their separate ways--leaving the bone there.

So Hausas who are clever at words, if they see a
dog with a bone, and another dog come up to him, they'll
use their imagination and tell you that that is what
they're saying. So much for that one.

Here's another about a dog and his son. The father
had gone and lain down in the fireplace, while the son
was outside wandering round. The latter saw a hyena,
a n d began to say "I see a black thing, black, black,
black; I see a black thing, black, black, black." Says
the father, from where he lay in the fireplace "Have a
good look." So the youngster stopped--and still saw a

black thing, black, black, black, and went on saying
so, and presently came in past his father. At which
the father rose. The young one went into a hut, and
the father began saying "Get over there, get over
there please; get over there, get over there please."
At last, he too went into the hut.

So when a dog and a puppy start to bark, on seeing
a hyena, Hausas, such ones as are witty speakers, will
affirm that this is what they are saying.

A MALAM AND HIS PUPIL (II/95)

(LNDDN (p. 54) has a more elaborate version
of this, in which the boy also disguises his
remark that the meat is done, saying that he
had lost the place in reading, and substituting
the Ar. mamun for the H. nuna "is done".)

There was once a malam had pupils, and he bought some
meat. He picked out one of the pupils, a sharp lad and
said to him "Go and grill this meat for me." "Right"
said the boy and off he went and began grilling the
meat. Meanwhile some other malams came to the first
and they began reading together. But the boy kept on
grilling the meat.

Presently he went back to tell the malam that the
meat was done. But when he got back he found the malam
surrounded by the other malams, to whom he was expounding
the passage. And the boy left them and went away again.
But shortly after he returned, and though the other
malams were still there, the boy said to the malam "Malam,
the meat is done." To which the malam replied "Take it
off and spit it on the tankalladhina amanu (purlin-of-
those-who-believe)*." "OK" said the boy, and went off,

*He would have said "purlin of the hut" but broke off
to go on with the Koran, alladhina amanu being a
ubiquitous phrase in that book. The lad, however,
was smart enough to take his meaning.

and took the meat off the fire and spitted it on the
purlin of the hut. That's all.

THE GUINEA-FOWL AND THE HARE (II/96)

The guinea-fowl was out for a walk when he met the
hare. He began to mock the hare saying "Well! So
you've come this way, hare!*" But the hare answered
straight away "Oh, even the other day I came this way**."
Says the guinea-fowl "What! How dare you abuse me so
shamelessly, hare!" "But, guinea-fowl" protested the
hare, "It was you started being personal. And now, when
I get my own back, are you going to start getting upset?" "Well" says the guinea-fowl, "In any case, I
don't like these sort of games." "All right" replied
the hare, "If you don't like them, don't use those
words to me again!" And that's the end of that one.

LADI AND SULE (III/139)
(A tongue-twister, playing on the syllable
sul-.)

Ladi and Sule climbed the wastrel's (?) rock. Then
Sule slipped down from there, leaving Ladi, making
spindles (?)+.

THE MAN, HIS CHILDREN AND HIS WIFE (I/131)
(There is a slightly different version at
LNDDNY, p. 55.)

A man once had a wife and four children. He went to

---

*The H. puns, being approximately "so there are ears
   here".
**"even the other day" puns on "that horny excrescence"
   on the guinea-fowl's nose.
+Presuming sulli = sille; the expression tana kayan =
   "she is making" is also somewhat dubious.

market and bought the head and feet of a goat. And he
had them cooked.

When they were done, the mother of his children,
said "Boys, the goat's head is done, how will you tell
your father?" Then the youngest said "Send me. I know
what I'll tell him." "Very well" says she.

When he reached the entrance hut, he found that
there were a lot of people with his father, so he said
"Dad, the business of the head has come up." "That's
true" said his father, "There are four of you. Let
each one take to his feet. As for me, hearing and seeing
and speaking are enough for me, thank you. And, even
if she hasn't a carrying-pad, let her carry the load."

Then the youngest went quickly back and told his
mother "Dad says we are each to take a foot, and you're
to put aside the tongue and the ears and the eyes; and
you're to have the brain."

THE MISERLY MAN (III/161)
(This is a variant of the last.)

There was a mean man that bought the head and feet of
a goat and took them home to have them cooked for himself. While these were being cooked, some meal-cadgers
came to visit him, and settled down.

Their greed prevented them going, and presently
the head was cooked. His wife wished to take the pot
off, but wasn't sure whether her husband was ready. So
she said to her son "I want to take the pot, but your
father has people with him." "Leave it to me" said the
boy, "I'll go and ask him." "But what will you say?"
she asked. "What concern is it of yours?" he answered.

And he went to his father and said "Dad, which
year was I born in?" "The year of the removing.*"

Then the boy went back to his mother and said "Dad
says to take the pot off." So she took it off and presently it was cool. She wished to divide the food out

_____
*Or "of our move".

and said "I want to divide out the contents of the pot; but your father has people with him." "I'll go and ask him" said the boy. "What will you say?" she asked. "What concern of yours is it?" he answered.

Then the boy went back to his father and said "Dad." "Yes" said the other. "Mother wants to go out to one of the villages." His father answered "Feet of your mother; ears and eyes yours; you see a son of the head of your father.*"

The boy went back into the compound crying. "What's the matter with you?" asked his mother. "Dad says you're to take the feet for yourself**." "Is that why you're crying?" she asked. "He abused me ears and eyes*." "Is that why you're crying?" "He abused me head of my father*." "Well" she said, "Isn't he your father?" "Yes" he said, "It's true. I was crying because my share was so little."

Then she divided it out, gave the boy the ears and the eyes, took out the feet, and kept the head for the father.

---

*The H. makes little more sense than the English. The point being to introduce the names for the different parts somehow or other.
**Or, perhaps, "lift your feet up".

XVI
Riddles

For other examples of these guessing games, see
Fletcher, R. S. Hausa Sayings and Folklore (Oxford,
1912). A selection of the original Hausa versions
with notes is included in Skinner, Neil, Hausa Readings
(Madison, 1968) pp. 74-78. Some of the answers are
fairly logical and can be deduced by anyone having a
knowledge of a Hausa household; for the others, the
meanings are lost in the mists of the early tales.

Confusingly, a "riddle" is tatsuniya, equally with
a tale. It is also sometimes ka-cinci-ka-cinci, which
invites the interlocutor to have a guess. And the usual
challenge and reply is also the same as for a tale, viz.

Questioner: ga ta ga ta nan	Here she is!
Guesser: ta je ta dawo or	Let her go!
ta zo ta wuce or	Let her pass!
ta zo mu ji ta etc.	Let's hear her!

Questioner then states the riddle, and the guesser has
to guess it. "I give up" is na ba ka gari ("I give you
the town"). If you get it right, it is your turn to ask.

The last four are longer and not in the traditional
form. They may perhaps be translations from the Arabic.

265

(II/IV)

Beneath, a bamboo; above gold.
  That's bulrush-millet.

Dad's calabash-basins, too big to be contained by any
  roof.
    That's heaven and earth, which never meet.

I put the pot on at Mecca, but it wasn't done till Medina.
    That's a pot of dambu*.

Two peanuts in the shell, one on the other.
    That's a pot of dambu*.

(I/LXXXIV)

1. Sets of threes that every one sees--
     the stones of the cooking-place.

2. A youngster's hut without a door--that's an egg.

3. The bush is full of rustling, but the big one stands
     silent--that's an ant-hill.

4. I see the amata** charms far off--that's a locust-
     bean tree.

5. The red one falls, the red one picks it up--a
     deleb-palm and a Filani.

---

*This may describe the appearance of one pot set above
  another on the fire. Dambu is prepared by steaming
  a mixture of flour and herbs in this way, a very slow
  process.
**Origin unknown, but now (BARG) used as synonym for
  dorowa (= locust-bean tree), cf. 27 . Possibly
  the name of a fabulous character.

6. I hear the voice of my girl-chum far off--that's the <u>dundufa</u> drum.

7. Dangling dangling--you can't come in*--that's a string door curtain.

8. And when you came in, girl, what did they give you?-- Or, what comes in but never gets anything?--that's a door.

9. My farm came to fruition, and when I reaped, the crop made one handful--that's the hair of the head.

10. An Arab among Arabs--that's the tongue and teeth**.

11. Dad's turban that can't be wound on the head-- that's a road.

12. Dad's wooden bowl that can't be licked clean--a borrow-pit.

13. I had a farm, and it came to fruition, and I reaped the guinea-corn, and grasped it all in one hand-- that's the hair of the head.

14. An Arab among Arabs--that's the tongue between the teeth.

15. The old woman in our home is bending down and praying God--that's a grass booth.

16. The wren-warbler has fallen to the ground and his loin-cloth has split--that's the fruit of the desert-date.

---

*Or, as we might say, what dangles but doesn't come in?
**Perhaps because of the colors, white and red.

17. Though there are very many in our compound, we
    bought five cowries worth of food, and ate and
    were satisfied--that's peppers (i.e. a little
    goes a long way).

18. If you go to the market, buy me something that
    hasn't been touched by a fly--that's fire.

19. If you go to the market, buy me what's west of the
    market--that's meat*.

20. Mother's round gourd full of bits that won't go
    through the sieve--that's a bitter tomato.

21. The bending of a bow** much looked at--that's bul-
    rush millet.

22. The little bow on the ant-hill--that's a toe-nail.

23. I have two roads: if I take the first, I come out;
    if I take the second I come out--that's trousers.

24. Mother has gone round; father has gone round--and
    they haven't met--that's ears.

25. I've given it you, what are you looking at me for?--
    that's a dog.

26. Thin and flimsy--you can't come in!--that's a
    string door curtain.

27. I see the amata[+] charms far off--that's a deleb-
    palm.

28. Snow-white--like tuwo exposed on a faifai--that's
    the stars.

---

*The abattoir is always in this position.
**By the farmer, to see whether it is ripe.
[+]Cf. 4. above.

29. I washed out my calabash and threw it up, and when it fell to the ground it didn't break--that's paper.

30. I have a thousand thousand cattle, with but one rope to tie them--that's a broom.

31. I have a thousand thousand cattle, but you can't see their dust--that's black ants.

32. Cattle lying down, a bull standing up--that's stars and a full moon.

33. Father's donkeys with the white mouths--that's pestles.

34. Luxuriantly leafy but not for eating--that's indigo.

35. I saw father's beard far off--that's smoke.

36. The little itinerant trader that trades in the market of the next world--that's a bucket.

37. A harlot all bedecked, the men run away--that's an arrow.

38. There's a hubbub going on, but the big fellow is outside--that's a mortar.

39. My flock of raw cotton is white as snow, and none touches it but God--that's the stars.

40. A supple stick on the road that lays low both great and small--that's hunger.

41. A young maiden with beautiful hair--that's sugar-cane.

42. Mother's calabash marked by the Prophet--that's a guinea-fowl.

43. Mother's calabash with the bits that won't go
    through the sieve in it--that's a bitter tomato.

44. The big bull that roars in the middle of the com-
    pound--that's the grindstone.

45. The girls of your compound who always clap when
    they set off for the bush--that's doves.

46. Super*-pestle, super*-mortar, super*-pounding--
    that's a smithy.

47. I heard the voice of my big brother far off--that's
    a _kalangu_ drum.

48. The youngster's sleeping hut that has no door--
    that's an egg.

49. Only Mamurada** can wear Mamurada's shoe--that's
    a scorpion.

50. God gave him a saddle, but not for riding on--
    that's a scorpion and its sting.

51. Flour in the hut, but still the children go to
    bed hungry--that's ashes.

52. Big and wide on top of very big, with a bat and
    a basket[+]--that's a hut with a small, thatched
    roof.

53. All the town has a strolling minstrel (_dan kama_[++])--
    that's the tuft on top of the thatch of a hut.

---

*Or, perhaps, "naked".

**Emending by making it a proper name and altering
  takalmi to _takalmin_--but it remains obscure. It
  seems more like a proverb than a riddle. Probably
  Mamurada = Namarudu = Nimrod, legendary hero.

[+]The second phrase seems redundant.

[++]'_yan kama_ wear a cap which may give rise to this
  metaphor.

54. I travel with my sister but I can't hear her movement--that's my shadow.

55. Convolvulus clinging round the edge of the well--that's a woman's private parts.

56. A little club and a spider--that's a penis.

57. I have a thousand cattle, but the grey dog has sweeter milk than they--that's sugar-cane.

58. Potash*, not bone--that's potash.

59. Very dark, but not from indigo--that's an over-clouded sky.

60. The little one with his lips stained with cola-nut, who goes right through the waters of the Niger--that's a leech.

61. The old woman died with her cloth tied up round her waist--that's a fence.

62. Legs apart, a frog prevents the river from flowing--that's a fishing-net**.

63. She sits with her legs apart[+] to meet God--that's a grass booth.

64. The Zabarma girl who builds a wall with her rear[++]--that's a scorpion.

65. The chief Maguje opens his mouth and prays to God--that's a mortar.

---

*But using a special word.
**Emending kundu to kwaḍo and taro to taru.
[+]Apparently the posture of pleading.
[++]Perhaps there is some reference here to a joking relationship with the Zabarma tribe.

66. The chief Maguje with rolls of fat--that's a comb-
    in with a purlin round the thatch.

67. The chief Maguje with a tiny head--that's a hut.

68. Malam-open-the-book--that's a moth.

69. Three things resemble three other things were it
    not for yet three more things--sleep is like
    death, were it not for breathing; a guinea-hen
    is like a pepper-and-salt pattern cloth, were it
    not for the horny excrescence on her head; marri-
    age is like slavery, were it not for freedom.

70. A hatched hawk flew off with a hatched chick, perched
    on an ant-hill and chewed it tappingly in his
    tapped beak*--that's a smithy.

71. I went to the bush, the bush was laughing at me--
    that's cotton.

72. A forked post with a stirrup-iron on top and a bat
    hanging--that's an empty hut with a narrow roof
    and something hanging from it.

73. A little stream going round the hill--that's tuwo
    and miya.

74. I washed my calabash a gleaming white, then I went
    to Kano and to Daura and came back, but it hadn't
    dried--that's a dog's nose.

75. The deep well of adornment--that's a dye-pit.

76. All the young men of our compound have white mouths--
    that's pestles.

77. There's a maiden in our compound who is always
    washing--that's a dipping gourd.

---

*The same H. word covers "hatch" and "tap", the four-
fold repetition seems to be the main point.

78. Quickly from the nest, welcome the bird of the
     <u>geza</u> tree--that's a needle.

79. Sets of two that everyone knows--that's eyes.

80. The little earthenware pot that crosses the fence
     (or that escapes quickly)--that's a hedgehog*.

81. Life below, life above, but no life in between--
     a horse, the one who is on him, and the saddle.

82. The boys in our compound have all got caps--that's
     the fruits of the <u>dinya</u>.

83. There's an old woman in our compound who gives us
     each a cowrie-shell every morning when she gets
     up--that's goat's excrement.

84. I slaughtered my ox, but it was all fat and I took
     nothing except the skin--that's a bottle gourd.

85. Brightly adorned** with the designs (patterns) of
     God--that's a guinea-hen.

86. If you go to the market, buy me some liver without
     blood--that's cola-nuts.

87. If you go to the market, buy me some of the market
     dust--that's tobacco powder.

88. A youngster's hut without a door--that's an egg.

89. A stump on the road that fells young and old--that's
     a stumble.

-----

*In popular belief, the hedgehog is credited with
  remarkable powers.
**Reading <u>k̉yari k̉yari</u> for <u>k̉ari k̉ari</u>. There may be
  onomatopoea here, referring to the bird's noise.

90. Super-soft the slaves' grave*--that's chaff.

91. I washed my calabash spick and span, then I went
    to Katsina and to Daura, but it hadn't dried--
    that's a dog's (or "an ox's") nose.

92. Down stream, let's go to Zaria--that's a head-pad**.

93. Mother's⁺ sewing, Namaridu's⁺⁺ pattern--that's a
    mat calabash-cover.

94. There's an old woman in our compound who gives us
    each a cowrie-shell every day when she goes to
    market--that's a goat.

95. Shady but not proper shadow--that's rainclouds.

96. Something faintly seen (or "something very small")
    in the thicket--that's a fingernail.

97. I saw the charm worn by the king's wife afar off--
    that's a locust-bean tree.

98. The king danced but he didn't penetrate the ground--
    that's excrement.

99. The Galadima danced and he penetrated the ground--
    that's urine.

100. All the girls of our compound have white mouths--
     that's pestles.

---

*? a cheap one, requiring no digging? Also, place
where they labor--the threshing floor.
**? because it makes for ease? Also play on gan-.
⁺Presuming iyya = iya.
⁺⁺See 49. Nimrod is made responsible for many things
in legend and poetry. His name occurs in a number
of riddles here too, e.g. saƙan N. ("the weaving of
N" = "honey").

101. A prince on a grass mat--that's cola-nuts.

102. I washed my calabash very clean and threw it up,
     and when it fell to the ground it didn't break--
     that's paper.

103. The little ball of paste that spreads all over
     the river--that's the full moon.

104. Mother's <u>faifai</u>, plaited by Namaridu*--that's a
     guinea-hen's feathers.

105. Tread on life and pluck the fruits of death--that's
     treading on a king's mat and taking his cap.

106. Tread on a branch and pick the fruits of death--
     that's treading on a king's mat and taking off
     his cap.

107. Travelling snakewise, bearing twins--that's a
     bottle-gourd.

108. I hear chopping, but not the sound of falling--
     that's a town (i.e. the sound of pounding).

109. Tread on me, that I may grow taller than you--
     that's corn.

110. A thin thing, a broad thing, a thing with small
     fruits (?)--that's a deleb-palm.

111. Tiny dripping drops', trickling trickles--that's
     an ash-sieve.

112. Hen-bird with a backside like a mortar, oboe that
     is a long time coming to birth--that's a chicken.

113. Mother's <u>faifais</u>, all alike--that's sky and earth.

---

*See 93.

114. A long thing, but it won't collect gum--that's
      rope (because it is not stiff like a stick).

115. I've mounted the roan, give me a whip--that's
      I've climbed on the corn-bin, give me some rope.

116. Taut on top, taut underneath, and the inside tied
      tight too--that's a loom.

A HAUSA SUM (II/XXXV)

There was a man had a chicken. She laid forty eggs,
and she hatched out forty chicks. And the forty chicks
each one laid forty eggs. And the mother of the chicks
hatched out her forty eggs. Well, how many chickens
were there altogether? Answer--one thousand, six hundred and eighty one chickens.

HAUSA RIDDLES (II/XXXVI)

What is one in the world? There is no other save God.
     What is two in the world? There is no two in the
world, save only night and day.
     What is four in the world? Four in the world: four
are the wives that you may marry. Any who marries more
than four breaks the law.
     What is nine in the world? Every man in the world
is nine, nor will he attain ten. For if a man is nine
months in the womb, then--if it is a normal pregnancy*--
he will be born.
     If the tops of nine city buildings each have nine
cattle-egrets perched on them, and each egret is holding
nine locusts, how many locusts are there altogether?
Answer--seven hundred and twenty-nine.

---

*Perhaps a reference to the H. belief that a pregnancy
  could last a year--witness the name "Shekarau",
  given to such a child.

WHEN SEVEN THINGS ARE LACKING (II/LXXI)

Seven things lacking mean seven other things lacking.
The man who lacks a home lacks the wherewithal to cover
himself; he who lacks food, lacks strength; he who lacks
a son. lacks joy; he who lacks a wife, lacks religion;
he who lacks clothing, lacks respect; he who lacks
clothing also lacks comeliness; he who lacks patience,
lacks wisdom.

A TOTAL OF FOUR PEOPLE WHICH EXCEEDS
FORTY-FOUR PEOPLE (II/LXVIII)

Four people exceed forty-four people. And this is
really so, as you will see when you hear the explanation.
One married man exceeds eleven bachelors. One seeing
man exceeds eleven blind men. One man with fingers
exceeds eleven lepers. One man with legs exceeds eleven
cripples. Now you know why I said that four people
exceed forty-four people. That's all.

XVII
Proverbs

Again, a selection of the originals, with notes, is to
be found in Skinner, Neil <u>Hausa Readings</u> (Madison 1968)
at pp. 79-87.

(I/LXXXV)

Numbers in brackets after a proverb refer to the page
of Whitting, C.E.J., <u>Hausa and Fulani Proverbs</u> (Gregg
reprint, 1967), on which it, or a closely similar one
appears. For a modern selection of Hausa proverbs,
see <u>Hausa Ba Dabo Ba Ne</u>, Kirk-Greene, AHM (Ibadan 1966).
There is also a collection of 6407 unpublished proverbs
(also collected by Edgar) in the Regional Archives,
Kaduna.

1. The (appointed) day will never be untrue, but the
    girl's mother may. (91)

2. The crown of a brave promise is fulfillment.

3. Washing with flour is no cure for hunger--you have to imbibe it. (71)

4. Espying something in the distance won't bring it-- it still has to come. (58)

5. If a man doesn't swallow his greed, his greed will swallow him. (135)

6. Greed opens the doors of trouble. (136)

7. He who is greedy for other people's things will undergo shame before he dies; but not everyone who is greedy--only he who is greedy and dishonest too.

8. Keep an eye on the road for me (ABR "you'll be wise to accept my advice"). (82)*

9. By courtesy of the chicken, the lizard drinks the water in the potsherd. (39)

10. I did some frying, but forgot the onions (i.e. the essential ingredient). (71)

11. However big a madman may be, he is useless, a little fellow in his right mind is worth more than he. (60)

12. "What use is mere size?"--the fat penis wouldn't stay hard.

13. However big the grass, it's useless for thatching unless it's prepared. (118)

14. The dirt in the water-bottle is accepted by the stomach. (82)

15. He who buys corn needn't try to compete with the man who grows it on his farm.

------

*Whitting adds "as the blind man said, when he wanted to indulge in malicious gossip".

16. The rich man is he who has enough.

17. You don't begin to feel shame, till you cease feeling hunger (lit. only when the mouth eats does the eye know shame).

18. A black bull spoils the herd. (28)

19. Get acquainted with the ferryman during the dry-season (i.e. before you need his services). (122)

20. I fried some oil but forgot the onions (see 10). (71)

21. Two at once--Baidu's catching bandicoots (see I/124).

22. The mat of shame gets rolled up in madness (= act crazy to hide your embarrassment. See I/112 and III/158).

23. In communal contributions the elephant has the bigger family (cf. I/35). (16)

24. "Don't relax your guard!" won't stop a thief thieving.

25. Trickery is no use to the man who has gone down the well. (119)

26. We're sick of hearing "Beware of the bull*"--let's see some horns! (129)

27. Even if you're long away from a man, don't trouble to inquire about his nature (because it won't change).

28. Even if you're long away from a man, don't trouble to inquire about his nature, but about his circumstances.

---

*Called out by butchers dragging a bull to slaughter.

29. Character is an etching on stone. (4)

30. It's no good laying your head down away from the woman dressing it.

31. One doesn't hide one's navel (<u>or</u> umbilical hernia) on bath-day. (46)

32. One who leaves the domestic doves alone is already replete with meat. (35)

33. "Just leave it for a minute to cool" gives someone else a chance to take his share.

34. If the ear hears, the throat will escape cutting (i.e. "forewarned is forearmed"). (50)

35. If you don't listen to "Leave off!", you'll listen to condolences. (43)

36. One doesn't fry oil unless one adds onions (see 10). (71)

37. One doesn't uncover the head away from the woman who is to dress it.

38. A camel's tail is a long way from the ground*. (21)

39. The stomach was not made for corn (but vice versa).

40. To love one who loves another is to have one's fill of trouble. (93)

41. I don't lay my eggs, unless (they've been fertilized) by a rooster. (36)

42. I don't drink water that has grass in (ABR a. "bite off more than I can chew", b. "get detected in extortion", c. "get syphilis").** (14)

---

*<u>Abr</u>. "Fancy his thinking he's up to doing it!"
**Whitting says "look before you leap".

43. If you see a mare with a saddle*--she's thrown someone (ABR e.g. an attractive woman no longer married suggests some hidden fault). (22)

44. A hare doesn't come into the market for nothing. (107)**

45. (The state of) markets and of rivers is unpredictable. (129)

46. Night, that hides all secrets. (1)

47. Night, the great shadow. (1)

48. At night I take a staff, during the day a cornstalk suffices me as support.

49. From his trade you can judge a man--even though it be drinking beer. (116)

50. A path can't leave its proper place (ABR "What's bred in the bone comes out in the flesh"). (5)

51. The mark of a true son is to inherit from his father.

52. The best dancing comes from short chaps. (56)[+]

53. The best swaggering is done by tall fellows. (56)[+]

54. "Girl come here!" says the newly rich wife to her slave, but God hates ostentatious boasting (see ABR under bude).

55. God is the helper of those that strive.

---

*Mares are not normally ridden. (For the metaphoric use of "mares" and "saddles" for "wives" and "marriage", cf. I/100.)

**Whitting is wrong here.

[+]Whitting adds conditions to both these. Hausas commonly only quote the beginning of a well-known proverb (as we might say "a stitch in time") and this is what the scribe has done here.

56. Those who strive shall obtain.

57. The evening sun, which gives the world no warmth
    (ABR "said of a useless person").

58. You can't lose an eye and then use antimony to
    revive it. (49)

59. You prefer that the gazelle rather than the goat
    should be well fed (i.e. one who neglects his
    family for others).

60. "Leave off!" and "I won't leave off" have had a
    son--but you haven't noticed it (i.e. a dig at a
    short-sighted man who doesn't notice what is in
    front of his nose).

61. Night the cloak of wickedness. (1)

62. Night, which limits a stranger's wandering. (1)

63. Everyone reaps what he has sowed.

64. The superior man is he who drives out greed from
    his heart, or who keeps it there for no more than
    a day; then his self-respect--quite apart from any
    superiority--makes him keep his desires to himself (?).

65. Even if he speaks the truth, whoever loses his
    temper before his king, he'll* have him killed.

66. Whoever is miserly with his wealth, does not give
    it to himself--but to the man who marries his wife.
    For when he dies it will be given to her and she
    will marry again.

67. Whoever uses truth in his conversation, is the
    better for it.

---

*Emending <u>a</u> to <u>za</u>.

68. Whoever gives away his wealth will be honored, but whoever gives away his self-respect will be despised.

69. Whoever commits oppression, his destruction is not far off.

70. Whoever digs a well for his brother to fall into, will fall into it himself.

71. Whoever speaks words that he shouldn't, will hear things that he won't like.

72. Whoever is eternally* lying at rest, won't get what he seeks.

73. One wears a boy's loin-cloth to enter the water ("When accused one blames one's subordinate"). (68)

74. The repentance of the cat with the chicken in his mouth.

75. Where a four-footed beast falls, how much more so a two-footed one! (30)

76. Bone but no meat--of no interest to the dog!

77. The meddlesomeness of the itinerant trader who ate nakiya, i.e. the poor can't afford luxuries. (111)

78. Perforce--like the burden of testicles: a son may see his father's but the father has to carry them. (92)

79. Chicken, eat and still scratch for more! (i.e. pecking the hand that feeds it).

80. The top of the tree--where the crow lives.

81. A skillful tongue will make a thief laugh, even when he is in the corn bin (and therefore with maximum temptation to concentrate on remaining unperceived). (129)

---

*Deleting the comma after tutut.

82. One egg in the soup-pot is worth a chicken loose.

83. You'd outfight a hyena! (ABR said to a broker trying to distract attention from his defalcations by incessant talk).

84. Whoever gives to rope, rope will give to him = (ABR "If you deposit something with a trustworthy man, you'll get it back").

85. A hyena has a cure for diarrhoea but doesn't use it on herself. (14)

86. If the hyena had the cure for diarrhoea, she would have taken it herself. (14)

87. You don't begin to feel shame till you cease feeling hunger (same as No. 17). (48)

88. Anyone who just sits* and slacks, gets nothing.

89. Whoever "rides the horse of hurry," will stumble.

90. You don't take on a dog on the morning of the hunt.

91. One makes friends with the cow before one starts milking it. (21)

92. "Get it for yourself" is the cure for greed.

93. The stomach shouldn't turn its nose up at the liver (i.e. the pot shouldn't call the kettle black).

94. Only Fanna can take on Ari's affairs (? only a Kanuri** can put up with this sort of thing).

---

*Deleting the comma after zama--cf. (72).
**Abr makes it more general in application--but I think that, in any case originally, the meaning is as given here. The point being that these are two Kanuri names.

95. Only the young hyenas make a home in a hyena's den.

96. Even though you tread on a grasshopper, or on any sort of ant or insect--you don't know it.

97. A limp stomach means hunger; wind means cold; and something said but not done means a lie.

98. The _fura_ porridge took a bath and went back into the flour container (i.e. extremely improbable sequence, beginning again _ab initio_).

99. The _fura_ took a bath and went back into the bag.

100. The calf of another won't stop you milking.

101. "In the name of God"--that means someone has started two malams off quarreling with each other, (i.e. ? malams will quarrel at the drop of a hat).

102. Truth upon truth, the malam has bought himself a malam.

103. If your feet can't manage to jump over the stream, then go round.

104. Once done, never again! Like climbing the date-palms of Kalu (_or_ "Kalu's climbing the date-palm).

105. Horn--useless except for blowing! (ABR epithet of a miser).

106. Length of years does not make a wise elder, but consistency in what one says.

107. People in grass houses don't like people who light fires for fun.

108. If the chick is nothing to write home about, the egg-shell won't be either.

109. If you see a long mouth--it has an argumentative owner.

110. If you relax your attention, the world will discover that someone has planted rama* behind your hut (i.e. a stranger doing what belongs properly to the householder).

111. It's impertinence when someone asks you if you've seen the king's horse to say "No, but I'll pay its price".

112. The deaf parakeet whom the farmer shouts at--you don't start spinning till you've chalked your fingers. (? two separate proverbs: the first half, according to ABR, refers to one who talks so much himself that he never listens to what others say).

113. You don't eat the fruit of the date-palm, until its sharp points have pricked you.

114. Rudely interrupted--which prevented Barka having intercourse with his daughter**. (Probably a reference to the incestuous habits of non-Muslim peoples, cf. 234.)

115. "You know it and I know it too" (a mutual secret) won't disconcert a Kano man (? ability to ferret out secrets).

116. Losing, and making a profit--you get both, if you trade.

117. He who sells, makes a profit.

---

*The fiber Hibiscus cannabinus.
**Reading cin 'yarsa for chinyas sa ("a leg of beef"), but there may be a double entendre.

118. a. No trouble--like the bachelor's Fast Month--
        (Ramadan means extra expense for the normal,
        married household, but this is quite unnec-
        essary for a bachelor).

     b. Don't wear your cloth like Dadi's mother*. (She
        modestly covered the rest of herself but left
        her bottom bare.)

119. The census of the horses of Rano--live ones <u>and</u>
     dead ones.

120. Iron only rises in price when the rainy season comes.

121. Quarrelling is for those who can talk, a deaf-mute
     must forbear.

122. An elephant doesn't bite--it's that trunk you have
     to watch.

123. It's not saleable--even Kundila couldn't sell it,
     even at Kano.

124. "I have one of my own" as the corn-seller replied
     when they invited her to a party.

125. The hand of the writer has no eyes. (117)

126. However severe the fine, leave the householder
     his dog (? to guard the compound).

127. A virile man is like a guinea-fowl--he sleeps off
     the ground.

128. "Allah, God of Pleasure!" as the man stealing sugar-
     cane said. (72)

---

*Reading <u>Dadi</u> for <u>dadi</u>, and making it a separate proverb
 from the last.

129. "God has done a godlike thing!" as the pagan said when he found a dead monkey on his farm (unexpected good luck). (15)

130. It is known that even Maradî* will go to distant Bauchi (to buy slaves).

131. What has the period of washing after child-birth to do with males?

132. That's the world--if one woman doesn't like you, take another.

133. The water dried up on the young crocodile before he had finished growing.

134. A Gwari's axe--used for chopping and for building, and, if you take the shaft off, as a missile too.

135. It's not quarrelsomeness one dreads in an old woman-- it's harping.

136. For some clashes only a ram will do--a ewe has no true strength (?).

137. May God preserve an axe from hoeing! (ABR "What have we in common?")

138. Madness is a relative relative--everyone has his own type. (60)

139. Sour milk may like millet paste, but millet paste likes sour milk too! (i.e. mutual benefit).

140. The death didn't take place at Mecca, it took place in a raised sleeping-platform**.

---

*See I/LXV.

**The point appears to be the pun of Makka and makani-- but there is also comparison between the meaningful and the pointless. Mecca is the best place to die.

141.   However long the tether, being loose is pleasanter.

142.   A half-gourd for dipping isn't a variety but an
        exploitation of a gourd (i.e. they don't grow in
        halves, but have to be processed--ABR, quoting
        only the first half, says, perhaps too specifically,
        "There is no harm in appointing a person to an
        official position even though not hereditary to
        him").

143.   You don't fill the bed, but you fill the hut like
        a noisy bell.

144.   The offspring of a gazelle won't fail to be swift.
        (14)

145.   The man with offspring need never despair. (92)

146.   If the drum beat changes, then the dance must change
        too.

147.   Whoever takes the way that is not his, will get
        lost.

148.   We despise the intelligence of the hyrax--because
        it hasn't a tail!

149.   If you must swing, swing from a tamarind-tree--if
        you catch hold of the sabara* shrub, it'll break.

150.   The spot the load was dropped--that's where you
        look for a headpad.

151.   Others see an invading army, you just see a cloud
        of dust.

152.   If you see a road, you know it leads to a home. (5)

153.   A donkey won't pass by ash (but roll in it) (ABR
        "This is just in your line!"). (23)

---

*Guiera senegalensis.

154. Punishment does not destroy--it reforms character.

155. An indication is sufficient for the wise man. (54)

156. One sip isn't drinking--no man is satisfied by one drink.

157. What is a goat doing with a large hide-bag (for a donkey) on its back?

158. Comfort is what one is used to, i.e. one's standard of living is a matter of habit (but see ABR p. 164).

159. Those that are prisoners have no choice in the matter of their work. (117)

160. It doesn't happen that a gazelle is a swift runner, but her son a crawler (cf. 144). (14)

161. Big bull! You get a separate tethering-post!

162. However nearly right he may do it, the hasty man will not be free of mistakes.

163. Absorbed eating--like boys knocking back grass-hoppers (?).

164. Plants that grow from roots left in the ground-- they're the ones that win to next year.

165. Even if you don't like the thatching-needle, you'll like it on the day you're fixing the thatch.

166. If you ask a prisoner for the truth, he'll say "Let me be released".

167. In avoiding a sprain you've got a fracture. (52)

168. If you see <u>kainuwa</u>* on dry land, you know it's withered.

---

*<u>Pistia stratiotes</u>, a floating plant.

169. A frog won't go a whole year without touching damp.

170. Selling perforce but hoping to buy back one day--
      since there's no money.

171. Anyone who tells a lie will find someone from
      his own compound turn up (and expose it).

172. If anyone says he'll swallow an axe, let go of
      the handle for him! (to facilitate his task) (52)

173. Long years of slavery don't add up to freedom.

174. Profit's profit--even in Mecca.

175. Who goes short today tomorrow shall have plenty.

176. However much the sickle cuts, it's still grass.

177. Success in twenty-four hours--like the growth of
      gamba* grass.

178. Contrary one, you're a bad guest! One sees you on
      your way, and then you return.

179. They've got what they wanted--someone's thrown a
      hoe at the farmer's daughter.

180. Hot weather before the rains, killer of the king's
      horses!

181. "Let bygones be bygones" as the calabash-mender**
      said when he became king. (117)

182. An important woman--one who doesn't have salt
      bought for her (? because she doesn't cook).

183. Spouting from the corner of the roof, you irrigate
      the bush! (Wasted effort) (121)

---

*Andropogon Guyanus.
**The most despised occupation.

184. Cadging is a matter of opportunity--you can even do it in your own mother's hut.

185. We all have the same skin to our bodies--but each to his own nature.

186. The mouth is a drum that prevents the skin's loss (talking oneself out of a difficult situation).

187. I despise the boxing skill of a blind man, even if he's actually got his fists up.

188. I am sorry for you, trying to manage two pots full of water at the same time--you've got losses coming.

189. Kill him who would harm you before he kills you.

190. Some sorts of speech will bring cola-nuts out of (the hearer's) pockets.

191. Buying a dog for his barking--then, when he arrives, he refuses to bark!

192. Seeing the Kware men again, even if you don't see Jega (?).

193. If the eating isn't just right, the repletion won't be!

194. The hyena doesn't think of it as night--but it still has to endure walking in the dark.

195. When the shave reaches the front of the forehead, it hurts.

196. There's no profit in retailing bean-cakes (no margin on home-made cookies; ABR "Love's labor lost"). (71)

197. A splinter can kill an elephant.

198. You must do the decoration on a mud building before it dries.

199. Dog, you don't get a warning (? just a kick or a
stone).

200. Hawking strips of dried meat like a hyena--eat
them and have the money too.

201. A fire's been lit in two places--which will you
cook on?

202. Let's pray God that we may behold a dog with a
hyena slung on its back (i.e. an impossibility).

203. (?) A hawk setting its sights at an elephant, a
fly swooping on a large calabash-full (? excessive
greed).

204. "'Tis God and God alone" as the ground-squirrel
on the rocky hill said--he didn't dig his own hole,
but found a refuge.

205. "'Tis God and God alone" as the man said as he
sowed bran. "It may grow, it may rot, but by God's
grace the bran won't rot."

206. Wheat on a rock--God waters it and the Prophet
waters it too.

207. If your road lies among enemies, take it in the
name of God; whether there are thorns or not, God
will bring us through.

208. "I fear my head is inhabited" (?) as the wife of
the man with ringworm said.

209. If you're going to expel a guest, make sure he
takes his mat with him.

210. Roaming round with no work--the prevailing wind
of the hot season before the rains.

211. Quilted armour for a knight, worthy of a better
     fate than to be carried round on a salesman's
     shoulder! (109)

212. It may not be for a century--but it's reached a
     hundred days!

213. Going round and round the subject--like weaving
     a basket.

214. A waste of time--like locusts arriving at Garko
     during the dry season. (43)

215. The farmer lives a lie--the answer to weeds is
     (not hoeing but) the dry season.

216. The seedling that has God's favor will grow even
     if it's not watered.

217. The prisoner who has escaped doesn't fear the dark.

218. The month of the Festival--season for gazing at
     spectacles.

219. Even if God rejects the prayer of the man lancing
     the abscess, it'll still burst of its own accord.

220. Twice futile is the marriage where there is no
     affection.

221. "I'm too busy" means you're looking for someone
     who isn't.

222. (Repetition of 123.)

223. An invitation to partake of tuwo gives more
     pleasure than the actual eating of it.

224. Useless work's better than sitting idle--as the
     hyena said.

225. May God guide the monitor to the haulm--even if he doesn't eat it, he can make his bed in it.

226. A big farm is an insurance against having to buy corn next year.

227. However severe the dry season it doesn't prevent the silk-cotton tree from sprouting.

228. If the world were just, the spindle would not be left naked.

229. A cheap article is bound to have some flaw in it.

230. Pawpaw tree--whoever climbs you falls!

231. If I think little of a chicken, then I won't even want to drink broth made from it.

232. Earthenware basin--too heavy for a peg in the wall!

233. Even if a medicine won't go down the throat, it'll pour on to the floor!

234. What does a Gwari want with a husband? "Father'll do" says she. (96)

235. The green (of)------*, which draws angry glares from those who are unclothed. The old woman may see you, but has to pass a cold night.

236. The old hyena, who grabs at things without getting up.

237. I haven't even made an opening bid for it--let alone been prevented from buying it by the high price demanded.

238. Glares are not blows--let the eye do what it will, it has no effect.

---

*Madarunfa?

239. It's the pitcher that wanders abroad--you'll always find the storage pot in the hut.

240. Stupidity--like trying to put a halter on a duiker.

241. Pound in the hut, winnow in the hut (ABR "It's purely the concern of the family circle").

242. Liberally dipping out corn, liberally measuring out corn (ABR "said of generous market woman").

243. "I won"--boxing against a leper! (a walkover).

244. Snatching dum-palm fruit from the hand of a leper is nothing to make a fuss about.

245. Even if you have a charm to deflect arrows, you'll dodge as well.

246. Once and for all--like a Malle* man getting the tattooing on his temples done (? presumably they have heavy marking).

247. The same king who gave the guinea-fowl her markings also gave the bush-fowl hers.

248. If it weren't for the night, the mouse (rat) wouldn't get any further than the guest's loincloth.

249. It's the man with meat who wants the grilling fire. (71)

250. **Stepping on cattle excrement, wet inside, dry outside.

251. Hot temper won't achieve the paying back of a malicious trick. (57)

---

*Reading Malle for malle.
**Cf. the Nupe kirari in I/LXV.

252. I despise the boxing skill of a blind man, even when he clenches his fists (same as 187).

253. When the elephant gets up, the man with the dog looks at her from a respectful distance.

254. The time when the bats come out is not the time when the crows come out.

255. Haste--like the fellow who had a bundle of corn and said "Give me some gravy" (without any of the many intermediate steps in the preparation of tuwo). (71)

256. Young monkey! Your tail is the same length as the tails of your elders!

257. Festival-time is dressing-up time for everyone.

258. Meddlesomeness--no affair of yours.

259. A covered wooden bowl attracts many eyes.

260. (?) Syphilis, cure for the mother of twins!

261. (?) A relative of a relative, like the creeper garafuni* and the fence (i.e. connected by circumstance rather than by relationship).

262. Think little of the size of the baobab tree--the bagaruwa** is worth more. (9)

263. Give a stranger some water if you want to hear what he has to say.

264. One's thoughts only turn to tobacco after one has had one's fura.

---

*Momordica balsamina.
**Acacia arabica.

265. One <u>sees</u> the article before one buys it.

266. If what is being discussed doesn't concern you, don't interfere.

267. A basket full of thorns doesn't get sat on.

268. Impatience is what makes a maid lose her virginity before she is married.

269. A leper's a bad guest.

270. Fouling your own nest, like a chicken. (37)

271. Communal work gets the job done quicker.

272. We'll put <u>one</u> day aside to help with the communal work (ABR "we'll try anything once").

273. Thank God--which is better than thanking an in-law.

274. However pleasant <u>gumba</u>* may be, <u>nakiya</u>** is pleasanter

275. Incessant copulation, like when the wizard got married (if my translation is correct, I think the point here is the double meaning of <u>ci</u>, viz. copulate and bewitch--but it also means a myriad of other things).

276. The hawk doesn't employ a charm--he just keeps on hovering (but you would--ABR "Nothing is obtained without effort").

277. Wheat on a rock--you're watered by God (cf. 206).

277a. The envious man still sleeps, but not by the wish of his enemies.

---

*Pounded millet and water.
**Sweetmeat made from flour, honey and peppers.

278.   (Practically a repetition of 245.)

279.   Impatience is what makes a maid lose her virginity prematurely. If she is patient, she'll dispose of it properly.

280.   What was far off has come near--the pains in the hyena's joints have reached his neck (?).

281.   The snake's head is battered, but they've left its tail still moving.

282.   A throat with a goiter can't escape supporting it.

283.   (?) Picking out with the fingers or ladling out, both have the same mother.

284.   The game that gets killed by the hunt hasn't heard the drums of the hunt.

285.   Seeing isn't eating--or the dog would be replete.

286.   You may speak truth to a fool when you're joking.

287.   Shame belongs to the eye--not to the back of the head.

288.   Thresh in the hut, winnow in the hut (cf. 241).

289.   If you lay by that which you want--that's pleasure; if you lay by what you don't want--you lay by nothing.

XVIII
Muslim Legends

Moses said "My Lord, God, I am in fear of the punishments of the grave," and again "I am in fear of the
pains of death," and again "I am in fear of taking my
place in the crowd at the last judgment."

God said "Moses, I will give you the remedies for
these fears. I command you to perform the mid-morning
prayers*, for they are the remedy for the punishments
of the grave. I command you to perform the prayers
twice between sunset and the last prayers at night--
these are the remedy for your fears of taking your
place in the crowd at the last judgment. And I command you that when you pray in the middle of the night,
as you perform the prayers, prolong your standing as

---

*Presuming luha = walha.

303

you recite from holy writ. Then when you clasp your
knees (?), prolong your obeisance; and when you touch
the ground with your forehead, then too prolong your
obeisance--these are the remedies for the pains of
death."

MOSES AND SATAN (III/XXXII)

The prophet Moses met Satan with five donkeys, laden
with goods. Says Moses "Satan, where are you going to?"
He answered that he was away hawking his hide-bags of
stuff. Says Moses "What's in them?" Says Satan "The
donkey in front has oppression in his; I'm taking that
to the rulers; the second donkey has pride in his--that
I'm taking to the sons of rulers; the third one has envy
in, and I'm taking that to the malams; the fourth donkey has hatred in, and I'm taking that to a rich merchant;
while the fifth donkey has 'Had-I-but-known" in--that
I'm taking to women."

THE DOVE, THE HAWK AND MOSES (II/CVI)

Once a dove entered the right sleeve of the gown of the
prophet Moses, at the same time as a hawk entered his
left sleeve.
        Said the dove to Moses "I pray you in the name of
God and of the Messenger of God, preserve me from that
hawk, which says that it will kill me and eat my flesh
and drink my blood. But if he kills me here, in the
sleeve of your gown, God will judge between us on the
last day.
        But the hawk said to Moses "I pray you in the name
of God and of the Prophet of God, that you do not keep
me from my property, which I have sought under God's
heaven for seven years, seven months, seven days and
seven hours. For if you keep me from it, and I die of
hunger here, in the sleeve of your gown, God will judge
between us on the last day."

Moses was at a loss for words, for, considering,
he saw that they both spoke truly. At length he said
to the dove "Well now--come out, and go to the hawk
here that wants to kill you. Thus your blood will be
on his head, and when he has killed you, you will turn
into one of the birds of paradise."

"I won't" said she. "Why did you run away when
Pharaoh was after you? Why didn't you stand so that
he could kill you? If you had died, you would have
turned into one of the men of paradise."

And Moses acknowledged that she spoke truly, and
said to the hawk "Well, hawk, come out and take this
knife and cut off flesh from my body and eat your fill;
and drink of my blood till you are satisfied."

Then said the hawk "I'll not eat of your flesh nor
drink of your blood. For I am not a hawk, and nor is
that one a dove. I am Michael, and that one is Gabriel,
and God has sent us to come to you, and, reaching you,
discover if you were a man of forbearance. Now we have
come and we have found that you are such a man." Then
they both vanished. This with peace.

THE PROPHET SOLOMON AND THE OWL (III/XXIII)

In the days of the prophet Solomon, to whom God gave
dominion over spirits and jinns and birds and horses,
once at night he was lying down in his hut, when an owl
came and alighted on top of the prophet's hut, and began
pulling out the thatch of the hut with his beak.

Then said the wife of the prophet Solomon "Husband,
do you hear there's something moving on top of the hut?
Therefore, if God brings us safely to the morning, you
must have all the birds summoned, and slaughter them,
and make us a hut from their feathers." But he said
"No! For how could I bear the responsibility of all
those lives?" But she persisted that he should make
them a hut in that way, and at last he said "Very well--
God bring us safely to morning." "Amen" said she.

But the owl had been listening, right from the time
when the prophet Solomon's wife first began talking, to
the end of their conversation. Then the owl flew off.

Next day when it was light, the prophet Solomon
sent a messenger to the birds, to the marabou-stork;
to the pelican; to the crested-crane; to the greater
bustard; to the lesser bustard; to the large black and
white stork; to the sacred ibis; to the hawk; to the
kite-hawk; to the kwarikwakko*; to the Senegal fire-
finch; to the glossy starling; to the spotted weaver-
bird; to the scarlet bishop-bird; to the black-headed
weaver-bird (or lesser hammerhead); to the racquet-
tailed, purple-rumped sunbird; to the heron; to the
cattle-egret; to the crow; to the speckled pigeon; to
the common pigeon; to the dove; to the griffon; to the
vulture; to the rhinoceros-bird (?); to it's larger
brother; to the sambona'i**; to the tawny-flanked wren-
warbler; to the black-bellied bustard; to the lily-
trotter; to the whistling teal; to the goose; to the
ostrich; to the Bateleur eagle; to the bush-fowl; to
the guinea-fowl; to the night-jar; to the Abdin's stork--
to all the birds of the world. The prophet Solomon summoned them all and they all alighted on the ground.

Then word was brought to him, saying "The owl hasn't
come." "Let someone go and summon her" said he. So
someone went and told her "Owl, the prophet Solomon has
summoned all the birds of the world, and they have all
arrived--except for you." Then she went along and came
before him.

Then said the prophet Solomon "Owl, what is the
reason that when I brought together all the birds, and
they all came, you didn't come--not until I had sent a
messenger three times." "Prophet" she answered, "I am
deeply sorry, but the reason that I took a long time in
this way is that I had guests, and they were quarrelling
and it looked as though they were going to fight, and I

---

*Also called ɗan sarkawa (English not known).
**Also called tsita, for which BARG gives no specific
  English name, said to be a very small, grey-green
  bird (Fulani gainel).

stayed to hear the quarrel." "What did you hear them
quarrelling about?" asked the other. "Well, prophet
Solomon--one of them said that a woman had given him
resourceful counsel, but the other said to him 'No, my
friend, don't allow yourself to accept the counsel of
a woman. A woman's counsel is not to be followed. If
you do follow it, you're usurping to yourself heavy
responsibilities from God, our Lord, to kill someone or
to allow him to live--no, it is God that gives one life.'"
She finished "There now, prophet Solomon, now you've
heard what the people were quarrelling about." Says the
prophet Solomon "Yes, owl, you have surely had guests"
and he went on "I was going to kill you all, but now,
owl, fly away. For a woman's counsel is no counsel.
Your guest spoke truly, that anyone who follows the
counsel of a woman will perish. But you must say nothing
of this to anyone! Be off!" And the owl flew away.
Then the prophet Solomon said "Go and tell the birds,
every one of them may fly away home." And they flew
off after the owl, flapping their wings against her and
asking her what had passed between her and the prophet
Solomon.

   And that is why the owl doesn't go out during the
day--only at night. If she comes out in the daytime
and one of the birds sees her, he'll come after her,
beating her and crying at her. But it's not just crying
that he is doing, he's calling the others to come and
seize the owl and question her about what passed between
her and the prophet Solomon. And even today, if any
birds see an owl, she'll only escape by getting into a
hole in a tree. And that is the end of what I know of
that story. That's all, I've told you.

THE PROPHET SOLOMON AND THE JINNS (II/CV)

In his time the prophet Solomon was given by God the
rule over spirits and jinns and horses.

   One day he had set off to war. He had mounted in
the morning after he had performed the pre-dawn prayer.
And from the time he mounted, from early morning, until

it was well past noon, white horses kept coming forth
(?). And, looking, he saw that he had been so pre-
occupied with the horses, that the time of the afternoon prayer had just passed without his performing the
prayers.

Then he commanded the angels to hold the chains
of the sun, till he had performed the prayers. And they
did so while he prayed.

And afterwards he said to his people "Let every
man kill his horse, since these horses so occupied my
attention, that the time for prayer nearly passed without my performing the prayers. Every one of you kill
his horse, and let the townspeople too cut down theirs."
And so they killed all their horses.

Then he ordered "Let every man, when he would go
forth to war, take his bed, get on it and be seated.
The spirits will take us to war, and bring us back again."
Obediently they all took up their bedding, their woollen
blankets, and got on to them. And the spirits took them
to war and brought them home again. And so it continued.

He returned home. And he took some jinns to his
farm, and there they were working for him. And taking
his staff he set it up in the farm. Now the jinns thought
that it was the prophet Solomon himself there. And even
when he died, forty years passed and they went on working
the farm, not knowing that he had died. For there was
the staff, which they could still see in the farm.

Presently along came a termite and ate through the
staff, which toppled over. And the jinns saw it and
came over. Said the termite to the jinns "Oh, didn't
you know, the prophet Solomon is dead. He's been dead
this last forty years!" "Well, termite!" said the jinns,
"We certainly thank you, and now we will make you a
promise: wherever you build, we'll bring you water."

And that's the reason why, wherever termites have
built, you'll find moisture. It's the jinns that have
brought them water, just as they promised, and they
still do so even today.

THE BUILDERS OF THE KA'ABA (II/CX)

First, the angels. Second, Adam. Third, Abraham.
Fourth, Qoreish. Fifth, Abdullah, son of Zubair.
Sixth, Hajaj, son of Yusuf. The length of the building
is fourteen cubits, and the breadth, thirteen cubits.

THOSE WHO SHALL NOT DIE (III/XXXIX)

Among the prophets, these are they--five of them--who
are alive to this day. First, Idrisu, he's in Paradise,
he hasn't died. Second, Haliru, he's in the river--he
hasn't died. Third, Yunisu (? Jonah), he's inside the
fish, and he hasn't died. Fourth, Ilyasu, he's in the
mountain and he hasn't died. Fifth, Isa (Jesus): he's
between heaven and earth, and he hasn't died.

SOME WORDS OF ALI, THE COMPANION (II/CXII)

These are the words of Ali, who had them from Muhammad.
    He who fasts on the ninth day of Muharram, that
which is called "Ashura'a", to him shall God give the
rewards of ten prophets. Firstly, the prophet Adam,
who repented on that day and was forgiven by God.
Secondly, Idris, who was exalted to a place of honor
on that day. Thirdly, the prophet Noah, who was preserved from the Flood on that day. Fourthly, the prophet
Solomon, who was restored to his throne on that day.
Fifthly, the prophet Job, who was delivered from his
ills on that day. Sixthly, the prophet Joseph who was
taken from the well on that day. Seventhly, the prophet
Moses, who with his people was delivered from Pharaoh on
that day. Eighthly, on that day God created ten things
of glory: first, the Heavens; second, the Throne;
third, the sky; fourth, the earth; fifth, the writing-
board (slate); sixth, the pen; seventh, the beasts;
eighth, the rivers; ninth, paradise; tenth, fire and
rocks.

A KING AND THE MEN OF CHINA (III/XXXVIII)

There was once a king called Dhu'l Karnain (the one
with the horn*), who came to a place called China. And
he found that the men of China had five characteristics:
they had no king, no one who was ignorant, no paper,
no paupers, if a man died he was buried at the entrance
of the hut, and their temples** were far from their
homes.

Then he asked them their reasons for being thus,
listing these things one by one. And the men of China
answered him "We have no king, in order to prevent
oppression--and so there is among us, no oppressor;
there is no one who is ignorant among us, for we do
not lie with our wives, saving only on a Friday, a
Monday or a Thursday; the reason why we have no paupers,
is that we are not envious of one another; the reason
why we make our graves at the entrance to our huts is
that each day, when we leave the hut and see the grave,
we may remember death; and the reason we make our
temples far from our homes, is to prevent our carrying
on the traffic of life close to the house of God."

WOMEN WHO HAVE DESTROYED THEIR
COMPANIONS (III/XLI)

The prophet Adam was turned out of Paradise and sent
to earth--because of woman. Habilu (Cain) killed Abel
(Kabilu)--that was the sons of Adam--because of woman.
The people of the prophet Lot were destroyed--because
of woman. Salihu's female camel was stabbed--because
of woman. God destroyed the men of Ada--because of
woman. Haruta and Maruta, angels of God were given the
punishments of hell--because of woman. The prophet

---

*The parenthesis is the scribe's--this is, of course,
  Alexander the Great.
**The H. is also the word for "mosque".

Solomon was removed from his throne for forty days before being restored--because of woman. The prophet David was caused great trouble--because of woman. The prophet Zakariya killed Yahaya--because of woman. Hamza was killed--because of woman. The prophet Joseph was imprisoned--because of woman. Ali(yu), Commander of the Faithful, was killed--because of a woman. God reproved the Prophet Muhammad--because of woman.

THE ANGEL GABRIEL (III/XXVI)

Here's an account of the visits that the Angel Gabriel made to the Messengers, when God sent him to tell them not to do something, or to do something. He came to Idrisu eleven times. Gabriel came to Noah twenty-three times. He came to Abraham forty-eight times; to Joseph, four times. To Shu'aibu he came seven times. To Moses Gabriel came four hundred and eighty times. To David, six times. Two hundred times Gabriel came to Solomon; to Isa (Jesus) thirty-two times. To Muhammad, Gabriel came a hundred thousand and twenty-four times. And he who preserves them (? keeps them in memory) shall have great reward: he shall not see the pains of Munkari and Wanakiri (Angels of Death); worms shall not eat the flesh of his body; neither shall the earth; nor shall a reckoning be made of him at the Day of Resurrection.

Through the blessed power of Muhammad and the blessed power of all these prophets that we have mentioned, Muhammad said "Four men have made Arabic into a clear utterance (?)--Abdullah, son of Umar; Abdullah, son of Zubair; Abdullah, son of Mas'ud; and Abdullah, son of Abbas."

Other than these, there were: Abubakar, Umar, Uthman, son of Afanu, Aliyu, son of Talib, Abdurrahman, son of Aufu, also the son of Ka'abu, and Zubair, son of Thabit, also Tanimuddari, and Mu'azu, son of Jabal. As well as those first four, these others also made the Koran their study.

This account is no fable nor idle tale, but is taken from the Hadiths of the Prophet.

THE CREATION OF THE WORLD (III/XXVII)

This is the order of the creation as God sent things
down. God created the world, and for seventy years it
was empty. Then God created the earth, and two thousand
years passed. After that God created the men of Atam,
and two thousand years passed; then He created the men
of Bahun, and two thousand years passed; after them God
created the men of Yahun, and another two thousand years
passed. Then God created the first jinns, and two
thousand years passed. Then He created the second jinns,
and two thousand years passed. After them He created
seventy Adams, each one of whom had a thousand years.
After them God created (another) Adam, and then the
world was set up, seven thousand years (? ago). I
obtained this account from the Hadiths.

THE PROPHET MUHAMMAD, THE HUNTER AND
THE GAZELLE (II/CIV)

A hunter once went into the bush and set his trap.
Then along comes a gazelle. Now it happened that she
had recently given birth to a young one, which she had
left, to come and feed. And the trap closed on her
foot.

    Presently along came the Prophet, and as he passed
by he saw the gazelle, who had been caught by her foot,
in the trap since morning. Says the Prophet "Hey,
gazelle, what's the matter with you?" Says she "Oh
Messenger of God, I came here to have my feed, and now
I have been caught in this trap ever since the morning.
And I have a baby at home wanting his milk. Could I
but get to him to give him his milk, I would return
here on my own feet for the sake of the Most Excellent
One."

    Whereupon the Messenger, son of Amina, said "Very
well, gazelle, but if I let you go now, I shall have to
answer for it to the man who set it. If I let you go,
will you really return again?" The gazelle answered

"I will follow my very footprints to come right back
here." So the Prophet released the gazelle's foot from
the trap. Now it happened that there were people there
who saw it.

And the gazelle went off to feed her son. Says
the young one "Mother where have you been away, grazing
today?" Says she "I was over there feeding, and a trap
caught my foot and held me, ever since morning. And
now it's because the Prophet released the trap that I
have been able to come. So drink up quickly, for I have
to go back. My lord is there, waiting for me." But
the young gazelle said "Be off then, mother, for I give
up my milk, for the sake of the Exalted, the Most Excellent, the Almighty, for the sake of Our Lord, son of
Amina, the first of men."

Then the gazelle retraced her steps and reached
where the Prophet was. Along comes the hunter, the
owner of the trap. Says he "Be off, gazelle, for I
resign this meat for the sake of the son of Amina, our
Messenger, the first of men."

Then the Messenger, the son of Amina, spoke, saying
"Hunter, may God grant you his mercy--but bring me your
quiver and bow that I may make prayer for you." And
presently the Prophet, the Messenger, the son of Amina,
said again to the hunter "Now go your way. Any beast
that you see, and which you point your weapon at, shall
be yours. None shall escape, for the sake of our
Father, Most Excellent, Almighty."

And the hunter took again his bow and his quiver,
and before long he laid low a bush-cow; and very soon,
again, a roan antelope; and after that, an elephant.

And moreover the hunter received salvation from
the Lord God, who is beyond and above all men. That's
all. This with peace.

THE COMPANIONS OF THE MESSENGER
OF GOD (III/XXVIII)

Abubakar, Umar, Uthman and Aliyu: Abubakar ruled for
sixty years and two months; Umar for ten years and ten

months; Uthman for twelve years and ten months; Aliyu
for four years and nine months. When Muhammad, the
Messenger of God died, these were they who succeeded
him.

XIX
Muslim Lore, Explanations and Precepts

THE WORLD (II/CVII)

This is how the world is: it is on the back of an
angel, who is on the back of a wilderness, which is on
the back of a bull, which is on the back of a fish,
under which is water, under which is air, under which
is darkness. And under the darkness is that which none
save only God knows. Finis.

THOSE WHOM GOD SHALL SEND TO
THE FIRE (II/CVIII)

Three there are whom God shall send to the Fire, even
though they sin not. First is the ignorant man, who,
till he dies, never asks what are the laws of God.
Second is the rich man, who, till he dies, never uses
his wealth to benefit another. Third is he who through
pride does not ask what is the will of God.

THINGS THAT YOU SHOULD HASTEN TO DO (II/CIX)

They are seven. First, repent while you are young and
leave off all the things that God forbids. Second,
hasten to pay off your debts, while you still have
life. Third, hasten to arrange the marriage of your
daughter, before she reaches puberty. Fourth, hasten
to inter him who has died. Fifth, to do honor to your
guest, to give him food and drink. Sixth, hasten to
drink water after the sun has set in Ramadan. Seventh,
hasten to give tithes from your wealth.

LIVING IN A METROPOLIS (II/LXXXII)

God has prescribed living in a metropolis for men--even
though there be scarcity of food there. God has prescribed the path of peace* for men--even though it be
a long one. God has prescribed that men should marry
maidens (virgins)--even though they are ugly.

THE GRIEVOUS THINGS OF THIS WORLD (II/LXXIII)

There are five of them. The death of a loved one. Loss
of wealth. Public abuse from an enemy. A lengthy fever.
An evil wife. We find all this in the Hadiths.

THINGS WHICH MAKE A MAN'S
FACE BLACK (II/LXXIV)

They are five. Childlessness. Miserliness. To be
rendered lame or blind by God. A propensity to mischief-
making. An evil neighbor.

------

*Or "the smooth way".

THINGS WHICH IMPROVE A MAN'S VISION (II/LXXV)

They are five. Anointing with antimony. Gazing into
the waters of a river. Anointing with perfume (or
incense). Gazing at a beautiful woman*. Gazing at
something of a vivid green.

THINGS WHICH MAKE A MAN'S
VISION WORSE (II/LXXVI)

They are five. Too much blowing up a fire. Gazing at
the sun. Drinking the milk of an old female. Lying
with an old woman. Eating forbidden things.

GOD'S CREATURES (II/LXXIX)

The sons of Adam thank God they were created sons of
Adam and not donkeys. Donkeys that they were created
donkeys and not dogs. Dogs that they were created dogs
and not wart-hogs. Wart-hogs that they were created
wart-hogs and not thieves. Thieves that they were
created thieves and not misers. Misers that they were
created misers and not infidels. Infidels that they
were created infidels and not·liars. For God's curse
is on all liars.

NINE SORTS OF PEOPLE IN THIS WORLD (II/LXXX)

Three whom you must love whether they love you or hate**
you--your father, your mother and your teacher. Three
whom you should love if they love you, hate if they
hate you--your wife, your slave and the king of the
town. Three whom you should hate whether they love
you or hate you--a thief, an immoral man and one who
betrays a trust.

---

*Cf. II/CII (No. 223).
**Or "reject".

WASHING CLOTHES (II/LXXVII)

If someone washes his clothes on a Sunday, he will
regret it and the clothes will be unblessed. But he
who washes them on a Monday--his clothes will be
blessed. If a man washes them on a Tuesday, they*
will be stolen or burnt in a fire or sunk in the river.
If he washes them on a Wednesday, he will soon die**.
But as for the man who washes his clothes on a Thursday--
God will bestow upon him wealth and position. The man
who washes them on Friday will have long life. But if
he does so on Saturday, he will suffer from some illness, and either die or endure prolonged ill-health.

THE INFANT IN ITS MOTHER'S WOMB (II/LXXVIII)

If God so wills it, the seed of a man will join with
the woman's ovary and become a slimy fluid for a period
of forty days; this solidifies, and another forty days
pass; this becomes a lump, and another forty days pass;
in the next forty days the bones are formed; then the
flesh is formed and covers the bones; then life is blown
into the fetus and it begins to move about in its
mother's womb. The blowing in of life takes ten days.
After this four months pass, and then God moves the
embryo forward in its mother's body, during the night,
to l e t her eat and drink. Then the period of months
is fulfilled and the child is born. Thus it is with all
God's creatures. Every one of them was for a time in
the womb. But there are twelve exceptions, which had
no mother: Adam was never in the womb, nor was Eve;
nor were the staff of the prophet Moses, the female
camel of the prophet Salihu, the ram of Abraham, the
sword of Ali, Paradise, fire, the world, the next world,
the heavens, the earth. This account is no fable or
story, for we have it from the Hadiths.

---

*The H. pronoun could refer to the owner.
**Or "the clothes will soon wear out".

DAYS ON WHICH HEADS SHOULD NOT
BE SHAVED (II/LXX)

Heads should not be shaved on a Thursday; on Fridays,
if evening has come, a man who shaves his head then will
die without delay, or have his head cut off. A woman
shouldn't have her head shaved on a Sunday; for if she
does, her husband will die. When the first of Muharram
is a Thursday, one should not have one's head shaved on
that day. If you do, you will soon die. Again, when
Sunday is the first of the month, or a Thursday the
twelfth, if a man has his head shaved on either of those
days, he will die within the year. And if Friday is the
first of the month or Wednesday the twenty-seventh and
a man has his head shaved on either of those days, he
will die within the year. Every month has four days in
it, on which heads should not be shaved. He who fails
to observe them will die. This account of the days on
which one should not have one's head shaved comes from
the Hadiths.

THE SCHOOL, THE SLAUGHTER-PLACE AND
THE COURT (I/XLIV)

There are three places where it is useful to stay--the
school, the slaughter-place and the court of a king.
    For if you are in a school, even though you're not
taking part in the lessons, you will benefit by hearing
talk of the Muslim religion. If you're by the slaughter-
place when an ox is being skinned, you'll pick up some
trifle of meat. And if you're at court, even though
you acquire nothing, you will gain in wisdom through
the conversation of the elders--for all people gather
at the court.

THE CAUSES OF POVERTY AND
FORGETFULNESS (III/XXIX)

The things that cause a man to become poor or forgetful
are eighteen. These are they: he who commits fornica-
tion, will not prosper; second, neither will he who eats
his food with dirt, not washing; third, he who lets the
back of his head lie (?) on the ground; fourth, he who
bites his fingernails; fifth, he who faces east when he
urinates or excretes; sixth, he who eats his tuwo, without washing his hands; seventh, he who bathes on a
Saturday or a Wednesday; eighth, he who urinates on to
ashes; ninth, he who mixes hot and cold, that is, he
who eats hot tuwo and then drinks water; or who excretes
in the heat of the day over a cesspit, so that the moist
air from the pit rises up against him and penetrates him;
tenth, he who sews his clothes while he is still wearing
them; eleven, leaving a spider's web on the wall; twelve,
one who spoils food by using his left hand; thirteen, he
who puts his finger into his wife's vagina, before
sleeping with her (but stroking with the hand is per-
missible); fourteen, he who goes to sleep in the evening;
fifteen, he who puts a rosary round his neck; sixteen,
he who eats during the day during the month of Ramadan;
seventeen, he who sews up a white gown with dark thread,
or he who sews up a dark gown with white thread; eighteen,
he who puts his trousers at his head and rests his head
on them, to go to sleep. This account is no fable nor
is it an idle tale--we have it from the Hadiths.

EIGHT SORTS OF MEN (II/XC)

The malam (learned man); the ignorant; the Muslim; the
believer; the hypocrite; the polytheist; the immoral;
and the infidel. A malam is he who has studied the
Koran and the writings of wisdom, and knows both. An
ignorant man is he who has studied the Koran, but not
the writings of wisdom. A Muslim is he who refrains
from devouring the wealth of others and from shedding

their blood. The believer is he who knows that there
is only one God and believes in the Day of Judgment.
A hypocrite is he who has studied the Koran and the
writings of wisdom, but continually breaks God's laws.
A polytheist is he who has studied the Koran and also
the writings of wisdom, but still practices fetish
worship. An immoral man is he, who has studied the
Koran and the writings of wisdom, but is still sexually
immoral. The infidel is he who knows nothing of God's
laws; nor does he perform the prayers to God.

SIX MEN WHO WILL NOT CROSS THE NARROW BRIDGE
ON THE DAY OF JUDGMENT (II/XCI)

First, the profiteer. Second, he who does not perform
the five daily prayers: early afternoon, evening, sunset, night and that before dawn. Third, the liar.
Fourth, he who rejects the friendship of his fellows.
Fifth, he who refuses to pay tithes from his wealth.
Sixth, he who, summoning his wife, sends her out to the
market.

THE DOG TELLS ITS BEADS (II/XCII)

How the dog makes prayer to its maker*. Then its
master* gives it food, it will eat it and say "My thanks
to thee, oh God, for that thou madest me the humblest
of all thy creation. May God have mercy on them that
pity me!"

THINGS THAT CAUSE PREMATURE DEATH (II/LXXXV)

They are four. Failing to empty one's bowels regularly,
that is complete evacuation. Second, omission of the
last, night prayers. Third, incessant copulation. Fourth,
tying a turban round one's head**.

---

*The same word in H. Perhaps I should have made it the
same in translation.
**? i.e. the responsibilities of high office?

MEN WHOSE PRAYERS GOD WILL
NOT HEAR (II/LXXXVIII)

God has said that there are three of these. First,
the man who eats what is forbidden. Second, he who
is continually slandering others. Third, he who is
envious of his brothers.

THE GUESTS OF THIS WORLD (II/LXXXIX)
(Bako connotes both "stranger" and "guest".
A further vagueness of this piece is that it
is genitivally connected with the following
words and "guest of a king" could mean that he
was staying with the king or was sent by the
king. Perhaps the main idea of "guest" is that
such is the responsibility of God, the Prophet,
etc.)

Such are five, nor is there a sixth. First, God's
guest. Second, the Prophet of God's guest. Third,
the king's guest. Fourth, Satan's guest. Fifth, your
own guest.
    That first one, God's guest, is a malam. The
Prophet's guest is a student of the Koran. The king's
guest is an oppressive official. Satan's guest is a
thief. And your own guest is the Angel of Death.

THE FINGERS OF THE HAND (II/LXXXVI)

The first belongs to the prophet Ali. The second to
the prophet Moses. The third to the Prophet Muhammad.
The fourth to the prophet Joseph. The fifth to the
prophet Noah.

HUSBAND AND WIFE (II/LXXII)

God only permits a husband to strike his wife on three
occasions. If a wife insults her husband, he is permitted to strike her. If she goes out without his
knowledge, he may strike her. If he is instructing
her in matters of religion, and she refuses to learn,
he is permitted to strike her. We find these details
in the Hadiths.

WOMEN (II/XXXI)

Hausa women, if they wish to follow the Way of God and
His Messenger, will be obedient wives. If one of these
dies, she will receive God's mercy. But if she does
not follow the Way of God and His Messenger, when she
dies, she will go to the Devil and be taken to the well
of fire. The one who is obedient to God and His Messenger, when she dies will be taken into the presence
of God and enter Paradise. As for the one that will be
taken to the Devil, to the fire, she is the one who
vexes her husband and fails to do what makes him content; she is the one who is always causing her husband
distress of mind. Her portion is the fire.
      But the woman who, when her husband instructs her
to do something, gets up and does it, without any sign
of reluctance; when she brings him water, kneels before
him to give it; and so too, when he asks her to bring
him fura; and so too when he asks her to bring him tuwo;
who from the day she first comes to his compound, never
runs off in a temper and leaves him; never commits
adultery; says the prayers, before dawn, after midday,
evening, sunset and after dark--that woman, when she
dies, the Devil won't get a glimpse of her. Even if
she must enter purgatory, God will make it light for
her. So now you know how things are for women! That's
all.

WHAT GOD HAS ENJOINED UPON WIVES (II/LXXXI)

Eight things. First, to guard her chastity. Second,
to guard her tongue, not to abuse her husband. Third,
to remain in her husband's compound. Fourth, to hold
fast to her husband's precepts. Fifth, to show a
pleasant countenance when she sees her husband approaching.
Sixth, if he goes out, to guard herself, not to hold
converse with any other man, and to guard his wealth.
Seventh, if her husband gives her anything, though it
be something small, let her rejoice and be pleased.
Eighth, let her show patience.

And if a wife does these eight things, day and
night, her husband must feed her, clothe her, house
her; nor may he abuse her or beat her--God has not
said*.

THE WIFE WHO MENTIONS HER HUSBAND'S
NAME (II/LXXXVII)

If she does so--unless it be of necessity--then the
curse of God is on her; and the curses of the Prophet
and the angels. Nor, if she is divorced, should the
marriage-payment be returned to her.

THE MODESTIES (II/LXXXIII)

There are ten in the world--a woman has nine, and a
man one. When you marry a woman and sleep with her,
and morning comes and she sees you clearly and you see
her clearly--then she has thrown three of them away.
Remain six. When she has born your child, she has
thrown three more away. Remain three. Then, on the
day she commits adultery with another, none remain--
not one.

---

*The last sentence appears to be corrupt.

THE MARRIAGE PAYMENT (II/LXXXIV)

There is dispute whether a father may spend the marriage
payment that he receives for his daughter. Well, God
has spoken and forbidden that any man--even a father--
touch a marriage payment. If a man do so in ignorance,
let him refund the amount and let him express his
repentance. Then he may be pardoned.

MEN AND WOMEN (III/XVII)

There are three sorts of men and three sorts of women,
and if the right sort isn't paired off with his fellow,
their marriage won't last. They are: the highly sexed
man (lit. "of bone"), the man of medium sexual inclina-
tions (lit. "of spleen" ?) and the man that is lightly
sexed (lit. "of flesh").

The man "of bone" is so called because of his extreme virility. If he gets an erection, he will be wild
until he can find somewhere to put it.

Whereas the man "of spleen", if he gets the opportunity, he welcomes it, and uses it when he gets it.
But if he doesn't, he is able to wait until the chance
comes.

But the man "of flesh", if he has to do with a
woman who is herself highly sexed, or if they marry--
they will quickly separate, for his lack of zeal.

As for the three sorts of women, first she with an
excessively developed clitoris: if she doesn't get a man
"of bone" as a husband, the marriage won't last.

The woman of medium sexual desire, (whose clitoris)
is neither much exposed nor deeply set in--the husband
for her is a man "of spleen". But if she doesn't get
one, marrying rather a man "of bone", the marriage won't
last. Nor will it, if she marries a man "of flesh".

As for a woman of little sexuality, whose clitoris
is set in deeply, unless she gets for a husband a man
"of flesh", her marriage won't last, that is to a man
"of bone". Nor will it to a man "of spleen". No, the

only man for her is a man "of flesh". If she marries
him, the marriage will succeed.

Nor does a woman want a man like a rooster, who
ejaculates very quickly and then gets up. No, she
doesn't like that.

Nor again, does a woman like a man "of bone", who
goes on and on at it for a long time, without getting
off. A woman likes a man to be moderate--not too hasty,
nor too protracted.

Nor again do women like a man to sleep with them
night after night without paying them attention. They
like copulation every night, even if only once.

However old a woman is, she will never dislike
sexual relations, though a man may grow tired and leave
a woman. But if a woman says that she doesn't want a
man to sleep with her, even if they go to the judge's
compound, the judge will not put her to the oath, for
she is not speaking the truth. It is, in fact, the man
who has rejected her.

All this is most certainly not a fable, but it is
veritably so and the truth. And if anyone denies it,
let him think calmly about it, and he'll see that it is
so in every detail. Moreover, if a man denies it, let
him read the words of wisdom, let him look in the Book
of the Hadiths, and he will see it. That's all. This
with peace.

MORE FROM THE HADITHS (III/XXXI)

It is no sin for a man to look at his wife's genitals,
even when he is sleeping with her. Nor is it a sin for
him to lick them with his tongue--it is not forbidden,
but it is disapproved of. And if one sleeps with his
wedded wife right until morning, and she gets water and
heats it and gives it to him so that he may wash--her
reward is great.

MEN AND WOMEN (III/XXXVII)

The Messenger of God taught his Companion, Aliyu, not to lie with his wife while looking at the sun. If he got a son* on that day, he would be a very small child.

And he enjoined upon him not to lie with his wife in the. open compound, looking at the stars. If he got a son then, he would be a thief.

Again he taught him not to lie with his wife, while in her menses, or while still not healed after childbirth. If he got a son then, it would be a leper, or a pustular leper.

Again he taught Aliyu that he must not lie with his wife by force, when she was unwilling. If he got a son then, he would be one who abused his parents.

Again he taught him not to lie with his wife within the hearing of others. If he got a son then, he would be an ignoramus, knowing nothing.

Again, that he should not lie with his wife, while looking at her genitals. If he got a son then, it would be one who sinned against God.

Again, that he should not lie with his wife on the eve of a Festival, or on the morning of the Festival. If he got a son then, it would be an evil child, a spiller of the blood of men.

Again, that he should not lie with his wife on a Wednesday. If he got a son on that day, he would be a rogue, a hater of God; a hater of the angels, both above and below, a hater of himself, and a hater of all men.

Again, that he should not lie with his wife on the first of the month. If he got a son then, it would be mad.

Again he taught Aliyu that he should not lie with his wife, while she was sleeping. If he got a son then, he would be a heretic.

Again, that he should not lie with his wife in the middle of the day. If he got a son then, there would be permanent enmity between the child and his father.

---

*Throughout this account, "son" might also be "child".

Again, that he should not lie with his wife with
excessive violence (?). If he got a son then, it would
be a prisoner (?)*.

Again, that he should not have intercourse with
her from behind. If he got a son then, the child would
be a liar.

Again, he taught Aliyu not to lie with his wife
and touch her genitals with his hand the while. If he
got a son then, the child would be a simpleton.

Again, he taught Aliyu that when he lay with his
wife, he should stroke her genitals, before reaching
her. If he got a son then, the child would love his
father and his mother.

Again he taught him to lie with his wife on a
Thursday or a Friday or a Monday. If he got a son then,
the child would be a malam, a king, a wealthy man or a
saint.

Again he taught him to lie with his wife on the
eve of a Friday. If he got a son then, the child would
be fortunate, or a brave warrior.

We have this account from the Hadiths of Ali(yu),
the Companion of Muhammad, the Messenger of God.

MARRIAGE TO AN OLD WOMAN (III/XXX)

Don't marry an old woman. Even though she gives you a
thousand dinars each day, don't marry her. She has ten
faults: first, you'll become less handsome (or possibly
"less virtuous"); second, you'll shorten your life;
third, you'll exhaust your strength; fourth, your virility will die; fifth, your muscles will atrophy; sixth,
don't be surprised at what she will give you; seventh,
she is lustful, that is wishful (for one) to sleep with
her (?); eighth, she is lazy, that is she has a worm in
her vagina; ninth, the moisture of her vagina is poison,
deadly, for which there is no remedy; tenth, her snoring
is poison. We have this account from the Hadiths.

————————
*Masajuni is Ar. rather than H., and a little unusual,
 I think. Perhaps majanuni "pixielated" might have
 been what was meant.

XX
Hadiths (Traditions of the Prophet)

In fact, it seems likely that many of these are not
Hadiths, but proverbs and sayings translated from
the Arabic, e.g. No. 14. The Hausa is in a markedly
Sokoto dialect.

HADITHS OF THE PROPHET MUHAMMAD (II/CII)

1. The essence of work is resolving to do it.

2. The only pleasant abode is where there is no war.

3. A man of wise counsel has a possession that will
   not spoil.

4. A promise is a debt.

5. It is a pleasant thing to pay a debt.

6. Strife is guile.

7. To live among other men is pleasant.

8. To live where there are no other people is torment.

9. Trust is true wealth.

10. One of the virtues of Islam is clemency.

11. Only he who has wealth has relatives.

12. In the field of war children inspire fear; at home, miserliness.

13. Living out in the bush is folly*.

14. Thrift is the half of food; love, of wisdom.

15. Much grief is the portion of old age.

16. A paucity of dependents makes this life an easy one.

17. First say "May peace be upon you" and then you may proceed to other greetings.

18. The child absorbs character with the milk that it sucks: suck from a quarrelsome woman, and you will be quarrelsome.

19. The prosperity of a child rests with its elders**.

20. To be good, work should be completed.

21. Religion is rightly practiced when one avoids eating forbidden foods.

22. No book is great that is not complete.

23. The most important thing to do is to avoid eating forbidden foods.

---

*= 280
**Cf. 96, 124.

24. To keep one's own money safely at home and go forth and beg from another is to deal oppressively.

25. If a man works for you for wages and you fail to pay him, that too is oppression.

26. It is thanks that God delights in.

27. Chastity in a woman, continence and avoidance of immorality--these are what God wishes.

28. Fasting is a shield against the fires of the next world.

29. Payment falls on the man who stands surety.

30. Clemency to a brother is wisdom.

31. The good character is the obedient one.

32. Youthful folly is kin to madness.

33. Women are Satan's trap. If he digs it, he catches every man.

34. Drinking alcohol is the greatest of sins that a Muslim can commit.

35. Drinking alcohol is the chiefest of sins that a Muslim can commit.

36. Who consumes the proceeds of oppression consumes coals of fire.

37. Only the ignorant lament death.

38. Fever is death's scout.

39. The heat of a fever is the red-hot fire of the other world.

40. A fever means a reduction in the torment of the next world.

41. Contentment is wealth that will not be consumed away.

42. To discharge a trust faithfully is to invite prosperity.

43. To betray a trust is to invite poverty.

44. Slumber prevents prosperity.

45. Immorality prevents prosperity.

46. The eye of every man pursues immorality.

47. The eye's immorality is--to look.

48. The dignity of Arabs is--their turbans!

49. Modesty is good for all men.

50. Modesty will bring prosperity.

51. A mosque is God's house.

52. Speech has a fault--falsehood.

53. Knowledge has a fault--forgetfulness.

54. Virtue has a fault--pride.

55. Religious observance has a fault--omission to perform it.

56. War has a fault--oppression.

57. Generosity has a fault--telling of it.

58. Wealth has a fault--miserliness.

59. Kingship has a fault--excessive pomp.

60. Looking has its fault--looking at the wives of other men.

61. Almsgiving has its fault--telling others of it.

62. Religion has its fault--selfishness.

63. The prosperous man has prosperity for his lot from the time he was in his mother's womb.

64. The wealthy man is he who observes others like himself.

65. The rogue has roguery for his lot from the time he was in his mother's womb.

66. If you would seek God's clemency, repent.

67. Friday is a pilgrimage for those who are crippled or blind.

68. Every man's pilgrimage is--to be without power.

69. A woman's pilgrimage is to obey her husband and protect her chastity.

70. To seek out what is lawful--that is the Jihad.

71. The death of a stranger is <u>shahada</u>* (i.e. = a death fighting for Islam).

72. For a malam to hide his wisdom, and not expound it to another, is forbidden.

73. He whose death is <u>shahada</u> will obtain merit.

74. He, at whose instance good has been done, shall be treated as if he had done it himself.

---

*Cf. 293.

75. He, at whose instance evil has been done, shall
    be treated as if he had done it himself.

76. He who gives others something to drink, shall him-
    self drink later.

77. Who speaks words of excellence shall obtain merit.

78. He who visits his brother in order to see* him
    shall obtain merit.

79. Cases where blood has been shed should have prior
    hearing in court.

80. The giving of alms begins with your brother.

81. The giving of alms lengthens the life of the giver.

82. The giving of alms forestalls an evil death.

83. The giving of alms privily will suppress the wrath
    of God.

84. Maintaining the ties of kinship will lengthen life.

85. If you eschew what God dislikes, you will escape
    the next world.

86. A man in the next world will be under the shade of
    the alms that he has given.

87. The giving of alms puts out the fires of God, as
    water extinguishes the fires of this world.

88. He who opposes the giving of alms incurs God's
    wrath.

89. He who sins, and then repents, shall be as if he
    had not sinned.

---

*The H. word may have some additional connotation.

90. Oppression is the darkness of the next world.

91. Excessive laughter kills a man's spirit.

92. Give food to every man alive*, and you will acquire merit, even though you despise (him).

93. Malams are the friends of God.

94. The love of God will consume all the strength of a Muslim.

95. Paradise is the home of those that have acted well.

96. The paradise of a child rests with its two parents.**

97. Paradise is the home of those who have modesty.

98. The Fire is the home of the miserly.

99. Requests made to God during the prayers will be accepted.

100. It is an obligatory duty to have an occupation whereby to obtain one's food.

101. That woman deserves the greatest respect, for whom a small marriage-price is given.

102. Believers are brothers to each other.

103. Believers will consort with other believers.

104. Call him a believer, who knows a thousand men and is known by a thousand.

105. Call him a believer, who is trusted by men; who does not covet their wives; or slander them; or spill their blood; or consume their wealth. He is a believer.

*Lit. "owner of liver", a translation of the Ar.
**Cf. 19, 124.

106. Call him a believer who is of excellent character.

107. Call him an evil man, who is deceitful.

108. A believer stands to others as does the head to the body.

109. The believer will have to consume but one spleen* (<u>sic</u>) in the next world.

110. But the infidel will consume seven spleens* in the next world.

111. Call him an evil man who consumes the wealth of others; spills their blood; slanders them; and covets their wives.

112. The believer's profit is a hundredfold--for the day is short, but the night is long.

113. Prayer is the sword of the believer.

114. The daily prayers are the light of the believer.

115. The world is the believer's prison, paradise the evil man's.

116. What the believer intends is the test of what he does.

117. What the infidel intends is the test of what he does.

118. The believer lives in anticipation of death: in the morning, he does not expect to see the evening, and in the evening he does not look to see the morning.

119. A believer's zeal is shown by his keeping vigil into the night.

---

*= "life", cf. 92, above.

120. Excellent character is the friend of a believer.

121. Wisdom is the believer's brother.

122. Knowledge is the believer's vizier.

123. Good deeds are the abode of the believer.

124. Whether or not things are easy for a son depends on his parents*.

125. Obedience is the believer's brother.

126. Patience is enjoined upon the believer--this is his chief warrior.

127. Modesty should be part of the religious man.

128. Acceptance of predestination is the part of the religious man.

129. Patience is the half of any task.

130. Patience is the half of wisdom.

131. The religious man is a respecter of persons.

132. The Muslim is the brother of other Muslims.

133. To be a Muslim is to cooperate closely with other Muslims.

134. Death mitigates sin.

135. It is an obligatory duty upon the Muslim to seek knowledge.

136. A Muslim should not spill the blood of another Muslim, or put him to shame or consume his wealth.

---

*Cf. 19, 96.

137. God has forbidden the wrongful taking of the wealth of Muslims, even as he has prohibited the spilling of their blood.

138. God loves the man who loves Him*.

139. God abhors the man who abhors Him.

140. He who is zealous to follow God is zealous in his own behalf.

141. The evil man is he who follows the desires of his own heart.

142. A man is compassed by the religion of his own nature.

143. The excellent man is he who wishes for his brother that which he wishes for himself.

144. Men are like those who use silver to build a house of gold.

145. Men without a king are like a hundred camels with no herdsman.

146. **Wisdom is the only basis for work of excellence.

147. **Let there be friendship towards other men.

148. He is wealthy who resigns his desires for the things of men, and retains only his desires for the things of God.

149. The true brother of every man is his own wisdom.

150. That which is coming is as if it had just come.

---

*Cf. 286.

**Probably one tradition: "The head of wisdom is good work and love towards others".

151. All things have an end, save only the kingship
of God.

152. Everything has its support; the support of religion
is the study of holy writ.

153. Whatever is consumed and intoxicates, is forbidden,
is contrary to religion.

154. Ye people all—you are shepherds!

155. Ye people all—God will ask from you an account
of that which he has entrusted to you to herd.

156. All men follow the religion of their ruler.

157. The first reckoning that will be made for the sons
of Adam in the next world is of blood spilt.

158. The first question that will be asked of the sons
of Adam in the next world is about the daily prayers.

159. The first thing that will be weighed of the works
of the sons of Adam is good character.

160. The first things that God takes away from worldly
people are their modesty and trust.

161. Friendship is an inherited thing.

162. Hatred is an inherited thing.

163. If a man desires something, if one shows him the
evil of it, he will not hear; if one tells him,
he will not hear.

164. If a man desires something, he loses his hearing
and his wits.

165. Prosperity lies in the head of a horse, evil in
the horse's hair (?). Journeying is half torture,
if you are on a horse; but torture itself, if you
are on foot.

166. The excellence of woman rests in her obedience
     to her husband.

167. Calamities will surely come if you summon them.

168. Fasting is half of patience.

169. Everything has its tithes: the tithes of blood-
     shedding are fasting.

170. God receives the prayer of him who fasts.

171. Fasting during the cold season is profitable for
     it cools the blood (?) (or perhaps merely...because
     of the cold).

172. Rubbing the teeth will increase a man's eloquence.

173. The better a man at speaking, the better will be
     his life*.

174. A king acquires merit from the good deeds of his
     subjects.

175. A king incurs sin from the evil deeds of his
     subjects.

176. Muezzins will have longer sufferings than other
     men in the next world.

177. Muezzins are God's trusted.

178. Muhammad alone is the salvation of the doers of
     evil deeds, in the next world.

179. God's benevolence is upon men.

180. Silence is speech to a wise man.

-----

*Or, possibly, vice-versa.

181. Prosperity seeks out a man--even as death seeks him out.

182. A farmer is more useful than a trader.

183. A wealthy trader is a stone (rock).

184. A wealthy trader will acquire merit for his prosperity (wealth).

185. The good angels are those whom God has ordained to bring rain.

186. The bad angels are those who refuse rain.

187. The shame of this world is a small thing compared with that of the next.

188. The grave is a stage of the stages of the journey through the next world.

189. It is better to be patient and to take from your wealth and to give alms.

190. If you have female children and they die and you bury them--this is a relief for you.

191. The mortal span allotted the men of these times is between sixty and seventy.

192. The hypocrite--God will send him to the Fire.

193. He who swears falsely in God's name has his home in the Fire.

194. The liar shall obtain the profits of his false-hood--the world.

195. An oath with solemn intent by one who knows what God is is sufficient, even though no Book is available.

196. It is evil to fail to greet one's brother.

197. Knowledge not used is as wealth not used.

198. He who feeds the hungry acquires merit.

199. The mosque is the house of those that fear God.

200. What divides the infidel from the Muslim is the daily prayers.

201. Saying the prayers seated acquires half the merit of saying them standing.

202. Women's perfume--revealing what she is like, hiding her smell (?).

203. Men's perfume--revealing both his smell and what he is like (?).

204. Throwing away profits (?)--as children will, at play.

205. Lives joined are like wars.

206. He who denies a statement, argues.

207. He who denies a statement, thinks that he has the truth.

208. Falsehood is profit.

209. The Koran is wealth.

210. One only acquires wealth the once.

211. The religious man is never unhappy.

212. To flee the world is profit.

213. He who desires worldly things will have unhappiness.

214. Wealth is harmful to the man who is not religious.

215. The malam and the pupil both acquire merit.

216. Something entrusted to a man is at his discretion until the day that it is again taken from him.

217. A child is the woman's responsibility.

218. It is lawful that a stranger be given food at his lodging-place.

219. It is forbidden for food to be given by one from the same town to a fellow townsman.

220. Give to a beggar, even though he comes on a horse.

221. No disease is harder of treatment than miserliness.

222. He who gives a present and later takes it back is as a dog that vomits and returns to its vomit.

223. Gazing at a beautiful young woman improves the eyesight*.

224. Wearing a dark turban improves the eyesight.

225. Muhammadu's people exceed all others in brightness, in the next world.

226. **He who performs the ritual ablutions shall shine brightly in the next world.

227. A woman's rosary is to fold her hands (in obedience to her husband).

228. A man's rosary is to say "Praise be to God!".

*Cf. II/LXXV.
**Cf. 458.

229. There is no more deadly poison in the hands of Iblis*--it dwells in three things: a woman, a horse and a house.

230. The two greatest blessings men can have are wealth and health.

231. The bitter pains of purgatory will be the lot of the Arabs.

232. Despite and anxiety and scorn--these are the lot of him whom God loves.

233. He who would escape the misfortunes and the ills of the world, let him give alms.

234. The most amenable son is he who resembles his father.

235. The most amenable man is he who performs good works.

236. He who does good in this world will benefit in the next.

237. The most truthful of men is the best loved of God.

238. Kings are the shade that God has given his land to protect those that are oppressed.

239. A word that a man speaks has life, for good or for ill.

240. To speak truth, to keep trust and to do good-- these are the half of prophethood.

241. Prophets are the friends of God**.

---

*Transposing the semi-colon to after <u>Ibilis</u>.
**Cf. 93.

242. Malams are the light of the world, and to live with them is beneficial.

243. He who eats his fill of forbidden food is as he who clothes himself with grass.

244. You should wash your hands before eating food.

245. Eating food without washing hands brings poverty.

246. Washing hands after food improves the sight.

247. The curse of God is certain for that judge who conceals the truth in return for a present.

248. The judge who speaks the truth for God's sake, will receive compassion.

249. The eyes of the rich merchant are on his wealth.

250. He who buys corn and stores it, praying that God will send a famine, so that he may sell it again-- his wealth is accursed by God.

251. The blessed of God is he who has a long life.

252. He who is not blessed by God dies while yet young.

253. The pains of purgatory are assured to him who leaves his family hungry while he has food.

254. There are three prayers that God accepts: the prayer of the traveller; the prayer for a child that parents make; and the prayer of him who is oppressed.

255. The prayer of the oppressor God will not receive.

256.   Of three judges, two have the Fire for their
       portion, one Paradise. The judge who has knowl-
       edge, but hides it in order to obtain money, his
       portion is the Fire; so too the judge, who is made
       judge though he has no knowledge, professing to
       have knowledge in order to obtain money; but the
       judge who has knowledge, and applies it as in
       God's sight, not for money, his portion is
       Paradise.

257.   There are two things that a hypocrite lacks--
       keeping silence for the sake of God (not for some
       wicked reason) and a knowledge of holy writ.

258.   There are two things that will not be found in
       the virtuous man--miserliness and evil.

259.   Two eyes will not be burnt by the Fire of the
       next world: the eye that weeps through the watches
       of the night for the fear of God; and the eye that
       closes not in sleep, watching lest an army come
       and kill the people.

260.   Two stomachs will never be filled: the stomach
       that hungers for a knowledge of holy writ, and
       the stomach that hungers for worldly things.

261.   An evil old man desires two things: long life
       and plenty of wealth.

262.   There are four men accursed of God: the trader
       who supports his falsehood with "By God"; the poor
       man who brings in the name of God, going up to
       some man who has a little wealth and saying "It
       is three days since there has been any food pounded
       in my compound--for God's sake help me"; the man
       who has grown old but not left off sexual immorality;
       and the evil king who eats of forbidden things.

263. Six men, three of whom God will destroy and three whom he will preserve: he will destroy the old man who sins against him; the man who follows his own selfish will even to sinning against God; the proud man who boasts that none are greater than he. Three people who shall escape the next world: he who fears God both secretly and publicly; he whom poverty has forced to resign himself to what is ordained; the rich man who acts justly.

264. He who farms on the edge of the bush is near destitution.

265. He who separates himself from other men, and goes off on his own, is near destruction.

266. He who feeds orphans shall eat in Paradise.

267. He who points with his finger at his brother sins against God.

268. Death is raiding among men at all times.

269. He who holds his tongue shall find salvation.

270. He who says that he is nothing in the eyes of God--him God will exalt.

271. But he who says that he is something--him God will belittle.

272. He who says that he is for paradise makes God a liar.

273. He who seeks pardon--him God will pardon.

274. He who seeks clemency from God--him God will pardon.

275. He who is patient in misfortune--God will give him his reward.

276.   He who exalts God--him God will exalt.

277.   Prosperity is at the direction of God.

278.   He who wastes his substance--him God will forestall.

279.   He who commits fraud--him God will grievously
       punish.

280.   Living out in the bush is folly*.

281.   He who pursues hunting is a fool.

282.   He who fixes his affection on the rulers of this
       world shall perish.

283.   He who is killed for (defending) his wealth--his
       death is shahada**.

284.   He who is killed for the sake of (? defending)
       his family--his death is shahada.

285.   He who is killed for his religion--his death is
       shahada.

286.   He who professes his love of God--him God loves[+].

287.   He who professes his love of God--let him defend
       God's religion.

288.   He who professes to love God--let him defend the
       rights of others.

289.   He who wishes to enter Paradise, let him be a
       doer of good.

---

 *= 13.
**See 71.
 [+]Cf. 138.

290. He who fears the Fire--let him desist from his evil desires.

291. He who fears death--let him cease enjoying the world.

292. He who would shun the world--let him avoid eating what is forbidden.

293. He who dies while away from his home acquires merit*.

294. He who ill-treats a slave--him God will ill-treat.

295. He who wears cloths and makes himself like a woman does not belong to the religion of Muhammad .

296. He who grows a moustache does not belong to the religion of Muhammad.

297. He who holds to the teaching of the Prophet will not take back a present that he has given.

298. He who delays--he may get his desire--or he may not!

299. He who sows good shall reap what he desires.

300. He who hastens--he may get it right--or he may get it wrong!

301. He who sows evil shall reap "Had I but known!"

302. He who knows God will never cease loving Him.

303. He who treats others with respect--God will respect him.

304. He who would that men should respect him, let him put his reliance on God.

*Cf. 71.

305. He who would not be overpowered by men, let him
      fear God.

306. He who wishes wealth, let him follow God.

307. He who is sorry for harm done--him God will forgive.

308. He who visits another, let him benefit him, even
      though only by a mouthful of _tuwo_.

309. He who wishes people to fear him, let him be silent.

310. He who is always talking will always be falling.

311. He who is always falling, will always be offending.

312. He who is always offending--him God will send to
      the Fire.

313. He who prospers in an occupation, let him continue
      in it.

314. He whom God has given prosperity, let him give
      thanks.

315. He who does not give thanks for small things,
      neither will he give thanks for great things.

316. He who gives respect to one of God's servants
      acquires merit.

317. He who gives food to a fasting man, to him God
      will give recompense.

318. He who gives respect to the Nation--to him God
      will give respect.

319. He who greets the one who has done him wrong
      acquires merit.

320. He who helps the man who has been oppressed--God will help him.

321. He who travels together with an oppressor is himself an oppressor.

322. He who behaves like any men has become one of them.

323. He who goes on a dark night to the mosque shall have illumination in the next world.

324. He who seeks knowledge of holy writ shall be given it by God.

325. He who is not benefited by his knowledge is harmed by his ignorance.

326. He who has done wrong, let him hasten to put it right.

327. He who becomes a judge cuts off his own head, though he uses no knife.

328. He who takes his occupation into the market place casts away pride.

329. He who desires something, let him zealously seek it.

330. He who says that the Prophet's saving power is false--he will* meet him on the Day of Judgment and then he will see.

331. He who does evil--do good to him.

332. He who fasts but takes forbidden foods, fasts in vain.

---

*Emending a-su to za su.

333. He who wishes to find himself a fine house in the
     next world, let him make improvements to it in this
     world.

334. He who wishes for respect in the next world, let
     him avoid violent desires in this world.

335. He who performs abundant prayers at night shall
     be of good countenance by day.

336. He who loves the world, makes worse his fate in
     the next world.

337. He who loves the next world, makes worse his lot
     in this.

338. He who belittles a king that is godly, shall be
     belittled by God.

339. He who gives respect to a king that is godly, shall
     be given respect by God.

340. He who sympathizes with people in their desires for
     what is good or what is evil, shares with them in
     their merit or in their sin.

341. He who seeks his defense from God--him God will
     defend.

342. He who seeks help from you in God's name--help him.

343. He who begs from you in the name of God--give to
     him.

344. He who calls you in God's name--answer him.

345. He who comes and visits you, when he departs,
     accompany him some way, though you give him nothing.

346. He who wishes you to know him, become acquainted
     with him.

347. If someone comes to your house by mistake (?), don't detain him, but send him on his way.

348. He whom God has granted long life is permitted sixty years* (?).

349. He whom the morning discovers without intent to oppress another, shall be pardoned by God.

350. If a man professes to like you, don't hide from him.

351. If a man does you evil, do him good.

352. If a man seeks pardon of you, pardon him.

353. He who fears God should fear what God has made.

354. He who fears not God, neither does he fear what God has made.

355. He who wishes to be joined with God is he with whom God wishes to be joined.

356. He who refuses to be joined with God is he with whom God refuses to be joined.

357. If a man asks you something that you know, tell it to him.

358. If a man knows the answer to a question put to him in the name of God, God has put a bit** of fire in his mouth.

359. He who has authority over you, let him be one that loves good works.

360. He who opens the door of virtue to other men, God will open a door for him in the next world.

---

*Transposing the comma to after rai.
**(i.e. curb).

361. A good man ought never to close the doors of goodness.

362. He who commits a great sin destroys his hopes of the next world.

363. He who hastens to eat food, let him give some to another.

364. That which you do not wish for yourself--don't wish it for your brother.

365. He finds a sure defense whom God defends.

366. He who errs over something that has been given into his safe-keeping, commits an error in this world and the next.

367. He who professes to love God, let him love God's people.

368. He who separates himself from other men ties a rope round his own neck.

369. He who separates himself from other men, loses his defender.

370. He who puts forth his hand to that which God has prohibited shall be without excuse in the next world.

371. He who, having separated himself from other men, dies, his death is the death of the ignorant.

372. He who wishes to dwell in Paradise, let him abide with God's people.

373. He who professes some occupation let him preserve it from evil.

374. He who preserves his tongue from slandering others and treating them with disrespect shall be preserved himself, by God.

375. He who is separated from his son in this world—
God will not allow him to have any pleasure on
the last day.

376. He who displays proudly that he is a Muslim (?)
shall have illumination at the Day of Judgment.

377. He who hastens to help a poor man—him God will
hasten to bring to Paradise.

378. He who ignores the poor shall not enter the shade
of God's throne.

379. He who is regularly double-tongued in the world—
him God will inflict with two tongues in the Fire.

380. He who looks at the book (? Book) of his brother
without his permission, him God shall cause to look
upon the Fire in the next world.

381. He who disciplines himself to goodness, him God
will cause to enjoy goodness in Paradise.

382. He who sanctifies God with heart and tongue for
forty days has God's approval.

383. He who professes to know God and to believe in
the next world, let him treat with respect a
guest (stranger).

384. He who professes to know God and the next world,
let him treat his neighbor with respect.

385. He who professes to know God and the last day,
let him not do wrong to his neighbor.

386. He who professes to know God and the next world,
if he is about to speak, let him speak what is
good, or keep silent.

387. He who trains another so that he follows God must enjoy Paradise.

388. He who helps his brother, him will God help in the next world.

389. He who neglects his brother, because he* enjoys wealth, professing not to know him--him will God neglect in the next world.

390. He who satisfies his brother's need shall have his own need satisfied by God.

391. He who clothes his brother shall be clothed by God in this world and the next.

392. God will help any servant of his who helps his brother.

393. He who builds a mosque, though it be but one cubit long--for him God will build a home in Paradise.

394. He who seeks knowledge and dies before attaining it, him will God give knowledge in the next world.

395. He who seeks knowledge and, getting it, dies, him God will reward in the next world.

396. He who waits for another to act, shall be deaf in the next world.

397. He who pursues the world at the expense of his chances of the next, shall not enjoy the next.

398. He who obtains knowledge, let him thank God.

399. He who hides knowledge has become an infidel.

---

*The H., I think, is not clear as to the antecedent; presumably the subject of the sentence.

400. He who has knowledge and guides his actions by
      it, let him thank God.

401. One of the sons of Abdul Muṭālib who was well-
      known in the world was predestined never to sin
      against God, and so has a place of honor in the
      next world.

402. He who does not betray the secrets of a brother
      who is dead, him will God clothe in his grave.

403. He who takes from his wealth and gives to God,
      him God will make wealthy, wherever he may be.

404. He who gives up all thought of this world shall be
      saved in the next.

405. He who praises others for sinning against God
      shall himself receive praise of others--in the
      Fire.

406. He who wishes God's approval, let him desist from
      sinning against other men.

407. He whom other men approve, is approved also of God.

408. He whom God approves, is approved also of men.

409. He who dies while engaged in good works shall
      obtain merit.

410. He who dies while doing evil is guilty.

411. Let no man give up hope of God's kindness.

412. He who sins against God in the world, him shall
      God bring to punishment.

413. God will never oppress his servants.

414. He who commits a great offence, let him hasten to repent.

415. He who never eats what is forbidden shall escape the punishment.

416. He who does not distinguish in his food between what is lawful and what is forbidden, but eats of everything indiscriminately--neither will God distinguish through which gate he will dispatch him to the Fire.

417. He who is punctilious with his prayers when he sees other men there, but, if he does not see them, does not pray--God will reveal his secret in the Fire of the judgment of the next world.

418. He who makes his prayers void--that is, while he is praying, shows disrespect, speaks, does something else or turns his back--him God will send to the Fire.

419. He who seeks after things that are not of God-- him God will consign to the Fire.

420. He who has inherited what is good or what is evil, on him God shall have mercy; that which is evil shall bring its reward, and that which is good shall do so likewise.

421. He who is blessed with virtuous subordinates shall enjoy shade--such as wives, or son, or slave.

422. He to whom God has given a hankering after women, or some other specious thing--for him a home is built in the Fire.

423. He who kills a living being, for no sufficient cause, his victim shall be brought (before him) on the Day of Judgment and will say "Behold the man that killed me for no fault of mine."

424. He who begs people for their wealth, shall be
sent by God to the Fire in the next world.

425. He to whom God has given three things, let him
give thanks for being set on the first step of the
road to Paradise--knowledge of holy writ, royal
office and wealth.

426. He who begs others for food when he already has
his own, eats poison.

427. He who comes to a meal, when not invited, is a
thief.

428. He who slanders his brother Muslim or sows mischief
between him and the king shall have no refuge in
the next world--the Fire is his lot.

429. He who, when the king is angry with a fellow
Muslim, begs him to spare the man for the sake
of God, and the king does so--God shall see him
safely over the Narrow Bridge.

430. He who plays with draughtsmen* shall play with
fire in the next world.

431. He who commits evil will be caught up by it in the
next world.

432. He who gambles and he who eats pork or drinks
blood shall be shackled, hand to neck, in the
next world.

433. He who is lodging with others (?), let him not
fast for merit, save only if it is the month of
Ramadan.

434. He who initiates a heresy, great destruction shall
ensue.

---

*The original Arabic word was perhaps more deserving
of such harsh condemnation.

435. He who harms a heretic shall increase his standing in God's eyes.

436. He who rises daily in fear of God, his body shall escape the Fire.

437. He who harms a Muslim--on him will God take vengeance.

438. He who is forgetful of God, then, turning back again, remembers him--him will God help.

439. He whom the people have chosen to exalt, let him not be oppressive to them.

440. He whom the people trust, let him not speak falsely to them.

441. He who treats others with grave respect shows his own sense of justice.

442. He who is endowed with the fear of God ought not to be kept hidden.

443. He who remains chaste, not committing immorality, and preserves his feet from following the path of sin against God, shall enter Paradise.

444. He who tells deliberate falsehoods has the Fire for his portion in the next world.

445. He who brings fear down upon men--him shall God debit with sin.

446. The likeness of Paradise is seen in those men who pay no heed to worldly desire.

447. The likeness of the Fire is seen in those with worldly desires.

448. It is your duty to love him who is wroth with you.

449. The rousing of men from the tomb shall be as the rising of locusts.

450. Help comes on the east wind.

451. The men of 'Ād* shall be destroyed by the east wind.

452. He who is surprised by God has lost his part in Paradise.

453. Your deeds are given you by your Lord, whether good or ill.

454. The rousing of men at the Day of Judgment shall be according to what were their intentions.

455. He who bears false witness, his tongue shall be long** in the Fire.

456. God will have mercy on the man who has a good tongue.

457. He who has a virtuous tongue, even though he obtains not (? Paradise), shall find salvation.

458. ⁺The mercy of God is on those who perform the ritual ablutions.

459. He for whom God has destined wealth, shall become wealthy.

460. God can enrich his servant wherever he will.

461. Falsehood brings bitter oppression in its train.

---

*Emending adawa to Adawa. The former (= "enmity") would make little sense.
**I.e. physically, not temporally.
⁺Cf. 226.

462. Hardness of heart shall make a man a pauper or an infidel.

463. He who gains the upper hand attracts envy.

464. God shall preserve him from evil who has knowledge of men.

465. Increase of years brings increased knowledge.

466. A believer shall be known by his character.

467. Be neither excessively nor insufficiently active.

468. Why did you start what you do not accomplish?

469. You seek what you don't know; and when you do know it, you don't perform it.

470. He who looks to tomorrow shall not be troubled by today.

471. I marvel at him who scrutinizes another, but does not scrutinize himself.

472. I marvel at him who seeks after the world while death is seeking him.

473. I marvel at him who is full of laughter, the while he is ignorant whether God approves of him or not.

474. I marvel at him who puts his faith in the house of falsehood, but forgets the house of truth.

475. I marvel at the believer who has not faith in the rule of God.

476. God will not judge a believer, except beneficially.

477. The Day of Judgment is at hand, and men have not yet made ready their provisions, except those for the satisfactions of their own desires.

Appendix

<u>Table of Cross References to the Hausa Edition</u>

1:, 2:, and 3: refer to the three volumes of this translation.

TATS	Page	TATS	Page	TATS	Page
I/1	2:51	I/37	1:279	I/73	1:297
I/2	2:191	I/38	1:279	I/74	2:470
I/3	1:3	I/39	1:280	I/75	1:97
I/4	2:191	I/40	2:447	I/76	1:297
I/5	1:58	I/41	1:252	I/77	1:252
I/6	1:5	I/42	2:447	I/78	1:99
I/7	1:8	I/43	1:159	I/79	1:408
I/8	1:407	I/44	2:469	I/80	1:161
I/9	1:10	I/45	1:176	I/81	1:225
I/10	1:289	I/46	1:97	I/82	1:409
I/11	1:227	I/47	2:51	I/83	1:14
I/12	1:157	I/48	1:294	I/84	1:410
I/13	1:69	I/49	1:160	I/85	1:71
I/14	1:240	I/50	1:243	I/86	1:72
I/15	2:65	I/51	2:469	I/87	1:277
I/16	1:290	I/52	2:448	I/88	1:100
I/17	1:182	I/53	2:449	I/89	2:218
I/18	1:89	I/54	1:183	I/90	2:431
I/19	1:158	I/55	1:209	I/91	2:222
I/20	1:59	I/56	3:243	I/92	1:73
I/21	1:184	I/57	1:258	I/93	1:299
I/22	1:11	I/58	2:52	I/94	1:6
I/23	1:278	I/59	2:196	I/95	1:91
I/24	1:279	I/60	2:196	I/96	1:302
I/25	2:215	I/61	1:179	I/97	2:53
I/26	1:222	I/62	1:259	I/98	1:410
I/27	1:178	I/63	1:179	I/99	1:411
I/28	1:251	I/64	1:180	I/100	1:162
I/29	1:381	I/65	1:295	I/101	2:450
I/30	1:293	I/66	1:189	I/102	1:207
I/31	1:13	I/67	1:295	I/103	1:243
I/32	1:241	I/68	3:248	I/104	1:246
I/33	1:242	I/69	1:194	I/105	2:197
I/34	1:257	I/70	2:196	I/106	3:110
I/35	2:447	I/71	1:224	I/107	1:280
I/36	2:52	I/72	1:204	I/108	1:247

TATS	Page	TATS	Page	TATS	Page
I/109	1:281	I/154	1:130	I/XXXVII	1:289
I/110	2:471	I/155	1:312	I/XXXVIII	3:114
I/111	1:303	I/156	1:61	I/XXXIX	3:248
I/112	1:260	I/157	1:17	I/XL	3:99
I/113	2:225	I/158	2:229	I/XLI	3:224
I/114	2:449	I/159	1:78	I/XLII	1:210
I/115	2:451	I/160	1:19	I/XLIII	1:206
I/116	2:54	I/161	1:169	I/XLIV	3:319
I/117	2:479	I/162	1:164	I/XLV	3:229
I/118	1:110	I/I	3:92	I/XLVI	3:255
I/119	1:74	I/II	3:65	I/XLVII	3:256
I/120	1:304	I/III	3:113	I/XLVIII	3:256
I/121	1:253	I/IV	3:95	I/XLIX	3:135
I/122	2:452	I/V	3:104	I/L	3:79
I/123	2:452	I/VI	3:107	I/LI	3:9
I/124	2:453	I/VII	3:150	I/LII	3:158
I/125	2:453	I/VIII	1:190	I/LIII	3:47
I/126	1:228	I/IX	3:57	I/LIV	3:7
I/127	1:306	I/X	3:80	I/LV	3:20
I/128	2:454	I/XI	3:230	I/LVI	3:81
I/129	1:75	I/XII	3:25	I/LVII	3:130
I/130	2:226	I/XIII	3:232	I/LVIII	*
I/131	3:262	I/XIV	3:102	I/LIX	3:249
I/132	1:98	I/XV	3:107	I/LX	3:249
I/133	1:242	I/XVI	3:61	I/LXI	3:20
I/134	2:472	I/XVII	3:101	I/LXII	3:19
I/135	1:308	I/XVIII	3:133	I/LXIII	3:236
I/136	1:309	I/XIX	3:134	I/LXIV	3:236
I/137	2:198	I/XX	3:70	I/LXV	3:238
I/138	1:310	I/XXI	3:125	I/LXVI	2:192
I/139	2:199	I/XXII	3:102	I/LXVII	3:258
I/140	1:276	I/XXIII	3:244	I/LXVIII	3:240
I/141	1:264	I/XXIV	3:229	I/LXIX	3:258
I/142	1:413	I/XXV	3:6	I/LXX	3:240
I/143	2:454	I/XXVI	3:129	I/LXXI	3:241
I/144	1:15	I/XXVII	3:119	I/LXXII	3:250
I/145	1:247	I/XXVIII	3:68	I/LXXIII	3:250
I/146	1:416	I/XXIX	3:3	I/LXXIV	3:250
I/147	1:77	I/XXX	3:23	I/LXXV	3:250
I/148	2:455	I/XXXI	1:181	I/LXXVI	3:251
I/149	1:229	I/XXXII	3:245	I/LXXVII	3:251
I/150	1:163	I/XXXIII	3:207	I/LXXVIII	3:251
I/151	1:129	I/XXXIV	3:55	I/LXXIX	3:251
I/152	1:311	I/XXXV	3:22	I/LXXX	3:252
I/153	1:16	I/XXXVI	3:221	I/LXXXI	3:252

*Not included.

TATS	Page	TATS	Page	TATS	Page
I/LXXXII	3:253	II/40	1:113	II/85	1:323
I/LXXXIII	3:254	II/41	2:390	II/86	2:333
I/LXXXIV	3:266	II/42	2:20	II/87	2:152
I/LXXXV	3:279	II/43	1:384	II/88	2:336
I/LXXXVI	3:253	II/44	1:386	II/89	1:80
I/LXXXVII	*	II/45	2:252	II/90	2:157
II/1	1:110	II/46	1:194	II/91	1:327
II/2	1:112	II/47	1:316	II/92	1:329
II/3	2:76	II/48	2:257	II/93	1:418
II/4	1:132	II/49	2:109	II/94	2:340
II/5	1:138	II/50	1:318	II/95	3:261
II/6	1:92	II/51	2:263	II/96	3:262
II/7	2:81	II/52	1:95	II/97	1:332
II/8	1:314	II/53	1:320	II/98	1:201
II/9	1:134	II/54	1:76	II/99	1:334
II/10	1:141	II/55	2:269	II/100	2:347
II/11	1:265	II/56	2:279	II/101	2:349
II/12	1:22	II/57	1:142	II/I	3:163
II/13	1:102	II/58	1:388	II/II	3:259
II/14	2:84	II/59	2:112	II/III	3:260
II/15	1:415	II/60	2:288	II/IV	3:266
II/16	2:85	II/61	2:297	II/V	3:257
II/17	2:92	II/62	2:132	II/VI	3:257
II/18	2:3	II/63	1:391	II/VII	3:258
II/19	2:93	II/64	2:299	II/VIII	3:258
II/20	1:141	II/65	1:26	II/IX	3:259
II/21	2:9	II/66	2:306	II/X	3:259
II/22	2:11	II/67	2:138	II/XI	3:240
II/23	1:24	II/68	2:143	II/XII	3:121
II/24	2:474	II/69	2:308	II/XIII	3:18
II/25	2:230	II/70	3:41	II/XIV	3:27
II/26	1:315	II/71	1:321	II/XV	3:27
II/27	2:238	II/72	1:41	II/XVI	3:163
II/28	2:480	II/73	2:314	II/XVII	3:169
II/29	2:245	II/74	2:146	II/XVIII	3:26
II/30	1:24	II/75	2:318	II/XIX	3:14
II/31	2:96	II/76	2:321	II/XX	3:16
II/32	2:14	II/77	2:22	II/XXI	3:17
II/33	1:103	II/78	2:323	II/XXII	3:167
II/34	2:66	II/79	2:149	II/XXIII	3:31
II/35	1:185	II/80	1:266	II/XXIV	3:62
II/36	1:196	II/81	1:115	II/XXV	3:64
II/37	2:72	II/82	2:130	II/XXVI	3:170
II/38	2:100	II/83	2:151	II/XXVII	3:186
II/39	2:104	II/84	1:144	II/XXVIII	3:29

*Not included.

TATS	Page	TATS	Page	TATS	Page
III/52	2:392	III/97	2:173	III/142	1:108
III/53	1:166	III/98	1:361	III/143	1:127
III/54	1:347	III/99	1:52	III/144	2:426
III/55	2:483	III/100	2:293	III/145	1:151
III/56	2:329	III/101	1:350	III/146	1:55
III/57	2:459	III/102	1:363	III/147	2:178
III/58	1:83	III/103	2:414	III/148	1:368
III/59	1:202	III/104	1:106	III/149	1:153
III/60	1:348	III/105	2:486	III/150	1:67
III/61	1:36	III/106	2:176	III/151	1:87
III/62	1:429	III/107	2:434	III/152	2:126
III/63	2:484	III/108	1:46	III/153	2:194
III/64	2:397	III/109	1:249	III/154	2:491
III/65	2:462	III/110	2:201	III/155	1:261
III/66	2:433	III/111	2:34	III/156	1:369
III/67	2:205	III/112	1:395	III/157	2:493
III/68	3:244	III/113	1:121	III/158	2:494
III/69	1:395	III/114	1:397	III/159	2:38
III/70	2:484	III/115	2:442	III/160	1:430
III/71	1:283	III/116	2:180	III/161	3:263
III/72	1:394	III/117	1:50	III/162	1:371
III/73	1:170	III/118	1:351	III/163	1:372
III/74	1:383	III/119	2:204	III/164	1:431
III/75	1:177	III/120	1:147	III/165	1:231
III/76	1:173	III/121	1:123	III/166	1:373
III/77	2:192	III/122	2:420	III/167	1:234
III/78	1:283	III/123	1:364	III/168	1:272
III/79	1:352	III/124	2:205	III/169	1:400
III/80	2:163	III/125	1:147	III/170	1:401
III/81	2:485	III/126	2:182	III/171	2:58
III/82*	1:248	III/127	1:398	III/172	1:273
III/83	1:271	III/128	2:489	III/173	1:274
III/84	2:402	III/129	1:255	III/174	1:421
III/85	1:354	III/130	1:215	III/175	1:432
III/86	1:355	III/131	2:421	III/176	1:128
III/87	2:168	III/132	1:84	III/177	1:128
III/88	1:357	III/133	1:124	III/178	1:284
III/89	2:405	III/134	1:126	III/179	1:284
III/90	2:408	III/135	1:232	III/180	1:284
III/91	2:140	III/136	1:86	III/181	1:285
III/92	1:282	III/137	2:184	III/182	2:203
III/93	2:30	III/138	2:186	III/183	2:203
III/94	2:32	III/139	3:262	III/184	2:464
III/95	1:359	III/140	1:366	III/185	2:437
III/96	1:40	III/141	2:202	III/186	1:275

*Wrongly referenced in Volume I.

TATS	Page	TATS	Page	TATS	Page
III/187	1:376	III/XII	1:399	III/XXVII	3:312
III/188	1:403	III/XIII	1:403	III/XXVIII	3:313
III/189	2:60	III/XIV	3:185	III/XXIX	3:320
III/190	2:207	III/XV	3:174	III/XXX	3:328
III/I	2:61	III/XVI	3:176	III/XXXI	3:326
III/II	2:495	III/XVII	3:325	III/XXXII	3:304
III/III	1:338	III/XVIII	3:137	III/XXXIII	3:188
III/IV·	3:10	III/XIX	1:403	III/XXXIV	3:191
III/V	3:74	III/XX	3:195	III/XXXV	3:192
III/VI	3:182	III/XXI	3:210	III/XXXVI	3:214
III/VII	3:115	III/XXII	3:85	III/XXXVII	3:327
III/VIII	3:39	III/XXIII	3:305	III/XXXVIII	3:310
III/IX	3:41	III/XXIV	3:228	III/XXXIX	3:309
III/X	3:226	III/XXV	3:98	III/XL	1:203
III/XI	3:86	III/XXVI	3:311	III/XLI	3:310